Career Issues
in
Human Resource
Management

D0075151

CAREER ISSUES IN HUMAN RESOURCE MANAGEMENT

RALPH KATZ, Editor

Sloan School of Management
Massachusetts Institute of Technology

Prentice-Hall, Inc.   Englewood Cliffs, New Jersey   07632

HF
5549
.C292

Library of Congress Cataloging in Publication Data
Main entry under title:

Career issues in human resource management.

     Includes bibliographies.
     1. Personnel management—Addresses, essays,
lectures.   I. Katz, Ralph.
HF5549.C292   658.8   81-15346
ISBN 0-13-114819-2   AACR2

Applied Management Series
Cary L. Cooper, *Series Editor*

Editorial/production supervision by Margaret Rizzi
Interior design by Anne Bridgman
Manufacturing Buyer: Ed O'Dougherty

©1982 by Prentice-Hall, Inc., Englewood Cliffs, N.J. 07632

All rights reserved. No part of this book
may be reproduced in any form or
by any means without permission in writing
from the publisher.

Printed in the United States of America

10   9   8   7   6   5   4   3   2   1

ISBN   0-13-114819-2

Prentice-Hall International, Inc., *London*
Prentice-Hall of Australia Pty. Limited, *Sydney*
Prentice-Hall of Canada, Ltd., *Toronto*
Prentice-Hall of India Private Limited, *New Delhi*
Prentice-Hall of Japan, Inc., *Tokyo*
Prentice-Hall of Southeast Asia Pte. Ltd., *Singapore*
Whitehall Books Limited, *Wellington, New Zealand*

101317

To my family:

Judy,

Daniel,

and

Elana

Contents

Part IV

ISSUES IN PROFESSIONAL
AND ORGANIZATIONAL ROLES

Contributing Authors

Professor Lotte Bailyn

Massachusetts Institute of Technology
Cambridge, Massachusetts 02139

Professor Gene W. Dalton

Brigham Young University
Provo, Utah 84602

Professor Thomas J. DeLong

Brigham Young University
Provo, Utah 84602

Professor C. Brooklyn Derr

University of Utah
Salt Lake City, Utah 84112

Professor Michael J. Driver

University of Southern California
Los Angeles, California 90007

Dr. Alan R. Fusfeld

Pugh-Roberts Associates, Inc.
Cambridge, Massachusetts 02139

Professor J. Peter Graves

California State College
San Bernardino, California 92402

Professor Ralph Katz

Massachusetts Institute of Technology
Cambridge, Massachusetts 02139

Dr. Raymond L. Price

Hewlett Packard Corporation
Palo Alto, California 94302

Professor Edward B. Roberts

Massachusetts Institute of Technology
Cambridge, Massachusetts 02139

Professor Edgar H. Schein

Massachusetts Institute of Technology
Cambridge, Massachusetts 02139

Professor Paul H. Thompson

Brigham Young University
Provo, Utah 84602

Professor John Van Maanen

Massachusetts Institute of Technology
Cambridge, Massachusetts 02139

Preface

This book focuses on a variety of career related issues associated with the management of human resources. By career related, I mean issues that concern the way individual perspectives and abilities unfold and change as they continue to work in their various organizations. In particular, how can internal work environments be created such that organizational members are provided with the kinds of experiences and opportunities that enable them to self-develop and grow—especially if one assumes that such personal development is necessary to cope more effectively with rapidly and unpredictably changing outside environments. The ten chapters presented here represent the current thinking of a number of researchers interested in building a richer understanding of the interplay between individual perspectives and organizational demands. Furthermore, all of the authors are still actively investigating the particular issues they have chosen to discuss. The ideas and frameworks presented, therefore, are primarily research-based in that the authors have drawn upon their own research findings and conclusions.

The idea for this volume grew from an Industrial Liaison Program Symposium conducted in Los Angeles by members of the Organizational Studies Faculty of the Sloan School of Management at the Massachusetts Institute of Technology. In organizing this symposium, it became clear that all of us were investigating concepts that described the way individuals come to define and structure their particular work settings. What are the processes by which employees formulate perceptions, assumptions, and expectations about their specific job situations? More interestingly, we were all concerned with how job perspectives change as individuals pass through different career stages. Shortly after this symposium, several of the faculty members also participated in a career symposium at the Western Academy of Management Meetings in which several additional career related issues were addressed. This volume is comprised of the research efforts presented at these two symposia.

In putting this material together, I decided not to organize by the familiar themes of early, middle, and late careers. Instead, the chapters are divided into four major parts, each representing an important set of problems commonly associated with the introduction and management of new and existing products or services. Perhaps this grouping simply reflects my early work experiences as a marketing research consultant. Nonetheless, I have felt for a long time that there should be some strong conceptual links between the way organizational behavioralists look at processes of human resource management and the way marketing researchers look at processes of product development. After all, the development of highly competent and responsive personnel should be viewed as one of the organization's most important products.

For some time, marketing strategies have been concerned with building product and service development systems; designing processes that meet organizational goals, are compatible with its organizational structure, and satisfy the demands and characteristics of its industry and marketplace. From a parallel point of view, Part I contains two chapters that deal with the design of better human resource planning models. In the first chapter, Schein presents a developmental model of human resource planning and development, and discusses how the major components of this system should be coordinated for maximum effectiveness. He then describes the roles that both line managers and staff specialists will have to play if the system is to be effective. In the second chapter, Driver presents a conceptual model for organizing certain structural elements involved in one's career. Based on this model, Driver outlines four contrasting types of career concepts (i.e., transitory, steady state, linear, and spiral) and shows how important differences among them can affect the appropriateness of different career related interventions.

Another set of issues in the area of marketing concerns product positioning and market segmentation—identifying which consumers either are or should be the primary target group for a given product. In the same vein, all three chapters in Part II try to identify important individual differences in the career orientations of organizational employees. Bailyn reports on a 1970 survey study of 1350 M.I.T. alumni, all of whom graduated in the 1950s. By comparing their outlooks at the midpoint of their lives and careers, she is able to identify six types of career orientations. To deal with this pluralism of orientation at midcareer, Bailyn argues that for technically trained professionals, organizations must develop a greater variety of organizational roles and career paths than those presently available. In the fourth chapter, DeLong reports on the development of an instrument for measuring managerial career orientations. Building on Schein's concept of career anchors, DeLong presents a questionnaire for measuring eight different types of career orientations. He further concludes that it would be mutually beneficial to both individuals and organizations if a proper match were maintained between the needs and capabilities of managers with particular career orientations and the skills required by their specific managerial roles. In the last chapter of Part II, Derr studies some 70 Naval officers and defines three different career orientations according to the importance one attaches to a second career. Derr goes on to describe the particular strategies and activities that differentiate among these orientations. The impact of such second career or career switching tactics are then discussed in a more generalized context.

Part III focuses on issues involving the entry and development of new organizational employees, just as marketing researchers have examined the effectiveness of different strategies for introducing new products and innovations. And just as marketing studies have shown how powerful social information processes can be in the successful diffusion of new products, the chapters here also emphasize the important influence of social processes in the development of individual work perspectives. In presenting a description of socialization practices, Van Maanen shows how certain agent designed "people processing" devices can have important consequences in the way employee perceptions are formed and in the way employee energies become directed. Van Maanen argues that by gaining a richer understanding of boundary crossings, the hidden consequences of certain organizational careers can be elaborated. In chapter seven, Graves contends that most organizations are not supporting the kinds of activities that supposedly help young managers in their careers; rather organizations tend to promote the opposite. After studying the managerial behaviors, performances, and reward successes of about 90 managers, Graves concluded that behaviors which bring tangible organizational rewards to young managers are not the same as those behaviors which get jobs done effectively. Career development programs, according to Graves, will only prove useful to both the organization and its younger managers when effective management is truly rewarded.

In pushing the concept of a product life cycle, marketing people have clearly recognized that products proceed through a progression of stages, and that organizations must take an active role to extend their life cycles. Similarly, the three chapters in Part IV present a variety of frameworks for looking at the career stages of individuals within organizations. Dalton, Thompson, and Price offer a four-stage model of technically-based careers to describe the set of expectations held by professionals inside the organization. Moreover, individuals who moved successfully through these four stages continued to receive high performance ratings, whereas individuals remaining in the early stages were more likely to have received low ratings. The authors conclude by discussing the usefulness of their longitudinal framework for helping individuals make their own career decisions and for helping organizations identify and overcome those factors that block transitions between stages. In chapter 9, Katz presents a different developmental framework for looking at the way individuals respond to their work environments over time. Specifically, he presents a three traditional stage model to describe how employee perspectives and behaviors can be significantly affected by the length of time individuals have been working at their same job position and by the average length of time project members have worked together, i.e., job longevity and group longevity, respectively. Using data from 50 R&D project teams, Katz illustrates the negative influence of longevity on project communication and performance and suggests that such dysfunctions could be better managed through improved staffing and career decisions. In the final chapter, Roberts and Fusfeld present a multistage view of the technology-based innovation process and argue that certain "people" functions are necessary to meet the demands of the complete process. They further suggest that different individuals may be needed to perform each of the critical functions most effectively and that a different mix of critical functions may be required at certain stages of the innovation process. To make sure such critical functions can be carried out, Roberts and Fusfeld describe the role requirements of each function and illustrate in great detail how organizations can assess and also improve the managerial development of these critical functions.

Represented within these ten chapters are a wide variety of career related issues. One should keep in mind, however, that I have not tried to cover the vast range of material that could be included under the umbrella label of career; nor have I tried to select the most critical issues—many of which still need to be researched. Nevertheless, the set of issues that has been included represents important areas of concern both to researchers and to organizational managers interested in improving the management of their human resources. And in drawing the analogies between marketing and organizational behavior, my intention has simply been to emphasize the proactive roles that organizations must take if they truly hope to make such improvements.

ISSUES IN HUMAN RESOURCE

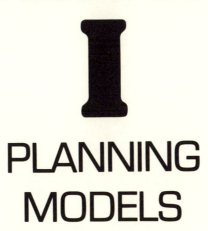

PLANNING MODELS

1

Increasing Organizational Effectiveness through Better Human Resource Planning and Development*

EDGAR H. SCHEIN

Massachusetts Institute of Technology

In this article I would like to address two basic *questions*. *First*, why is human resource planning and development becoming increasingly important as a determinant of organizational effectiveness? *Second*, what are the major *components* of a human resource planning and career development system, and how should these components be *linked* for maximum organizational effectiveness?

The field of personnel management has for some time addressed issues such as these and much of the technology of planning for and managing human resources has been worked out to a considerable degree.[1] Nevertheless there continues to be in organizations a failure, particularly on the part of line managers and functional managers in areas other than personnel, to recognize the true importance of planning for and managing human resources. This paper is not intended to be a review

*Reprinted by permission of *Sloan Management Review,* Volume 18, No. 3, 1977, pp. 1-20. Much of the research on which this paper is based was done under the sponsorship of the Group Psychology branch of the Office of Naval Research. Their generous support has made continuing work in this area possible. I would also like to thank my colleagues Lotte Bailyn and John Van Maanen for many of the ideas expressed in this paper.

[1] See Pigors and Myers [24] and Burack [10].

of what is known but rather a kind of position paper for line managers to bring to their attention some important and all too often neglected issues. These issues are important for organizational *effectiveness,* quite apart from their relevance to the issue of humanizing work or improving the quality of working life.[2]

The observations and analyses made below are based on several kinds of information:

- Formal research on management development, career development, and human development through the adult life cycle conducted in the Sloan School and at other places for the past several decades.[3]
- Analysis of consulting relationships, field observations, and other involvements over the past several decades with all kinds of organizations dealing with the planning for and implementation of human resource development programs and organization development projects.[4]

WHY IS HUMAN RESOURCE PLANNING AND DEVELOPMENT (HRPD) INCREASINGLY IMPORTANT?

The Changing Managerial Job

The first answer to the question is simple, though paradoxical. Organizations are becoming more dependent upon people because they are increasingly involved in more complex technologies and are attempting to function in more complex economic, political and sociocultural environments. The more different technical skills there are involved in the design, manufacture, marketing, and sales of a product, the more vulnerable the organization will be to critical shortages of the right kinds of human resources. The more complex the process, the higher the interdependence among the various specialists. The higher the interdependence, the greater the need for effective integration of all the specialities because the entire process is only as strong as its weakest link.

In simpler technologies, managers could often compensate for the technical or communication failures of their subordinates. General managers today are much more dependent upon their technically trained subordinates because they usually do not understand the details of the engineering, marketing, financial, and other decisions which their subordinates are making. Even the general manager who grew up in finance may find that since his day the field of finance has outrun him and his subordinates are using models and methods which he cannot entirely understand.

What all this means for the general manager is that he cannot any longer safely make decisions by himself; he cannot get enough information digested within his own head to be the integrator and decision maker. Instead, he finds himself increas-

[2] See Hackman and Suttle [13] and Meltzer and Wickert [21].

[3] See McGregor [20], Bennis [6], Pigors and Myers [24], Schein [29], Van Maanen [36], Bailyn and Schein [4], and Katz [18].

[4] See Beckhard [5], Bennis [6], Schein [28], Galbraith [12], Lesieur [19], and Alfred [1].

ingly having to manage the *process* of decision making, bringing the right people together around the right questions or problems, stimulating open discussion, ensuring that all relevant information surfaces and is critically assessed, managing the emotional ups and downs of his prima donnas, and ensuring that out of all this human and interpersonal process, a good decision will result.

As I have watched processes like these in management groups, I am struck by the fact that *the decision emerges out of the interplay*. It is hard to pin down who had the idea and who made the decision. The general manager in this setting is *accountable* for the decision, but rarely would I describe the process as one where he or she actually makes the decision, except in the sense of recognizing when the right answer has been achieved, ratifying that answer, announcing it, and following up on its implementation.

If the managerial *job* is increasingly moving in the direction I have indicated, managers of the future will have to be much more skilled in how to:

1. Select and train their subordinates.
2. Design and run meetings and groups of all sorts.
3. Deal with all kinds of conflict between strong individuals and groups.
4. Influence and negotiate from a low power base.
5. Integrate the efforts of very diverse technical specialists.

If the above image of what is happening to organizations has any generality, it will force the field of human resource management increasingly to center stage. The more complex organizations become, the more they will be vulnerable to human error. They will not necessarily employ more people, but they will employ more sophisticated highly trained people both in managerial and in individual contributor, staff roles. The price of low motivation, turnover, poor productivity, sabotage, and intraorganizational conflict will be higher in such an organization. Therefore it will become a matter of *economic necessity* to improve human resource planning and development systems.

Changing Social Values

A second reason why human resource planning and development will become more central and important is that changing social values regarding the role of work will make it *more complicated to manage people*. There are several kinds of research findings and observations which illustrate this point.

First, my own longitudinal research of a panel of Sloan School graduates of the 1960s strongly suggests that we have put much too much emphasis on the traditional success syndrome of "climbing the corporate ladder."[5] Some alumni indeed want to rise to high-level general manager positions, but many others want to exercise their particular technical or functional competence and only rise to levels of functional management or senior staff roles with minimal managerial responsibility.

[5] See Schein [31].

Some want security, others are seeking nonorganizational careers as teachers or consultants, while a few are becoming entrepreneurs. I have called these patterns of motivation, talent, and values "career anchors" and believe that they serve to stabilize and constrain the career in predictable ways. The implication is obvious—organizations must develop multiple ladders and multiple reward systems to deal with different types of people.[6]

Second, studies of young people entering organizations in the last several decades suggest that work and career are not as central a life preoccupation as was once the case. Perhaps because of a prolonged period of economic affluence, people see more options for themselves and are increasingly exercising those options. In particular, one sees more concern with a balanced life in which work, family, and self-development play a more equal role.[7]

Third, closely linked to the above trend is the increase in the number of women in organizations, which will have its major impact through the increase of dual career families. As opportunities for women open up, we will see more new lifestyles in young couples which will affect the organization's options as to moving people geographically, joint employment, joint career management, family support, etc.[8]

Fourth, research evidence is beginning to accumulate that personal growth and development is a life-long process and that predictable issues and crises come up in every decade of our lives. Organizations will have to be much more aware of what these issues are, how work and family interact, and how to manage people at different ages. The current "hot button" is *mid-career crisis,* but the more research we do the more we find developmental crises at *all* ages and stages.[9]

An excellent summary of what is happening in the world of values, technology, and management is provided in a recent text by Elmer Burack:

> The leading edge of change in the future will include the new technologies of information, production, and management, interlaced with considerable social dislocation and shifts in manpower inputs. These developments are without precedent in our industrial history.
>
> Technological and social changes have created a need for more education, training, and skill at all managerial and support levels. The lowering of barriers to employment based on sex and race introduces new kinds of manpower problems for management officials. Seniority is coming to mean relatively less in relation to the comprehension of problems, processes, and approaches. The newer manpower elements and work technologies have shifted institutional arrangements: the locus of decision making is altered, role relationships among workers and supervisors are changed (often becoming more collegial), and the need to respond to changing routines has become commonplace. . . .

[6] See Schein [32].
[7] See Bailyn and Schein [4], Myers [22], Van Maanen et al. [37], and Roeber [25].
[8] See Van Maanen and Schein [38], Bailyn [3] and [2], and Kanter [17].
[9] See Sheehy [33]. Troll [35], Kalish [16], and Pearse and Pelzer [23].

These shifts have been supported by more demanding customer requirements, increasing government surveillance (from product quality to anti-pollution measures), and more widespread use of computers, shifting power bases to the holders of specialized knowledge skills.[10]

In order for HRPD systems to become more responsive and capable of handling such growing complexity they must contain all the necessary components, must be based on correct assumptions, and must be adequately integrated.

COMPONENTS OF A HUMAN RESOURCE
PLANNING AND DEVELOPMENT SYSTEM

The major problem with existing HRPD systems is that they are fragmented, incomplete, and sometimes built on faulty assumptions about human or organizational growth.

Human growth takes place through successive encounters with one's environment. As the person encounters a new situation, he or she is forced to try new responses to deal with that situation. Learning takes place as a function of how those responses work out and the results they achieve. If they are successful in coping with the situation, the person enlarges his repertory of responses; if they are not successful the person must try alternate responses until the situation has been dealt with. If none of the active coping responses work, the person sometimes falls back on retreating from the new situation, or denying that there is a problem to be solved. These responses are defensive and growth limiting.

The implication is that for growth to occur, people basically need two things: *new challenges* that are within the range of their coping responses, and *knowledge of results,* information on how their responses to the challenge have worked out. If the tasks and challenges are too easy or too hard, the person will be demotivated and cease to grow. If the information is not available on how well the person's responses are working, the person cannot grow in a systematic, valid direction but is forced into guessing or trying to infer information from ambiguous signals.

Organizational growth similarly takes place through successful coping with the internal and external environment.[11] But since the organization is a complex system of human, material, financial, and informational resources, one must consider how each of those areas can be properly managed toward organizational effectiveness. In this article I will deal only with the human resources.

In order for the organization to have the capacity to perform effectively over a period of time it must be able to plan for, recruit, manage, develop, measure, dispose of, and replace human resources as warranted by the tasks to be done. The most important of these functions is the *planning* function, since task requirements are likely to change as the complexity and turbulence of the organization's environ-

---

[10] See Burack [10], pp. 402-3.
[11] See Schein [29].

ment increase. In other words, a key assumption underlying organizational growth is that the nature of jobs will change over time, which means that such changes must be continuously monitored in order to ensure that the right kinds of human resources can be recruited or developed to do those jobs. Many of the activities such as recruitment, selection, performance appraisal, and so on, presume that some planning process has occurred which makes it possible to assess whether or not those activities are meeting *organizational needs,* quite apart from whether they are facilitating the individual's growth.

In an ideal HRPD system one would seek to match the organization's needs for human resources with the individual's needs for personal career growth and development. One can then depict the basic system as involving both individual and organizational planning, and a series of matching activities which are designed to facilitate mutual need satisfaction. If we further assume that both individual and organizational needs change over time, we can depict this process as a developmental one as in Figure 1-1.

In the right-hand column we show the basic stages of the individual career through the life cycle. While not everyone will go through these stages in the manner depicted, there is growing evidence that for organizational careers in particular, these stages reasonably depict the movement of people through their adult lives.[12]

Given those developmental assumptions, the left-hand side of the diagram shows the organizational planning activities which must occur if human resources are to be managed in an optimal way, and if changing job requirements are to be properly assessed and continuously monitored. The middle column shows the various matching activities which have to occur at various career stages.

The components of an effective HRPD system now can be derived from the diagram. *First,* there have to be in the organization the overall planning components shown on the left-hand side of Figure 1-1. *Second,* there have to be components which ensure an adequate process of staffing the organization. *Third,* there have to be components which plan for and monitor growth and development. *Fourth,* there have to be components which facilitate the actual process of the growth and development of the people who are brought into the organization; this growth and development must be organized to meet *both* the needs of the organization and the needs of the individuals within it. *Fifth,* there have to be components which deal with decreasing effectiveness, leveling off, obsolescence of skills, turnover, retirement, and other phenomena which reflect the need for either a new growth direction or a process of disengagement of the person from his or her job. *Finally,* there have to be components which ensure that as some people move out of jobs, others are available to fill those jobs, and as new jobs arise that people are available with the requisite skills to fill them.

In the remainder of this article I would like to comment on each of these six sets of components and indicate where and how they should be linked to each other.

[12] See Dalton and Thompson [11]. Super and Bohn [34], Hall [14], and Schein [32].

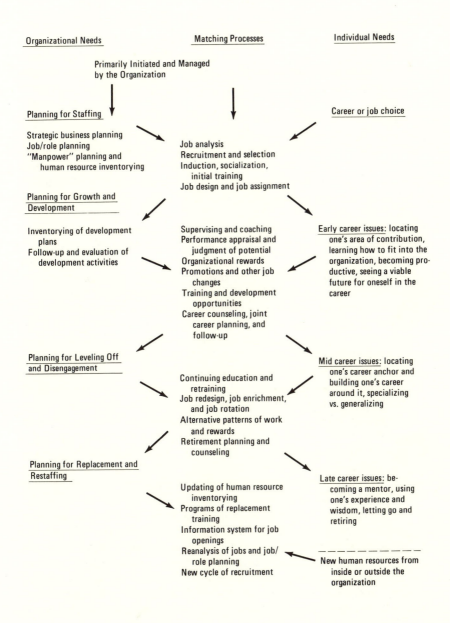

Organizational Needs   Matching Processes   Individual Needs

Primarily Initiated and Managed
by the Organization

Planning for Staffing   Career or job choice

Strategic business planning
Job/role planning   Job analysis
"Manpower" planning and   Recruitment and selection
    human resource inventorying Induction, socialization,
                                initial training
                           Job design and job assignment

Planning for Growth and
Development

Inventorying of development   Supervising and coaching   Early career issues: locating
    plans   Performance appraisal and   one's area of contribution,
Follow-up and evaluation of   judgment of potential   learning how to fit into the
    development activities   Organizational rewards   organization, becoming pro-
                    Promotions and other job   ductive, seeing a viable
                      changes   future for oneself in the
                    Training and development   career
                      opportunities
                    Career counseling, joint
                      career planning, and
                      follow-up

Planning for Leveling Off   Mid career issues: locating
and Disengagement   one's career anchor and
                    Continuing education and   building one's career
                    retraining   around it, specializing
                    Job redesign, job enrichment,   vs. generalizing
                    and job rotation
                    Alternative patterns of work
                    and rewards
                    Retirement planning and
                    counseling

Planning for Replacement and   Late career issues: be-
Restaffing   coming a mentor, using
                    Updating of human resource   one's experience and
                    inventorying   wisdom, letting go and
                    Programs of replacement   retiring
                    training
                    Information system for job
                    openings
                    Reanalysis of jobs and job/   New human resources from
                    role planning   inside or outside the
                    New cycle of recruitment   organization

Figure 1-1 A Developmental Model of Human Resource Planning and Development

Overall Planning Components

The function of these components is to ensure that the organization has an adequate basis for selecting its human resources and developing them toward the fulfillment of organizational goals.

Strategic Business Planning. These activities are designed to determine the organization's goals, priorities, future directions, products, markets growth rate, geographical location, and organization structure or design. This process should lead logically into the next two planning activities but is often disconnected from them because it is located in a different part of the organization or is staffed by people with different orientations and backgrounds.

Job/Role Planning. These activities are designed to determine what actually needs to be done at every level of the organization (up through top management) to fulfill the organization's goals and tasks. This activity can be thought of as a dynamic kind of job analysis where a continual review is made of the skills, knowledge, values, etc., which are presently needed in the organization *and will be needed in the future.* The focus is on the predictable consequences of the strategic planning for managerial roles, specialist roles, and skill mixes which may be needed to get the mission accomplished. If the organization already has a satisfactory system of job descriptions, this activity would concern itself with how those jobs will evolve and change, and what new jobs or roles will evolve in the future.[13]

This component is often missing completely in organizations or is carried out only for lower-level jobs. From a planning point of view it is probably most important for the highest-level jobs—how the nature of general and functional management will change as the organization faces new technologies, new social values, and new environmental conditions.

"Manpower Planning" and Human Resource Inventorying. These activities draw on the job/role descriptions generated in job/role planning and assess the capabilities of the present human resources against those plans or requirements. These activities may be focused on the numbers of people in given categories and are often designed to ensure that under given assumptions of growth there will be an adequate supply of people in those categories. Or the process may focus more on how to ensure that certain scarce skills which will be needed will in fact be available, leading to more sophisticated programs of recruitment or human resource development. For example, the inventorying process at high levels may reveal the need for a new type of general manager with broad integrative capacities which may further reveal the need to start a development program that will ensure that such managers will be available five to ten years down the road.

These first three component activities are all geared to identifying the *organization's* needs in the human resource area. They are difficult to do and tools are only

[13] See Schein [32].

now beginning to be developed for job/role planning.[14] In most organizations I have dealt with, the three areas, if they exist at all, are not linked to each other organizationally. Strategic planning is likely to exist in the Office of the President. Job/role planning is likely to be an offshoot of some management development activities in Personnel. And human resource inventorying is likely to be a specialized subsection within Personnel. Typically, no one is accountable for bringing these activities together even on an ad hoc basis.

This situation reflects an erroneous assumption about growth and development which I want to mention at this time. The assumption is that if the organization develops its *present* human resources, it will be able to fill whatever job demands may arise in the future. Thus we do find in organizations elaborate human resource planning systems, but they plan for the present people in the organization, not for the organization per se. If there are no major changes in job requirements as the organization grows and develops, this system will work. But if jobs themselves change, it is no longer safe to assume that today's human resources, with development plans based on *today's* job requirements, will produce the people needed in some future situation. Therefore, I am asserting that more job/role planning must be done, independent of the present people in the organization.

The subsequent components to be discussed which focus on the matching of individual and organizational needs all assume that some sort of basic planning activities such as those described have been carried out. They may not be very formal, or they may be highly decentralized (e.g., every supervisor who has an open slot might make his own decision of what sort of person to hire based on his private assumptions about strategic business planning and job/role planning). Obviously, the more turbulent the environment, the greater the vulnerability of the organization if it does not centralize and coordinate its various planning activities, and generate its HRPD system from those plans.

Staffing Processes

The function of these processes is to ensure that the organization acquires the human resources necessary to fulfill its goals.

Job Analysis.   If the organizational planning has been done adequately, the next component of the HRPD system is to actually specify what jobs need to be filled and what skills, etc. are needed to do those jobs. Some organizations go through this process very formally, others do it in an informal unprogrammed manner, but in some form it must occur in order to specify what kind of recruitment to do and how to select people from among the recruits.

Recruitment and Selection.   This activity involves the actual process of going out to find people to fulfill jobs and developing systems for deciding which of those people to hire. These components may be very formal including testing, assessment,

[14] See Schein [32].

and other aids to the selection process. If this component is seen as part of a total HRPD system, it will alert management to the fact that the recruitment selection system communicates to future employees something about the nature of the organization and its approach to people. All too often this component sends incorrect messages or turns off future employees or builds incorrect stereotypes which make subsequent supervision more difficult.[15]

Induction, Socialization, and Initial Training.   Once the employee has been hired, there ensues a period during which he or she learns the ropes, learns how to get along in the organization, how to work, how to fit in, how to master the particulars of the job, and so on. Once again, it is important that the activities which make up this component are seen as part of a total process with long-range consequences for the attitudes of the employee.[16] The goal of these processes should be to facilitate the employees' becoming productive and useful members of the organization both in the short run and in terms of long-range potential.

Job Design and Job Assignment.   One of the most crucial components of staffing is the actual design of the job which is given to the new employee and the manner in which the assignment is actually made. The issue is how to provide *optimal challenge*, a set of activities which will be neither too hard nor too easy for the new employee, and which will be neither too meaningless nor too risky from the point of view of the organization. If the job is too easy or too meaningless, the employee may become demotivated; if the job is too hard and/or involves too much responsibility and risk from the point of view of the organization, the employee will become too anxious, frustrated, or angry to perform at an optimal level. Some organizations have set up training programs for supervisors to help them to design optimally challenging work assignments.[17]

These four components are geared to ensuring that the work of the organization will be performed. They tend to be processes that have to be performed by line managers and personnel staff specialists together. Line managers have the basic information about jobs and skill requirements; personnel specialists have the interviewing, recruiting, and assessment skills to aid in the selection process. In an optimal system these functions will be closely coordinated, particularly to ensure that the recruiting process provides to the employee accurate information about the nature of the organization and the actual work that he or she will be doing in it. Recruiters also need good information on the long-range human resource plans so that these can be taken into account in the selection of new employees.

[15] See Schein [26] and [32].
[16] See Schein [27] and Van Maanen [36].
[17] See Schein [26].

Development Planning

It is not enough to get good human resources in the door. Some planning activities have to concern themselves with how employees who may be spending thirty to forty years of their total life in a given organization will make a contribution for all of that time, will remain motivated and productive, and will maintain a reasonable level of job satisfaction.

Inventorying of Development Plans. Whether or not the process is highly formalized, there is in most organizations some effort to plan for the growth and development of all employees. The planning component that is often missing is some kind of pulling together of this information into a centralized inventory that permits coordination and evaluation of the development activities. Individual supervisors may have clear ideas of what they will do with and for their subordinates, but this information may never be collected, making it impossible to determine whether the individual plans of supervisors are connected in any way. Whether it is done by department, division, or total company, some effort to collect such information and to think through its implications would be of great value to furthering the total development of employees at all levels.

Follow-up and Evaluation of Development Activities. I have observed two symptoms of insufficient planning in this area: one, development plans are made for individual employees, are written down, but are never implemented, and two, if they are implemented they are never evaluated either in relation to the individual's own needs for growth or in relation to the organization's needs for new skills. Some system should exist to ensure that plans are implemented and that activities are evaluated against both individual and organizational goals.

Career Development Processes

This label is deliberately broad to cover all of the major processes of managing human resources during their period of growth and peak productivity, a period which may be several decades in length. These processes must match the organization's needs for work with the individual's needs for a productive and satisfying work career. The system must provide for some kind of forward movement for the employee through some succession of jobs, whether these involve promotion, lateral movement to new functions, or simply new assignments within a given area.[18] The system must be based both on the organization's need to fill jobs as they open up and on employees' needs to have some sense of progress in their working lives.

[18]See Schein [30] and [32].

Supervision and Coaching.   By far the most important component in this area is the actual process of supervising, guiding, coaching, and monitoring. It is in this context that the work assignment and feedback processes which make learning possible occur, and it is the boss who plays the key role in molding the employee to the organization. There is considerable evidence that the first boss is especially crucial in giving new employees a good start in their careers,[19] and that training of supervisors in how to handle new employees is a valuable organizational investment.

Performance Appraisal and Judgment of Potential.   This component is part of the general process of supervision but stands out as such an important part of that process that it must be treated separately. In most organizations there is some effort to standardize and formalize a process of appraisal above and beyond the normal performance feedback which is expected on a day-to-day basis. Such systems serve a number of functions—to justify salary increases, promotions, and other formal organizational actions with respect to the employee; to provide information for human resource inventories or at least written records of past accomplishments for the employee's personnel folder; and to provide a basis for annual or semi-annual formal reviews between boss and subordinate to supplement day-to-day feedback and to facilitate information exchange for career planning and counseling. In some organizations so little day-to-day feedback occurs that the *formal* system bears the burden of providing the employees with knowledge of how they are doing and what they can look forward to. Since knowledge of results, of how one is doing, is a crucial component of any developmental process, it is important for organizations to monitor how well and how frequently feedback is actually given.

One of the major dilemmas in this area is whether to have a single system which provides both feedback for the growth and development of the employee and information for the organization's planning systems. The dilemma arises because the information which the planning system requires (e.g., "how much potential does this employee have to rise in the organization?") may be the kind of information which neither the boss nor the planner wants to share with the employee. The more potent and more accurate the information, the less likely it is to be fed back to the employee in anything other than very vague terms.

On the other hand, the detailed work-oriented, day-to-day feedback which the employee needs for growth and development may be too cumbersome to record as part of a selection-oriented appraisal system. If hundreds of employees are to be compared, there is strong pressure in the system toward more general kinds of judgments, traits, rankings, numerical estimates of ultimate potential, and the like. One way of resolving this dilemma which some companies have found successful is to develop two separate systems—one oriented toward performance improvement and the growth of the employee, and the other one oriented toward a more global assessment of the employee for future planning purposes involving judgments which may not be shared with the employee except in general terms.

[19] See Schein [26], Bray et al. [9], Berlew and Hall [8], and Hall [14].

A second dilemma arises around the identification of the employee's "development needs" and how that information is linked to other development activities. If the development needs are stated in relation to the planning system, the employee may never get the feedback of what his needs may have been perceived to be, and, worse, no one may implement any program to deal with those needs if the planning system is not well linked with line management.

Two further problems arise from the potential lack of linkage. One, if the individual does not get good feedback around developmental needs, he or she remains uninvolved in his or her own development and potentially becomes complacent. We pay lip service to the statement that only the individual can develop himself or herself, but then deprive the individual of the very information that would make sensible self-development possible. Two, the development needs as stated for the various employees in the organization may have nothing to do with the organization's needs for certain kinds of human resources in the future. All too often there is complete lack of linkage between the strategic or business planning function and the human resource development function resulting in potentially willy-nilly individual development based on today's needs and individual managers' stereotypes of what will be needed in the future.

Organizational Rewards—Pay, Benefits, Perquisites, Promotion, and Recognition.   Entire books have been written about all the problems and subtleties of how to link organizational rewards to the other components of an HRPD system to ensure both short-run and long-run human effectiveness. For purposes of this short paper I wish to point out only one major issue—how to ensure that organizational rewards are linked *both* to the needs of the individual and to the needs of the organization for effective performance and development of potential. All too often the reward system is neither responsive to the individual employee nor to the organization, being driven more by criteria of elegance, consistency, and what other organizations are doing. If the linkage is to be established, line managers must actively work with compensation experts to develop a joint philosophy and set of goals based on an understanding of both what the organization is trying to reward and what employee needs actually are. As organizational careers become more varied and as social values surrounding work change, reward systems will probably have to become much more flexible both in time (people at different career stages may need different things) and by type of career (functional specialists may need different things than general managers).

Promotions and Other Job Changes.   There is ample evidence that what keeps human growth and effectiveness going is continuing optimal challenge.[20] Such challenge can be provided for some members of the organization through promotion to higher levels where more responsible jobs are available. For most members of the organization the promotion opportunities are limited, however, because the pyramid narrows at the top. An effective HRPD system will, therefore, concentrate

---

[20] See Dalton and Thompson [11] and Katz [18].

on developing career paths, systems of job rotation, changing assignments, temporary assignments, and other lateral job moves which assure continuing growth of all human resources.

One of the key characteristics of an optimally challenging job is that it both draws on the person's abilities and skills and that it has opportunities for "closure." The employee must be in the job long enough to get involved and to see the results of his or her efforts. Systems of rotation which move the person too rapidly either prevent initial involvement (as in the rotational training program), or prevent closure by transferring the person to a new job before the effects of his or her decisions can be assessed. I have heard many "fast track" executives complain that their self-confidence was low because they never really could see the results of their efforts. Too often we move people too fast in order to "fill slots" and thereby undermine their development.

Organizational planning systems which generate "slots" to be filled must be coordinated with development planning systems which concern themselves with the optimal growth of the human resources. Sometimes it is better for the organization in the long run not to fill an empty slot in order to keep a manager in another job where he or she is just beginning to develop. One way of ensuring such linkage is to monitor these processes by means of a "development committee" which is composed of both line managers and personnel specialists. In such a group the needs of the organization and the needs of the people can be balanced against each other in the context of the long-range goals of the organization.

Training and Development Opportunities. Most organizations recognize that periods of formal training, sabbaticals, executive development programs outside of the company, and other educational activities are necessary in the total process of human growth and development. The important point about these activities is that they should be carefully linked both to the needs of the individual and to the needs of the organization. The individual should want to go to the program because he or she can see how the educational activity fits into the total career. The organization should send the person because the training fits into some concept of future career development. It should not be undertaken simply as a generalized "good thing," or because other companies are doing it. As much as possible the training and educational activities should be tied to job/role planning. For example, many companies began to use university executive development programs because of an explicit recognition that future managers would require a broader perspective on various problems and that such "broadening" could best be achieved in the university programs.

Career Counseling, Joint Career Planning, Follow-up, and Evaluation. Inasmuch as the growth and development which may be desired can only come from within the individual himself or herself, it is important that the organization provide some means for individual employees at all levels to become more proactive about their careers and some mechanisms for joint dialogue, counseling, and career planning.[21] This process should ideally be linked to performance appraisal, because it is in that context that the boss can review with the subordinate the future potential, development needs, strengths, weaknesses, career options, etc. The boss is often not trained in counseling but does possess some of the key information which the employee needs to initiate any kind of career planning. More formal counseling could then be supplied by the personnel development staff or outside the organization altogether.

The important point to recognize is that employees cannot manage their own growth development without information on how their own needs, talents, values, and plans mesh with the opportunity structure of the organization. Even though the organization may only have imperfect, uncertain information about the future, the individual is better off to know that than to make erroneous assumptions about the future based on no information at all. It is true that the organization cannot make commitments, nor should it unless required to by legislation or contract. But the sharing of information if properly done is not the same as making commitments or setting up false expectations.

If the organization can open up the communication channel between employees, their bosses, and whoever is managing the human resource system, the groundwork is laid for realistic individual development planning. Whatever is decided about training, next steps, special assignments, rotation, etc., should be jointly decided by the individual and the appropriate organizational resource (probably the supervisor and someone from personnel specializing in career development). Each step must fit into the employee's life plan and must be tied into *organizational needs*. The organization should be neither a humanistic charity nor an indoctrination center. Instead, it should be a vehicle for meeting both the needs of society and of individuals.

Whatever is decided should not merely be written down but executed. If there are implementation problems, the development plan should be renegotiated. Whatever developmental actions are taken, it is essential that they be followed up and evaluated both by the person and by the organization to determine what, if anything, was achieved. It is shocking to discover how many companies invest in major activities such as university executive development programs and never determine for themselves what was accomplished. In some instances, they make no plans to talk to the individual before or after the program so that it is not even possible to determine what the activity meant to the participant, or what might be an appropriate next assignment for him or her following the program.

I can summarize the above analysis best by emphasizing the two places where I feel there is the most fragmentation and violation of growth assumptions. First, too many of the activities occur without the involvement of the person who is "being developed" and therefore may well end up being self-defeating. This is particularly true of job assignments and performance appraisal where too little involvement and feedback occur. Second, too much of the human resource system functions as a

[21] See Heidke [15].

personnel *selection* system unconnected to either the needs of the organization or the needs of the individual. All too often it is only a system for short-run replacement of people in standard type jobs. The key planning functions are not linked in solidly and hence do not influence the system to the degree they should.

Planning for and Managing Disengagement

The planning and management processes which will be briefly reviewed here are counterparts of ones that have already been discussed but are focused on a different problem—the problem of the late career, loss of motivation, obsolescence, and ultimately retirement. Organizations must recognize that there are various options available to deal with this range of problems beyond the obvious ones of either terminating the employee or engaging in elaborate measures to "remotivate" people who may have lost work involvement.[22]

Continuing Education and Retraining. These activities have their greatest potential if the employee is motivated and if there is some clear connection between what is to be learned and what the employee's current or future job assignments require in the way of skills. More and more organizations are finding out that it is better to provide challenging work first and only then the training to perform that work once the employee sees the need for it. Obviously for this linkage to work well continuous dialogue is needed between employees and their managers. For those employees who have leveled off, have lost work involvement, but are still doing high quality work other solutions such as those described below are more applicable.

Job Redesign, Job Enrichment, and Job Rotation. This section is an extension of the arguments made earlier on job changes in general applied to the particular problems of leveled off employees. In some recent research, it has been suggested that job enrichment and other efforts to redesign work to increase motivation and performance may only work during the first few years on a job.[23] Beyond that the employee becomes "unresponsive" to the job characteristics themselves and pays more attention to surrounding factors such as the nature of supervision, relationships with co-workers, pay, and other extrinsic characteristics. In other words, before organizations attempt to "cure" leveled off employees by remotivating them through job redesign or rotation, they should examine whether those employees are still in a responsive mode or not. On the other hand, one can argue that there is nothing wrong with less motivated, less involved employees so long as the quality of what they are doing meets the organizational standards.[24]

Alternative Patterns of Work and Rewards. Because of the changing needs and values of employees in recent decades, more and more organizations have begun to

[22] See Bailyn [3].
[23] See Katz [18].
[24] See Bailyn [3].

experiment with alternative work patterns such as flexible working hours, part-time work, sabbaticals or other longer periods of time off, several people filling one job, dual employment of spouses with more extensive childcare programs, etc. Along with these experiments have come others on flexible reward systems in which employees can choose between a raise, some time off, special retirement, medical, or insurance benefits, and other efforts to make multiple career ladders a viable reality. These programs apply to employees at all career stages but are especially relevant to people in mid and late career stages where their own perception of their career and life goals may be undergoing important changes.

None of those innovations should be attempted without first clearly establishing an HRPD system which takes care of the organization's needs as well as the needs of employees and links them to each other. There can be little growth and development for employees at any level in an *organization* which is sick and stagnant. It is in the best interests of both the individual and the organization to have a healthy organization which can provide opportunities for growth.

Retirement Planning and Counseling.   As part of any effective HRPD system, there must be a clear planning function which forecasts who will retire, and which feeds this information into both the replacement staffing system and the counseling functions so that the employees who will be retiring can be prepared for this often traumatic career stage. Employees need counseling not only with the mechanical and financial aspects of retirement, but also to prepare them psychologically for the time when they will no longer have a clear organizational base or job as part of their identity. For some people it may make sense to spread the period of retirement over a number of years by using part-time work or special assignments to help both the individual and the organization to get benefits from this period.

The counseling function here as in other parts of the career probably involves special skills and must be provided by specialists. However, the line manager continues to play a key role as a provider of job challenge, feedback, and information about what is ahead for any given employee. Seminars for line managers on how to handle the special problems of pre-retirement employees would probably be of great value as part of their managerial training.

Planning for and Managing Replacement and Restaffing

With this step the HRPD cycle closes back upon itself. This function must be concerned with such issues as:

1. Updating the human resource inventory as retirements or terminations occur.
2. Instituting special programs of orientation or training for new incumbents to specific jobs as those jobs open up.
3. Managing the information system on what jobs are available and determining how to match this information to the human resources available

in order to determine whether to replace from within the organization or to go outside with a new recruiting program.

4. Continuously reanalyzing jobs to ensure that the new incumbent is properly prepared for what the job *now* requires and *will* require in the future.

How these processes are managed links to the other parts of the system through the implicit messages that are sent to employees. For example, a company which decides to publicly post all of its unfilled jobs is clearly sending a message that it expects internal recruitment and supports self-development activities. A company which manages restaffing in a very secret manner may well get across a message that employees might as well be complacent and passive about their careers because they cannot influence them anyway.

SUMMARY AND CONCLUSIONS

I have tried to argue in this article that human resource planning and development is becoming an increasingly important function in organizations, that this function consists of multiple components, and that these components must be managed *both* by line managers and staff specialists. I have tried to show that the various planning activities are closely linked to the actual processes of supervision, job assignment, training, etc., and that those processes must be designed to match the needs of the organization with the needs of the employees throughout their evolving careers, whether or not those careers involve hierarchical promotions. I have also argued that the various components are linked to each other and must be seen as a total system if it is to be effective. The total system must be managed as a system to ensure coordination between the planning functions and the implementation functions.

I hope it is clear from what has been said that an effective human resource planning and development system is integral to the functioning of the organization and must, therefore, be a central concern of line management. Many of the activities require specialist help, but the accountabilities must rest squarely with line supervisors and top management. It is they who control the opportunities and the rewards. It is the job assignment system and the feedback which employees get that is the ultimate raw material for growth and development. Whoever designs and manages the system, it will not help the organization to become more effective unless that system is *owned* by line management.

REFERENCES

Alfred, T. "Checkers or Choice in Manpower Management." *Harvard Business Review,* January-February 1967, pp. 157-69.[1]

Bailyn, L. "Career and Family Orientations of Husbands and Wives in Relation to Marital Happiness." *Human Relations,* 1970, pp. 97-113.[2]

Bailyn, L. "Involvement and Accommodation in Technical Careers." In *Organizational Careers: Some New Perspectives,* edited by J. Van Maanen. New York: John Wiley, 1977.[3]

Bailyn, L., and Schein, E.H. "Life/Career Considerations as Indicators of Quality of Employment." In *Measuring Work Quality for Social Reporting,* edited by A.D. Biderman and T.F. Drury. New York: Sage Publications, 1976.[4]

Beckhard, R.D. *Organization Development: Strategies and Models.* Reading, MA: Addison-Wesley, 1969.[5]

Bennis, W.G. *Changing Organizations.* New York: McGraw-Hill, 1966.[6]

Bennis, W.G. *Organization Development: Its Nature, Origins, and Prospects.* Reading, MA: Addison-Wesley, 1969.[7]

Berlew, D., and Hall, D.T. "The Socialization of Managers." *Administrative Science Quarterly* 11 (1966): 207-23.[8]

Bray, D.W.; Campbell, R.J.; and Grant, D.E. *Formative Years in Business.* New York: John Wiley, 1974.[9]

Burack, E. *Organization Analysis.* Hinsdale, IL: Dryden, 1975.[10]

Dalton, G.W., and Thompson, P.H. "Are R&D Organizations Obsolete?" *Harvard Business Review,* November-December 1976, pp. 105-16.[11]

Galbraith, J. *Designing Complex Organizations.* Reading, MA: Addison-Wesley, 1973.[12]

Hackman, J.R., and Suttle, J.L. *Improving Life at Work.* Los Angeles: Goodyear, 1977.[13]

Hall, D.T. *Careers in Organizations.* Los Angeles: Goodyear, 1976.[14]

Heidke, R. *Career Pro-activity of Middle Managers.* Master's thesis, Massachusetts Institute of Technology, 1977.[15]

Kalish, R.A. *Late Adulthood: Perspectives on Aging.* Monterey, CA: Brooks-Cole, 1975.[16]

Kanter, R.M. *Work and Family in the United States.* New York: Russell Sage, 1977.[17]

Katz, R. "Job Enrichment: Some Career Considerations." In *Organizational Careers: Some New Perspectives,* edited by J. Van Maanen. New York: John Wiley, 1977.[18]

Lesieur, F.G. *The Scanlon Plan.* New York: John Wiley, 1958.[19]

McGregor, D. *The Human Side of Enterprise.* New York: McGraw-Hill, 1960.[20]

Meltzer, H., and Wickert, F.R. *Humanizing Organizational Behavior.* Springfield. IL: Charles C Thomas, 1976.[21]

Myers, C.A. "Management and the Employee." In *Social Responsibility and the Business Predicament,* edited by J.W. McKie, Washington, D.C.: Brookings, 1974.[22]

Pearse, R.F. and Pelzer, B.P. *Self-directed Change for the Mid-career Manager.* New York: AMACOM, 1975. [23]

Pigors, P., and Myers, C.A. *Personnel Administration,* 8th ed. New York: McGraw-Hill, 1977. [24]

Roeber, R.J.C. *The Organization in a Changing Environment.* Reading, MA: Addison-Wesley, 1973. [25]

Schein, E.H. "How to Break in the College Graduate." *Harvard Business Review,* 1964, pp. 68-76. [26]

Schein, E.H. Organizational Socialization and the Profession of Management. *Industrial Management Review,* Winter 1968, pp. 1-16. [27]

Schein, E.H. *Process Consultation: Its Role in Organization Development.* Reading, MA: Addison-Wesley, 1969. [28]

Schein, E.H. *Organizational Psychology.* (3rd ed.) Englewood Cliffs, NJ: Prentice-Hall, 1978. [29]

Schein, E.H. "The Individual, the Organization, and the Career: A Conceptual Scheme." *Journal of Applied Behavioral Science* 7 (1971): 401-26. [30]

Schein, E.H. "How 'Career Anchors' Hold Executives to Their Career Paths." *Personnel* 52, no. 3 (1975): 11-24. [31]

Schein, E.H. *Career Dynamics.* Reading, MA: Addison-Wesley, 1978. [32]

Sheehy, G. "Catch 30 and Other Predictable Crises of Growing Up Adult." *New York Magazine.* February 1974, pp. 30-44. [33]

Super, D.E., and Bohn, M.J. *Occupational Psychology.* Belmont, CA: Wadworth, 1970. [34]

Troll, L.E. *Early and Middle Adulthood.* Monterey, CA: Brooks-Cole, 1975. [35]

Van Maanen, J. "Breaking In: Socialization to Work." In *Handbook of Work. Organization, and Society,* edited by R. Dubin. Chicago: Rand McNally, 1976. [36]

Van Maanen, J.; Bailyn, L.; and Schein, E.H. "The Shape of Things to Come: A New Look at Organizational Careers." In *Perspectives on Behavior in Organizations,* edited by J.R. Hackman, E.E. Lawler, and L.W. Porter. New York: McGraw-Hill, 1977. [37]

Van Maanen, J., and Schein, E.H. "Improving the Quality of Work Life: Career Development." In *Improving Life at Work,* edited by J.R. Hackman and J.L. Suttle. Los Angeles: Goodyear, 1977. [38]

2

Career Concepts —
A New Approach
to Career Research

MICHAEL J. DRIVER

University of Southern California

In talking to people about research on careers a rather serious problem has become clear to me: few seem to agree what the topic of careers really means. To some a career is a carefully worked out plan for self-advancement; to others it is a calling—a life role; to others it is a voyage of self-discovery; and to still others it is life itself.

When speaking with career researchers one sometimes has that feeling of being among the famous, blind wise men having their interminable discussions of the equally famous, multifaceted elephant. Educators seem to think in terms of vocational testing and training, business schools in terms of career paths and strategies, and psychologists in terms of varied life crises.

The primary purpose of this paper is to offer a model of career definitions which may aid in giving this research domain an underlying frame of reference. The intent is to offer a first pass at a set of career definitions which may be found across varied people. It is suggested that career concepts, like other cognitive phenomena, are subject to important individual differences in critical dimensions. These conceptual system differences may provide both an organizing rubric for the field of research and a topic of research in its own right.

*The author thanks Dr. Dianne Y. Sundby for her helpful comments.

I would like to represent four basic types of career concept as working hypotheses. This approach began with only two types; it may well be that there are types of career concept other than these four, or that a better framework exists. My purpose is mainly to encourage mutual exploration of the issues raised by career concepts.

In outline form I would like to:

1. Present the basic defining traits of each concept.
2. Speculate on possible historical origins of each concept.
3. Relate career concepts to deeper personality characteristics.
4. Tie the frequency distribution of career concepts to relevant career research concepts.
5. Relate career concepts to some practical organizational issues.
6. Present a sample of some pilot career concept research.

BASIC CAREER CONCEPTS

A *career concept* will be defined here as the conceptual structure underlying a person's thinking concerning his or her career. It does not necessarily refer to the content of one's career concept (i.e., the field chosen). Specifically, the structural elements refer to the way in which one's ideas on career are organized. The critical structural elements for defining career concepts used here are:

1. Time of career choice
2. Permanence of choice
3. Direction of career change

Using these three elements, four basic career concept systems are outlined in Table 2-1.

Table 2-1   Key Elements in Career Concepts

Concept	Time of Choice	Permanence	Direction of Change
Steady State	Youth	For life	None
Transitory	Continuous	Yearly changes	Usually lateral
Linear	Youth	For life	Upward mobility
Spiral	Cyclical	Five-to-seven-year cycles	Lateral mobility (often to new fields)

The *Transitory* concept is one in which no set job or field is ever permanently chosen. A person with a Transitory career concept simply moves along from job to job with no particular pattern. Rarely is there any upward movement in the sense of higher status.

In contrast, the *Steady State* career concept is that one selects a job or field early in life and stays with it for life. There is no concept of movement except perhaps to higher income or professional skill.

The *Linear* career concept is one in which a field is chosen fairly early in life. A plan for upward movement within that field is developed and executed. This upward movement can be in an organizational hierarchy or within a relevant reference group, such as a professional association.

The *Spiral* career concept involves a view that one develops in a given field for a period of time; then one moves on to a related or perhaps a totally new area. Preliminary indicators suggest that this cyclic movement may often fall in five- to seven-year intervals.

There is no necessary connection between these structural patterns of career concept and one's chosen field. Yet certain fields may historically be associated with a particular type of concept structure. For instance, the Transitory concept may be more frequently found among semiskilled laborers or among actors. The Steady State concept may turn out to be very common among established professions (e.g., physicians) and among skilled trades (e.g., carpenters). One might find the Linear concept strongly represented among corporate managers or among professors. Finally, the Spiral concept may be predominant among consultants or writers.

Such fits of concept content and structure would be due to the social structure of these occupations and the most frequent socialization process for the occupation. Exceptions could, and probably do, exist. There are undoubtedly doctors who seek high office in the AMA, as well as actors who seek the Presidency. There are professors who become "professional teachers," usually at the Associate rank, as well as laborers who see their work as a craft. There are undoubtedly consultants who have simply stumbled on this work by chance, as well as managers who have previously had rich careers as scientists. One of the initial interests of career research would be to develop a description of the distribution of career concepts across vocational fields.

A final illustration of the basic career concept might be to try to link each concept with a well-known career. Such an effort at this time can only be quite tentative. For instance, the folk singer Woody Guthrie seems to epitomize for me the Transitory concept, with is constant movement and pursuit of immediate feelings.

F. Lee Bailey comes to mind as a classic example of the master craftsman, Steady State concept—who remains year after year in trial law yet keeps his skill at a high peak. Henry Kissinger probably illustrated the Linear concept quite well, with his carefully planned rise through academia to the State Department; although where he goes now is something of a dilemma since the Constitution precludes his becoming President Kissinger.

Finally, as an example of a Spiral career, I offer John Gardner. He has moved from head of a foundation, to HEW, to Common Cause in roughly five- to seven-year cycles, developing each task to a fine pitch, but always moving on to new territory.

ORIGINS OF CAREER CONCEPTS

Career concepts appear to be learned in relation to societal or cultural norms. In simpler societies class or location might dictate one's concept. In more complex societies the impact of unique family values and of education is clearly very important. In the United States the impact of higher education on career concepts may turn out to be a socially crucial issue.

Looking back in time, probably the earliest career concept was the Transitory. It would fit quite well into a simple hunter-gatherer type of society in which there were no fixed roles. An example of a society with this orientation might be the pre-Columbian Eskimo or Cree Indian. Transitory subsystems can emerge in non-Transitory societies, however. For instance, the lowest strata of Western cultures often show a generalized Transitory pattern.

Somewhat later in time the Steady State concept may have emerged. It would seem particularly appropriate to settled agricultural societies or more static urban populations with fixed roles. The Steady State type of society may have first emerged in neolithic villages and seems extremely prevalent in most strata of medieval Europe. In many more-traditional developing societies today, (e.g., Latin America) the Steady State concept may still be the cultural ideal. However, the Steady State concept can persist even in nonprofessional cultures, as, for instance, the role of aristocracy in today's Europe.

The Linear concept seems somewhat more recent. It would seem to fit in an expansionistic capitalist or industrial society. Upward social mobility would be essential. Perhaps classical Athens and republican Rome first exhibited societies dominated by Linear career concepts. It is quite likely that in Western culture the Linear concept took root and flourished increasingly as the eighteenth and nineteenth centuries unfolded. In some ways the United States seems mainly Linear, even at its inception. Nevertheless, many career support functions operate, even today, as though we had a Steady State career concept dominating (e.g., career guidance primarily in high school).

The Spiral concept seems to be a fairly recent phenomenon on a mass scale. During the Renaissance, occasional individuals with a Spiral pattern stand out, but only recently has Spiral career shifting on the mass scale been reported in the United States—this may represent a new departure. At issue is whether this trend will continue or reverse. Cultural impacts on career concepts may prove a most vital research area.

CAREER CONCEPTS AND PERSONALITY

A very important issue is whether career concepts are rooted in more basic personality patterns, or whether they are more superficial, conceptual structures, easily learned and easily shed as situations change. When we think of the dilemma of people with career concepts at odds with their culture or organization, this issue becomes very critical.

Although it is far too early to resolve this question, a few emerging studies (Driver, 1976; Olson, 1976) are pointing in the direction that at least some deeper personality traits are linked to career concepts. Table 2-2 summarizes current hypotheses relating career concepts to at least two personality dimensions—motives and cognitive styles.

Table 2-2   Relation of Career Concepts to Motivation and Cognitive Styles

Career Concept	Motives	Cognitive Styles
Transitory	Independence	Flexible
Steady State	Security	Decisive
Linear	Achievement	Hierarchic
Spiral	Growth	Integrative

The motives associated with each career concept may form an integral part of the concept. For instance, it may be precisely because of their search for independence, of fear of commitment, that persons using the Transitory concept keep moving on. However, these ideas remain, as yet, conjectural. For instance, the Transitory concept might turn out to be at least as tied to a need for variety as for independence.

The Steady State concept may very well be rooted in a basic need for security, for a clear-cut, recognized, and valued role in society. Yet in many cases a Steady State career concept may be built on a love of family or even a desire for money.

The Linear concept would seem to be very aptly matched with need for achievement as McClelland (1961) defined it: that is, as a strong desire to move up, to score according to established "rules of the game." One of the clearest ways to achieve is to climb a socially defined hierarchy or organizational pyramid. Yet again, perhaps a need for power or desire to help others lies behind some Linear career concepts.

The Spiral career concept, as based on some pilot evidence, does seem to be related to the growth need, in the sense developed by Maslow (1962): that is, as maximum development of all inner potential. Each new career cycle may be in service of a new potential being developed. But again, perhaps some Spiral career concepts are fueled by achievement or variety needs. A clear linking of motivation and career concept would seem of great importance in clarifying career patterns.[1]

Cognitive styles refer to habits of thought. The Decision Style variable cited in Table 2-2 is based on a model presented by Driver and Mock (1975). The basic assumption of this model is that people learn different habits of decision making. Specifically, two dimensions are involved:

1. Amount of information used in decisions.
2. Focus or number of alternatives developed for implementation.

[1] The importance of motives is underlined by Van Maanen and Schein (1977) in their discussion of career anchors.

Based on these two dimensions, four basic Decision Styles can be defined, as seen in Table 2-3. The Flexible style is one in which just enough data is used to arrive at an acceptable decision, but then the decision can be successively reconsidered as new bits of information come in. The Decisive style also uses just enough data for a workable decision, but once an alternative is selected, it is retained.

Table 2-3   Decision Style Model

		Amount of Information Used	
		Minimize	*Maximize*
Focus (N of Alternatives)	*Single*	Decisive	Hierarchic
	Multiple	Flexible	Integrative

The Hierarchic style uses as much information as possible to develop an elaborate, multitactic, optimal solution. Once set, the Hierarchic style finds changing objectives hard, changing tactics more palatable. The Integrative style uses a maximum of data but simultaneously generates a set of alternative plans, which might be implemented in parallel or successively.

Preliminary findings suggest that Decision Styles (which are fairly stable, especially in older persons) do relate to career concepts.

For instance, the Integrative style seems to be linked to the Spiral career concept (Driver, 1976). Spiral career concepts might then be further defined as involving very large data bases for career decisions (e.g., counselors, trial and error). They employ these data continuously to develop either successive or parallel careers.[2]

The Hierarchic style is also linked to a concept—the Linear concept (Driver, 1976). This implies that the Linear concept user employs maximum data (perhaps reading, courses, vocational testing) to arrive at a choice of field, and then develops an elaborate, long-range game plan to reach the top of the pyramid in that area.

The connection of the Decisive style and the Steady State concept remains purely hypothetical at present. However, it would make sense that a Decisive decision maker would use minimal data (i.e., role models, advice of authority) to make an occupational choice which is then adhered to indefinitely.

Similarly, the Flexible linkage with the Transitory concept remains to be proven. Yet it would be reasonable to see a Flexible decision maker using minimal data (i.e., targets of opportunity, word of mouth) to arrive at a readily changed job decision.

It would be most interesting to determine what other personality factors (e.g., energy, emotional patterns) may also relate to career concepts.

[2] The parallel career pattern may represent a fifth concept.

RELATION OF CAREER CONCEPTS
TO CAREER RESEARCH

One of the most basic research directions suggested by this model is to measure the frequency distribution of career concepts in a given culture or region. The priority of research topics in the career area would, in part, depend on the predominant career concept found in a region or society.

For instance, in a society dominated by Transitory concepts, research on lifetime vocational choice, in the manner of Ginzberg et al. (1951), would seem nonoptimal. A rather more pressing problem might be the problem of anomie or nonidentity as developed by Erikson (1968).

In a society dominated by Steady State concepts, theories of change over life stages (Erikson, 1968; Van Maanen and Schein, 1977) might seem of less use than the one-time-only career choice research that originally lay behind the development of the Strong Vocational Interest Blank (Strong, 1943).

Clearly, where the Linear concept dominates, the key research issue becomes the problems of a lifelong unfolding in an increasingly demanding series of jobs. Stages of development become extremely relevant; so do studies of crises brought about by blocked upward mobility (plateauing)[3] or overextension (the Peter Principle). Symptomatic of Linear careers are midlife crises and retirement crises.

In a society dominated by Spiral career concepts, crises of the type described above are not likely since lateral movements and redirections are a way of life. However, problems now emerge as to how to facilitate growth in a production-oriented economy, how to foster self-renewal (Gardner, 1964) in the face of economic pressures, and how to retain Spiral career concept people in non-Spiral organizations.

If, indeed, the United States is moving from Linear to Spiral career concept dominance, then research priorities may require very careful analysis.

CAREER CONCEPTS AND POLICY ISSUES

To illustrate the possible pragmatic value of career concepts, in guiding research and organizational policy, consider the following set of questions and hypothetical answers.

1. What is the direction of career concept patterns in the United States today?

    Hypothesis: We are strongly Linear but moving toward Spiral patterns (e.g., Tarnowiewski, 1973).

---

[3] A sixth career pattern may be a downward spiral associated with a failure in a previously Linear pattern.

2. What is the source of this Spiral trend?

    Hypothesis: University-level education spreading to more and more people (see Astin et al., 1975).

3. What is the dominant model of careers in most organizations?

    Hypothesis: Linear.

4. What happens when non-Linear people enter a Linear organization?

    Hypothesis: A small percentage change their concepts and fit in; a larger percentage are discouraged, demotivated (see Dunnette et al., 1973).

5. What is the result of this nonfit?

    Hypothesis: Some of the best (i.e., most creative) employees leave (Driver, 1976); turnover increases.

6. What can be done?
   a. Remodel education to fit industry.
   b. Tailor organizational job design, training and reward systems to varied career concepts: for example,
       (1) For Transitorys, put emphasis on freedom (low structure) and use job enlargement to provide variety.
       (2) For Steady Staters, use pay, tenure, and skill improvement.
       (3) For Linears, use opportunities for promotion, achievement, and management by objectives.
       (4) For Spirals, use growth experiences, participation, job enrichment, and furloughs.

There are many other critical organizational issues that might be better understood and resolved given a career concept analysis. It is hoped that the suggestions listed above will be viewed simply as examples.

A SAMPLE OF CAREER CONCEPT RESEARCH

As reported by Driver (1976), a sample of 25 engineers in an aerospace firm took a career questionnaire, as well as measures of decision style, motivation, preference for job enlargement, and productivity and satisfaction.

Only Spiral and Linear concepts were assessed. The Hierarchic and Decisive styles were linked to the Linear concept, whereas the Integrative and, to a much lesser degree, Flexible styles were Spiral. Spiral-oriented persons were far more growth-oriented than were Linear people, but contrary to expectation, achievement need was not stronger for Linear people.

The Spiral-Integrative persons were extremely satisfied and productive and willing to be more so given counseling and job enlargement. The Linear-Hierarchics were depressed yet productive. They did not want counseling or job enlargement. The Decisives (Steady State?) were happy but not very productive. They did not want job enlargement, but liked the idea of counseling. The Flexibles (Transitorys?)

were neither happy nor productive, but were willing to try counseling and job enlargement.

It is, at present, impossible to categorize the dominant career concept in this organization. Yet it seems clear that Transitorys fit least well, Spirals most. Remedial actions vary, as might be expected, from the relationships of career concept to training-reward systems discussed above.

In an as-yet-unreported study of an advertising agency, rather similar results emerged: Integratives were more Spiral, highly productive; yet in this organization they were not happy.

CONCLUSION

So far we have measured at least two career concepts and linked them with motives and decision styles. We find provocative differences among people of different concepts in satisfaction and productivity. These differences may be mediated by organizational career concepts.

It seems a promising start. Yet it seems clear that before going too far into data gathering we need more careful thinking about the parameters of career concepts and about the usefully optimum number of such concepts. Hopefully, this paper will serve to focus thinking on this area, yielding a richer conceptualization of career concepts, and perhaps even some new career directions.

REFERENCES

Astin, A., M. King, and G. Richardson. "The American Freshman." Los Angeles: Cooperative Institutional Research Program, UCLA, 1975.

Driver, M.J. "Career Revolution in Aerospace Engineers." Paper given at Annual Conference, Society of Allied Weight Engineers, Philadelphia, May 1976.

Driver, M.J., and T. Mock. "Information processing, decision style theory, and accounting information systems." *Accounting Review,* 1975, *50,* 490-508.

Dunnette, M., R. Arvey, and P. Banas. "Why do they leave?" *Personnel,* 1973, May-June, 25-29.

Erikson, E. *Didentity: Youth and Crisis.* New York: Norton, 1968.

Gardner, J. *Self-Renewal: The Individual and the Innovative Society.* New York: Harper & Row, 1964.

Ginzberg, E., S.W. Ginsberg, S. Axelrod, and J.L. Herman, *Occupational Choice: An Approach to a General Theory?* New York: Columbia University Press, 1951.

McClelland, D. *The Achieving Society.* Princeton, N.J.: D. Van Nostrand, 1961.

Maslow, A. *Toward a Psychology of Being.* Princeton, N.J.: D. Van Nostrand, 1962.

Olson, T. "A proposed model of individual renewal and its relation to need for achievement, self-concept discrepancy, growth need strength, and career development." Unpublished doctoral disserttion, University of Southern California, 1976.

Strong, E.K. *Vocational Interests of Men and Women.* Stanford, Calif.: Stanford University Press, 1943.

Tarnowiewski, D. *The Changing Success Ethic.* New York: AMACOM, 1973.

Van Maanen, J., and E. Schein. *"Career Development."* In J.R. Hackman and J.L. Suttle, eds., *Improving Life at Work.* Santa Monica, Calif.: Goodyear, 1977.

ISSUES
IN CAREER
II
ORIENTATIONS

3

Trained as Engineers: Issues for the Management of Technical Personnel in Midcareer

LOTTE BAILYN

Massachusetts Institute of Technology

The majority of engineers that I have worked with have become disillusioned men. They feel they are hired hands, not professionals. They feel the "demand" for engineers is highly inflated by employers who want a cheap pool of labor. When I left engineering, the main comment I heard from my fellow workers was: "I wish I had your guts."

So speaks a 41-year-old graduate of M.I.T. who left his engineering job to become a securities and insurance salesman. Although many others like him stay with engineering, the complaint is by no means unique. Some versions of the same theme are rather mild:

Being a moderately successful but not enterprising engineer, I have to confess to a slight boredom. [Electronics engineer, 40 years old]

Others are more vehement:

Engineering is a "bad" profession. There is no pattern to the advancement of a professional as there is in architecture, medicine, law, business, brokerage, education, etc. [Vice-president of engineering, 36 years old]

Some engineers blame their education:

> The concept of engineering as a *profession,* as was taught me at M.I.T., bears little relationship to engineering as an *occupation.* M.I.T. engineers are the best equipped in the world to solve technical problems. Unfortunately, the *successful* solutions of most problems faced by engineers cannot be obtained solely by the application of elegant technology. [Supervisor of new product development, 33 years old]

But although the lack of "real-world" experience is a frequent complaint about engineering education at the top schools, engineers are particularly bitter about the way companies misuse their technical personnel:

> What a shock it is to an engineer to discover that the man who has developed leadership talents and has the ability to communicate is more promotable than the one who is primarily technically oriented. Even those entering the research lab are faced with this fact. [Assistant vice-president, 42 years old]

> Supposedly my company has a dual ladder system for advancement, the technical and the managerial. I have been most attracted to, and have concentrated my efforts toward, the technical path. But now, technical contributions comparable to my own can be bought at a lower price from a recent engineering graduate. Presumably, my years of *technical* experience with the company have little or no economic value to them. [Senior development engineer, 42 years old]

Some send a warning to students:

> The student is entitled to know how engineers often work on "production lines," are asked to join unions, are lured into "specialization," are utilized as high-grade technicians who can read and write; they should know that most engineers work at productive jobs for only a few years until they become managers of others—and management skills are required in addition to technical skills. [Unemployed, 44 years old]

> Engineers should be warned to go quickly into management or else stay out of industry for their own and their family's sake. [Development engineer, 40 years old]

Others want to reorganize the profession:

> Engineers either have to become true professionals (as doctors or lawyers) or unionize. We need the equivalent of the American Medical Association on a national level and something like "bar exams" that lawyers experience. A surprisingly large number of the engineers I know wish they had gone into medical or dental professions! [Group leader/staff engineer, 37 years old]

What is the source of this discontent? How can one explain it, and is there something that can be done to alleviate it? These are questions that have begun to be asked by engineers themselves (e.g., Bolz, 1975; Dubin et al., 1974). They are addressed, also, in a study of the career paths of engineering graduates from M.I.T., based on data collected some ten to twenty years after their graduation. What follows is a digest of some of the major findings of this study, and a discussion of the implications of these findings for the management of technical personnel.[1]

THE STUDY

The study from which the quotations above are taken is based on questionnaires sent to the graduates of the M.I.T. classes of 1951, 1955, and 1959.[2] These questionnaires were designed to elicit information about career paths, about current work attitudes and values, and about self-perceptions along a number of dimensions. The material proved rich enough to allow an analysis not only of the general character of careers in engineering, but beyond that, of the issues involved in providing these engineers with ways to work more effectively and to derive greater satisfaction from their jobs.

An initial detailed analysis of the current occupations of the entire M.I.T. alumni sample revealed two basic career patterns: one that is engineering-based and a second that is more scientific/professional. The former represents 71% of the sample, and it is the data from that large portion of the group as a whole that provide the information for this paper.

The engineering-based career pattern of M.I.T. graduates is characterized by the following modal tendencies: (1) graduation from the M.I.T. School of Engineering; (2) grades *below* the honors level; (3) termination of education *below* the doctoral level; and (4) career entry through an initial job in an engineering staff position. The midcareer occupations of the respondents in this pattern—the various roles in which engineers may find themselves some ten to twenty years after their engineering training—are given in Table 3-1, together with the number and percentage of the total sample in each. As can be seen, the bulk of the group are still performing technical jobs as staff engineers or engineering managers, but a sizable number have moved into more business-oriented careers as consultants, managers, or entrepreneurs.

Like most M.I.T. graduates, the alumni trained as engineers are concerned with the intrinsic character of their jobs. They value work that gives them freedom to adopt their own approach to the problems they deal with—to be creative and original; they seek work from which they can get a personal sense of accomplishment, and work that is challenging. They do so *less*, however, than do their peers in the scientific/professional pattern. Compared to them, those trained as engineers are considerably more concerned with organizational values. They value more the

---

[1] The data and conclusions presented in this chapter are based on *Living with Technology: Issues at Mid-career* (Bailyn, 1980).

[2] Questionnaires were sent to all members of these classes in 1970. Responses were received from 1351, a response rate of 61%. Fifteen (of 22) women alumnae responded to the questionnaire. Their data are not included here and have been analyzed elsewhere (Bailyn, 1980).

Table 3-1   Engineering-based Career Pattern

Current Occupational Role[a]	N	Percent of Total Sample
Entrepreneur	82	6.1%
Consultant	60	4.4
General manager	50	3.7
Functional (nontechnical) manager	157	11.6
Engineering manager	232	17.2
Business staff	70	5.2
Staff engineer	306	22.6
Total	957	70.8%

[a]This classification is based not only on job title but considers also a brief description of function, precoded job descriptors, and other information in the questionnaire. Managers are distinguished from staff on the criterion of whether or not the job centers *primarily* on responsibility for and supervision of people, whereas group leaders and first-level supervisors are included in staff categories. General manager is used for those who clearly occupy a position above functional or technical management, and applies only if the position was attained through promotion rather than by founding a company or joining a family business. Functional management and business staff refer to any function other than a purely technical one. The classification is described in Bailyn (1980).

opportunity to contribute to the success of their organizations; they are more interested in exercising leadership and in having jobs that have the potential for high earnings and advancement (Bailyn, 1980).

There is a certain homogeneity, therefore, in the engineering part of the overall M.I.T. sample. These alumni share a common educational background and similar early career experiences, and the occupational roles they fill are associated with a common set of value norms. But this homogeneity disappears when one looks at the way these respondents actually feel about their work.

REACTIONS TO WORK
IN ENGINEERING-BASED CAREERS

As is evident in Table 3-2, the reactions to work vary widely, despite the homogeneity in background and values. Staff engineers are the most negative: they are not very involved with their work, are least satisfied with their jobs, and are least likely to perceive themselves as successful. They are most often joined in these negative reactions by the small group in business staff positions. Both groups represent employees of large corporations (almost half—45% and 44%, respectively—are employed by organizations with over 10,000 employees) in which their positions are relatively low in the organizational hierarchy.

In contrast, the alumni in occupational roles at the top of the table show a much more positive reaction to work. The most work-involved, the entrepreneurs, are also the most satisfied with their jobs. And although they are not the group with the very highest perceived success, nonetheless over half perceive themselves to be very successful. Not unexpectedly, they are involved primarily in organizations employ-

Table 3-2   Reactions to Work in Engineering-based Careers

Occupational Role	Mean Work Involvement score[a]	Percent very satisfied with their jobs[b]	Percent who perceive themselves as very successful[c]
Entrepreneur (N = 82)[d]	3.17	63%	52%
Consultant (N = 60)	3.07	44	58
General manager (N = 50)	3.09	42	78
Functional manager (N = 157)	3.07	26	34
Engineering manager (N = 232)	3.02	25	32
Business staff (N = 70)	2.77	14	29
Staff engineer (N = 306)	2.79	12	17
Total sample (N = 1351)	3.02	27%	34%

[a]Work Involvement represents an index empirically derived from an analysis of a large set of questions dealing with work. The derivation is described in detail in Bailyn (1980). In its final form the index is based on a number of items dealing with a person's basic commitment to and satisfaction derived from his work; on the relative satisfaction he derives from his career as compared to that derived from his family; and on the relatively low importance assigned to family needs when considering crucial characteristics of his job. All of these items were shown by a factor analysis to load on a single factor, and hence could meaningfully be combined into one index. The index was normalized to go from 1.0 (low) to 5.0 (high).

[b]Job satisfaction was determined by responses to a direct, general question to be answered on a five-point scale. The figures given represent the response "very satisfied" (a rating of 5).

[c]Based on two questions: (1) At this point in your professional life, how successful do you think you are in your work? and (2) How successful do you think you will be at the height of your career? The figures represent those who rated themselves as "very successful" (5 on a five-point scale) now, or who rated themselves as somewhat successful (4) now, but indicated that they expected to be "very successful" (5) at the height of their career.

[d]N's are reduced where necessary by no answers to a given item.

ing fewer than 100 people; almost one-fourth (24%) are in organizations with fewer than 10 employees. They are similar in this respect to the consultants, who also work primarily in small organizations and whose reactions to work are also quite positive.

It is the general managers, among the M.I.T. graduates, as indicated in Table 3-2, who perceive themselves to be most successful. They are quite involved with their work and are generally satisfied with their jobs. The size of the organizations in which they work varies. About one-fourth (28%) are in organizations under 100, and another one-fourth (26%) are in organizations with more than 2500 employees. The modal size, in which 34% work, is between 100 and 500 employees.

Finally, there is the group of alumni who at midcareer are functional and engineering managers. They are involved, although not overwhelmingly, with their work; they are fairly well satisfied with their jobs; and they see themselves as fairly successful. They, like the staff groups, tend to be employed in larger corporations: about one-third (34% and 35%, respectively) are in organizations with more than 10,000 employees; over one-half (54% and 56%, respectively) are in companies with more than 2500 employees. But their positions in these organizations, being clearly managerial, are quite a bit higher.

From this basic information it is clear that those in higher organizational positions are considerably more positive to their work than are those in the lower staff positions.[3] They seem, also, to view their careers in a very different light. As the top of Table 3-3 shows, those in high organizational positions are more likely to have high career aspirations and to care very much about success at work; those in lower positions are much more concerned with job security. These data indicate that despite homogeneity in background, differences in organizational position are associated with very different career and life orientations at midcareer. Indeed, as is evident in the bottom half of the table, the modal orientation of those with low organizational positions is not toward work at all but more toward other aspects of their lives: family, community, or avocational concerns.

The orientations identified in the bottom of Table 3-3 permit one to ask additional and more subtle questions about these careers. In particular, this information allows one to shift the analysis away from modal patterns and to consider the fit between organizational position and each of the identified orientations. Which orientations for which positions are most likely to be considered effective by organizations? How do position and orientation combine when looked at from the point of view of the employee: which combinations are most likely to be satisfactory? The answers to these more interesting questions are by no means obvious. It turns out that organizational rewards and job satisfaction do not always go together, and the divergences reveal much about the strains that engineers experience in different occupational roles.

CAREER ORIENTATIONS, ORGANIZATIONAL REWARDS, AND JOB SATISFACTION

An initial point in this analysis is to note the various degrees of effectiveness shown by employees with different orientations at both high and low organizational levels. Since the data at hand do not include any direct evaluations of performance, salary information, adjusted to make it comparable across different occupational and age groups, is used as an indirect indicator of effectiveness. The adjustment was made by dividing the sample into the basic occupational roles, each of which was further subdivided into three graduating classes, a division that controls for age. The distribution of total professional income was then normalized for each of the resulting groups. By this means it was possible to assign each respondent a score indicating the number of standard deviations he falls above or below the mean of his occupational/age group: 15% of the respondents who gave information on income fall at around the mean of this normalized distribution, 42% have incomes above the

---

[3]To make sure that position is critical and that size is not the only factor, engineering managers were compared with staff engineers on all three measures of reactions to work. Differences are highly significant: $p < .001$ in each case.

Table 3-3 Career Orientations in Engineering-based Careers by Organizational Position

	Organizational Position		Total Sample (%) (N = 1351)
	High (%) (N = 581)[a]	Low (%) (N = 376)	
Percent with high success aspirations[b]	36*	15*	29
Percent who consider job security important[c]	23*	52*	35
Of those with unambiguous orientations[d]	N = 302	N = 196	N = 727
Percent technical	22	27	36
Percent people-oriented	44**	19**	30
Percent nonwork-oriented	34***	54**	34

Note: *Significant difference between high and low with $p < .001$.
**Significant residuals in 3 × 2 table ($\chi^2 = 34.7$) with $p < .001$.
***Significant residual with $p < .01$.

[a]These N's are reduced where necessary by no answers to particular items.

[b]Represents those who possess "high aspirations for your career" to a great extent (highest on a five-point scale) *and* consider it very important (5 on a scale from 1 to 5) to be successful in their work.

[c]Represents those who consider job security (steady work) very (5 on a scale from 1 to 5) or somewhat (4) important.

[d]The exact derivation of these measures is available in Bailyn (1980). Generally, the low end of the index of work involvement is used to identify a nonwork orientation. A people orientation is gauged by each respondent's reply to a direct question about the importance placed on working with people. Indication of a technical orientation, finally, is indirect, based on items in the questionnaire that previous analysis had shown to be related to a technical orientation. Cutting points were determined to equalize as nearly as possible the overall distribution, as is indicated by the total sample column. This column also shows that respondents in the engineering-based career pattern are less technically oriented than are scientific/professional respondents. The N's are greatly reduced in this analysis because only unambiguous orientations are considered. Because of measurement issues, respondents equally high on more than one orientation, or not high on any, had to be excluded from the analysis.

average of their occupational/age group, and 43% are below average. Employees whose salaries are above the mean by this criterion are assumed to be the more effective employees.

Table 3-4 indicates that in high organizational positions, respondents who are oriented toward people are most highly rewarded, although those who are technically oriented are very close. In these high positions, it is those with a nonwork orientation who are considered least effective. Thus, at this level a definite work orientation, whether directed to technical or to human problems and issues, is seen as most effective.

The situation in low organizational positions is somewhat different. As might be expected, high relative incomes clearly go to those who are technically oriented: 63% of this group have above-average incomes. But a nonwork orientation here is *not* penalized as much as a people orientation: 43% of the nonwork-oriented have above-average incomes, whereas this is true for only 29% of those who are people-

Table 3-4   Organizational Evaluation of Employees
with Different Orientations in Different
Organizational Positions

	Percent with Above-average Income	
Orientation	*High Org. Position*	*Low Org. Position*
Technical	37% ($N = 59$)	63% ($N = 49$)
People	41% ($N = 123$)	29% ($N = 35$)
Nonwork	26% ($N = 95$)	43% ($N = 94$)

Note: The percentages in the table refer to the percentage of those in each cell who are considered effective. Thus, of the 59 people in high organizational positions who are technically oriented (and for whom salary information is available), 37% fall into the above-average income category. As a guide to the reader, a difference of about 15% (given these N's) is significant at the $p < .05$ level.

oriented. It is the people-oriented employees, therefore, who are seen as least effective at this level—at least as judged by relative income. It is clear, therefore, that the organizational evaluation of employees as reflected in relative income depends less on orientation per se than on the congruence of orientation and organizational position.

But what about the individual's point of view: which orientations provide the greatest job satisfaction? In general, those in the sample who are technically oriented are most satisfied with their jobs. These respondents also tend to be among the most highly rewarded. Their job satisfaction, therefore, may merely be a response to their above-average incomes. The analysis of job satisfaction requires, therefore, that relevant income be controlled. Table 3-5 presents these data.

In the left half of the table are the data for those in high organizational positions. Here one can see that independent of income, those who are technically oriented are the most satisfied with their jobs.[4] In one way this is not surprising for people trained as engineers. On the other hand, the positions in this part of the table are centered on the management of people, and the modal orientation in this group is toward people, which is the orientation that is also most highly rewarded. What, then, is the meaning of these positions for the technically oriented respondents? It would seem, consistent with other findings on engineers (e.g., Ritti, 1971; Thompson and Dalton, 1976), that high organizational positions are satisfactory to the technically oriented because they give them the power to be autonomous in their technical functioning. It is the *autonomy* of high organizational positions that seems to be important for this group, not the prestige or status associated with the management of people. It is perhaps an indictment of organizations that this kind of autonomy is often not available to technically oriented employees without the accompanying duties of a manager.

[4]This is true for every engineering-based occupational role except the general managers. Only in this group are the people-oriented alumni more satisfied than those whose orientation is technical.

Table 3-5   Job Satisfaction by Orientation and Organizational Position with Relative Income Controlled

| | Percent Very Satisfied with Their Jobs | | | |
| | High Org. Position | | Low Org. Position | |
Orientation	Above-Average Income	Below-Average Income	Above-Average Income	Below-Average Income
Technical	62% ($N = 21$)	54% ($N = 26$)	13% ($N = 31$)	31% ($N = 13$)
People	39% ($N = 51$)	24% ($N = 50$)	10% ($N = 10$)	11% ($N = 19$)
Nonwork	28% ($N = 25$)	16% ($N = 51$)	10% ($N = 40$)	9% ($N = 44$)

Note: The figures in the table indicate the percentage in each cell who are very satisfied with their jobs. Thus, of the 21 technically oriented people in high organizational positions whose salaries are above average, 62% are very satisfied with their jobs.

The other side of the same picture is evident from the right side of Table 3-5, which gives the data for the low organizational positions. It has previously been seen that technically oriented respondents in these positions are, on the whole, very positively evaluated by their organizations—at least as judged by their having above-average salaries. But these relatively well-paid technically oriented employees in staff positions are *not* particularly satisfied with their jobs. On the contrary, the satisfaction level of this subgroup is no higher than that of respondents in these positions with other orientations. In fact, it is only among the technically oriented who are *not* highly evaluated by their organizations (who have below-average incomes) that one finds a sizable group very satisfied with their jobs. This is not an insignificant group for organizations, since they probably do the bulk of the routine technical tasks. Their relatively high satisfaction with their jobs, therefore, is important. Much more problematic for organizational policy is the fact that the best technically oriented people in engineering-based staff roles—at least those most highly rewarded—show so little satisfaction with their jobs. Staff positions held by those trained as engineers tend *not* to meet the needs of the most competent of those whose orientation at midcareer is toward the technical aspects of their work. For despite the fact that most of the technically oriented people in these jobs are evaluated positively by their organizations, they are not satisfied with their positions. The ablest technically oriented employees must either switch to managerial roles or remain in jobs that do not provide them with enough autonomy for satisfactory expression of their technical competence.

These findings make clear that there is a significant lack of congruence among organizational rewards, career orientations, and job satisfaction in engineering-based positions at midcareer. The essential facts are the following: (1) In high organizational positions it is the technically oriented M.I.T. alumni who are most satisfied with their careers, despite the fact that an orientation toward people is more consistent with the requirements of these jobs and is the modal orientation. (2) In low organizational positions, job and work satisfaction are generally low, but the few people who do show higher satisfaction are not the ones one might expect. At that level it is the technically oriented people with *below*-average relative incomes who have the highest percentage of satisfaction. Clearly, jobs at this level are not meeting the needs of the ablest of those whose orientations continue to be primarily technical.

IMPLICATIONS FOR THE MANAGEMENT
OF TECHNICAL PERSONNEL

To perceive the implications of these findings for management strategies, one should note that at midcareer trained engineers find themselves in a variety of organizational positions, and have evolved over the course of their careers a number of different orientations. Some of these M.I.T. alumni are not primarily involved in their work at all, and those who are may either continue to be oriented to technical work or may shift their orientation toward people. These differences are important, and should not be equated with differences in effectiveness. Indeed, as Table 3-4 showed, there are employees of all orientations whose normalized incomes are above the means of their occupational/age groups. In the management of technical personnel in organizations, therefore, it is not enough to consider employees' abilities and potential. The basic orientations of their lives must also be taken into account. Each combination of ability and orientation—each overall configuration—can contribute to an organization in different ways, and each requires different organizational responses. This is more than simply saying that employees are not only units of ability but in a full sense, people, and that an understanding of the psychological imperatives that shape career patterns is as important in maximizing their potential services to an organization as an accurate measure of their skills. It is also to suggest managerial strategies that can deal with the problems in concrete human terms.

The key to this way of looking at the issues is the matrix that results from combining each of the three orientations discussed above with two levels of effectiveness and potential. It is presented in Table 3-6, which indicates, also, in shorthand form, some of the organizational roles particularly suitable for each combination. The discussion will proceed through the table cell by cell.

Cell 1.   In cell 1 are technically oriented employees who are viewed as high performers by their employing organizations. In it one would find independent contributors of various kinds, including the "idea innovators" and "internal entrepreneurs" identified by Thompson and Dalton (1976). It is this group for which the "dual ladder" was originally invented, although the application of the concept has usually been limited to a small number of R&D specialists, or wrongly applied to certain cell 4 employees—to managers who are no longer seen as making valuable contributions to the organization.

A critical problem for the management of employees in this cell is to find a way for them to participate in the decision making of the company, particularly on technical matters which concern them most. The data have indicated that a number of people in this cell move into management because they see this as the only way to

Table 3-6   Midcareer Organizational Roles

	Organizational Evaluation of Effectiveness	
	High	*Low ("ordinary")*
TECHNICAL	**Cell 1** Independent contributor Policy specialist "Idea innovator" "Internal entrepreneur"	**Cell 2** Technical support Expert on "formatted" tasks "Master"
PEOPLE	**Cell 3** Top management Sponsor Development as policy "Successful" manager	**Cell 4** Mentor Individual development functions "Effective" manager "Coach"
NONWORK	**Cell 5** Specialist Internal consultant "Variance sensor" "Scanner"	**Cell 6** Routine tasks Reduced time commitment

(Row group label on left margin: Orientation at Midcareer)

contribute to the policy decisions that affect them. Such a move is probably not an optimal solution for them, at least not in the long run. *Temporary* assignments of cell 1 people to cell 3, however, might be of use. Such a strategy would ensure the high-performing technically oriented employees a central role in the organization. It would also help them and the organization test the degree to which they are continuing to orient their activities to technical work.

In general, if this group is to be provided with satisfactory life-long careers, and if they continue to be technically oriented, organizations will have to develop reward systems that are congruent with this orientation. One might imagine, for example, more emphasis being placed on recognition for technical accomplishments, more sharing of patent rights, more encouragement of attendance at professional meetings, more use of sabbaticals and company-supported educational efforts—rewards that are specifically meaningful to technically oriented people.

Cell 2.   Cell 2 consists of those technically oriented employees who are perceived as average in ability or potential by their organizations. It is a group that includes the steady, solid contributors to the organization, the ones who do the bulk of the day-to-day technical work. It is here that one finds the midlife engineers who are still technically challenged by their work, even though they may not be technical contributors at the highest level. How to keep such individuals from losing the work motivation they have poses a real challenge to managers. The obvious response to this challenge, which lies in organizing work for the specific purpose of keeping it technically challenging and involving, runs against some accepted organizational procedures. Because many of the people in this cell may be technically less up to date than recent graduates of technical institutions, and because younger employees are less expensive, organizations tend to be biased toward assigning the new and interesting projects to the recent graduate rather than to the more experienced but less formally up-to-date employee. Although such a strategy may make short-run financial sense, it may create serious long-run problems in the management of the technical work force.

First, it is likely to reduce the work orientation of midcareer cell 2 employees and effectively move them from cell 2 into cell 6. Second, evidence from studies of newly hired technical employees shows that their school-based knowledge is not sufficient for effective performance in a business organization (Jacobson, 1977). They must learn to integrate this knowledge with the needs and circumstances of the particular organization in which they are employed, and this takes experience and maturity of judgment. It is the experienced cell 2 employee who could best provide help here, and thus an apprenticeship-master pairing of the young and "old" in this cell might well serve the needs of both. Finally, obsolescence itself may be alleviated by proper concern for work assignments. One study has shown, for instance, that lack of participation in job-related decisions is associated with obsolescence (Shearer and Steger, 1975). There is increasing evidence also that necessary technical updating will be achieved by midcareer engineers on their own, if they are given a challenging assignment that requires new knowledge or skills (Dalton and Thompson, 1971).

It seems, therefore, that by ignoring the needs and experience of midcareer employees in this cell, organizations are underutilizing them and may be creating a group of disaffected employees where none need exist.

Cell 3.   Cell 3 consists of people-oriented alumni who are considered to be particularly effective by the organization. It is the group in which one is likely to find the future top executives of the company.

The incentives of high income and promotion which are typically available in organizations seem to fit well the career needs of employees in cell 3. In fact, human resource planning, reward systems, and performance appraisals are typically designed with this group of employees in mind, so much so, in fact, that there is a danger that senior managers will concentrate unduly on them and see the employees in the other cells as not worthy of receiving much serious concern and imaginative attention. The argument here, in contrast, is that employees in all the cells contribute significantly to organizational success and must therefore be provided with meaningful organizational incentives and rewards.

Cell 4.   In this cell are the people-oriented employees who are not seen as likely to rise in the organization. These are either employees whose technical orientation was never very strong or who have become more people-oriented in midcareer. They do not, however, possess the specific talents necessary to progress into top managerial jobs. It is this group that is most likely to be described as "plateaued" or "dead wood." What should be seriously explored for this group are assignments that draw on their technical background and experience but which have an interpersonal component to them.

There is some evidence, for instance, that technical careers are enhanced by mentors (Thompson and Dalton, 1976) and that being a mentor is in some ways a satisfying midlife stance (Levinson et al., 1978). Such a relationship requires, on the part of the mentor, much greater personal involvement than is usually the case when a top executive sponsors the person seen as most likely to succeed to his or her own top job. Midlife employees in cell 4 would seem to be uniquely qualified to play these roles, particularly for those employees—the majority in a company—who are not moving to the top. Thus, cell 4 employees could be the "effective" rather than the "successful" managers (see Chapter 7) who are critically important for the development of organizations. Further, as Rhoades et al. (1978) have recently noted, the innovation process in organizations involves a multiplicity of technical and interpersonal roles, and cell 4 people might be particularly suited to the interpersonal function ("coach") of project management.

Recognition that all people in organizations need to be developed—not only those headed for the top—will create more roles suitable for cell 4. And when such employees are performing functions that are congruent with their orientations and recognized as important by their organizations, the sense of "failure" that today often accompanies positions in this cell is likely to disappear.

Cell 5.   Cell 5 is the organization's major lost resource. It consists of high-potential people who have lost their work orientation or who never had very high work motivation in the first place. Within this group there are both technical- and people-oriented individuals capable of significant managerial or technical contributions, but who, for one reason or another, are more involved with activities outside the organization, such as their families, their hobbies, or their community.

Almost by definition, these are the employees who are least likely to follow the "rules of the game." The rewards and incentives associated with traditional organizational career paths are not likely to be effective here, since these tend to be rigid and unresponsive to "deviant" needs. Organizations that do not want to lose the contribution of these capable people must be willing to be flexible on work demands and to negotiate special roles for them. One person in this cell, for example, might want to have a consultant arrangement with the company, working intensively at certain times on certain problems, and then withdraw for a while. For another, a temporary assignment to cell 3 might be possible if paired with a sabbatical. Bennis (1976) suggests a number of roles necessary in modern organizations ("variance sensor"; "scanner") which might well be filled by people in this cell because they are likely to have the necessary distance from the organization—to have an insider's outside perspective.

In general, the optimal utilization of cell 5 employees acknowledges their particular situation and priorities and thus requires innovative arrangements between the organization and the employee based on individual negotiation. It would seem to be especially worthwhile to give thought to this cell because it is likely that as the present "youth" generation gets to the middle years, one will find more and more people in it. Hence, the proper organizational response to the needs of these people may become increasingly important.

Cell 6.   In cell 6 are found average employees whose orientations are toward something other than their work. The typical managerial response to this group is that they must be "remotivated," which is to apply to them the cell 3 managerial stereotype that low levels of work involvement are bad and must be "fixed." But the fact that involvement is low does not automatically mean that work is poor. Indeed, many tasks in organizations are pretty routine and might be best handled by less involved employees. This might be a group, also, that would respond well to opportunities for part-time work, job sharing, or various other arrangements for time off (see, e.g., Cohen and Gadon, 1978). Managers must recognize that efforts to "motivate" cell 6 employees may fail, but that high levels of work involvement are not necessary, indeed may be dysfunctional, for all members of an organization.

It is important, moreover, to point out that if the other cells are handled properly, cell 6 is likely to be small. As already indicated, it is often organizational policies, not "bad" employees, that augment the size of this group. Organizations may respond to employees in cells 2 and 4 in such a way that their work orientation disappears; or they may not provide cell 5 employees with the conditions under which their potential can be expressed and thus effectively push them into cell 6. In other words, by not looking at the varying orientations of midcareer people, and by not dealing as intelligently with the many employees of ordinary effectiveness as with their most able personnel, organizations unnecessarily increase the size of this problematic cell.

What can one conclude about engineering-based careers? Most important is the finding that despite common educational backgrounds, despite similar early career interests and experiences, and even despite consensus on job values, orientations at midcareer take a number of quite different forms. Indeed, some trained engineers in midcareer concentrate their lives outside work altogether. The successful management of technical careers, therefore, requires an appreciation of the whole range of possible orientations. It also requires an accurate assessment of each employee's capacities: an assessment in which both the employee and the employing organization must concur. But most important, the variations in orientation and in ability necessitate flexible personnel policies and multiple organizational roles. Only if these exist can organizations maximize the contribution of their technical personnel and provide them with satisfactory life-long careers.

REFERENCES

Bailyn, L. (in collaboration with E.H. Schein). *Living with Technology: Issues at Mid-career.* Cambridge, Mass.: M.I.T. Press, 1980.

Bennis, W. *The Unconscious Conspiracy: Why Leaders Can't Lead.* New York: AMACOM, 1976.

Boltz, R.W., ed. *The E/E at Midcareer—Prospects and Problems.* New York: Institute of Electrical and Electronics Engineers, Inc., 1975.

Cohen. A.R., and Gadon, H. *Alternative Work Schedules: Integrating Individual and Organizational Needs.* Reading, Mass.: Addison-Wesley, 1978.

Dalton, D.W., and Thompson, P.H. Accelerating obsolescence of older engineers. *Harvard Business Review,* September-October, 1971, 57-67.

Dubin, S.S., Shelton, H., and McConnell, J., eds. *Maintaining Professional and Technical Competence of the Older Engineer—Engineering and Psychological Aspects.* Washington, D.C.: American Society for Engineering Education, 1974.

Jacobson, R.C. The socialization of technology trained college hires in a computer company. Unpublished Master's thesis, M.I.T. Sloan School of Management, 1977.

Levinson, D.J., et al. *The Seasons of a Man's Life.* New York: Knopf, 1978.

Rhoades, R.G., Roberts, E.B., and Fusfeld, A.R. A correlation of R&D laboratory performance with critical functions analysis. *R&D Management,* 1978, *9,* 13-17.

Ritti, R. *The Engineer in the Industrial Corporation.* New York: Columbia University Press, 1971.

Shearer, R.L., and Steger, J.A. Manpower obsolescence: a new definition and empirical investigation of personal variables. *Academy of Management Journal,* 1975, *18,* 263-75.

Thompson, P.H., and Dalton, G.W. Are R&D organizations obsolete? *Harvard Business Review,* November-December, 1976, 105-16.

4

The Career Orientations of MBA Alumni: A Multidimensional Model

THOMAS J. DELONG

Brigham Young University

Over the past decade or so, there has been an influx of information appearing in books, guides, journals, and monographs concerning careers and career development (e.g., Gould, 1978; Levinson et al., 1974; Schein, 1978; Sheehy, 1976). In developing his concept of career anchor, Schein (1978) emphasized the need to create a model that would describe an individual's career development and would also reflect how values either determine or become determined by career experiences. Furthermore, Schein (1978) pointed out that one's own self-perceived talents lie at the foundation of one's career anchor. In one of the few studies of values applicable to this "career anchor" model, Scott (1965) concluded that values were extremely influential since people related them to certain life experiences.[1]

The current surge in career development literature emphasizes that individuals experience midlife crises. More and more individuals are changing employment in "midstream." Perhaps these crises and job changes are related to individuals

---

[1] A number of researchers (Bailyn and Schein, 1976; Bischof, 1976; Kalish, 1975; Kimnel, 1974; Troll, 1975) studied the relationship between values and career development and concluded that values significantly affect one's career decisions.

50

attempting to make career decisions that are inconsistent with their career orientations or values. Perhaps the midlife crisis is experienced because individuals perceive their career orientations to be in one specific area, whereas the organization has very different perceptions and expectations of the individual. Individuals as well as organizations need more insights into why individuals make the career decisions they do.

The career anchor model appears to have the potential to serve as a useful information base for either individuals contemplating a career change or for organizations seeking to aid managers in career planning. Although the career anchor model appears to be logical and potentially useful, the model is still evolving and needs to be carefully scrutinized before its validity can be determined. For this reason, this study was designed to evaluate part of Schein's model on career development.

CAREER ANCHORS

Schein asserts that certain motivational/talent/value self-images, formed through work experience, function to guide and constrain the entire career.[2] These basic self-images act, in effect, as "career anchors" that not only influence career choices but also affect decisions to move from one employer to another, shape what individuals are looking for in life, and color their views of the future. Schein suggested that although we continue throughout life to gain valuable data about ourselves in regard to our behavior, the first three to five years of work experience are particularly important for our career development and provide the groundwork for future career decisions.

Schein's career anchor model, however, is defined in broader terms than job values or needs. It emphasizes evolution, development, and discovery through actual work experience. It further emphasizes the importance of feedback to discover one's talents. The model also differs from McClelland's theory of motivation in that McClelland primarily focused on a person's motives and did not include elements such as talents and values (McClelland and Steele, 1973a, 1973b). More specifically, the concept of a career anchor tries to focus not only on what the person wants or thinks is important, but also on what the individual feels he or she "is good at."

The early career can be viewed as a time for mutual discovery between the new employee and the organization: how one fits into the organization, contributes to the organization, meets one's needs through the organization, and interacts and receives feedback from the organization. As a new employee gathers more informa-

---

[2] The career anchor model is not unique in its use of the developmental approach to career development. Ginzberg and his associates (1951), Super and Bohn (1970), and more recently, Gould (1978) and Thompson et al. (1977), have all taken a developmental approach to discussing career-related issues. More recently, Hall (1976), Driver (1976), and Van Maanen and Schein (1977) have emphasized the need for the organization as well as the individual to focus on the total life situation (i.e., the integration of self-development as well as family, career, and organization development).

tion about oneself, an occupational self-concept develops. This occupational self-concept has three components according to Schein (1978, p. 125):

1. Self-perceived talents and abilities (based on actual successes in a variety of work settings).
2. Self-perceived motives and needs (based on opportunities for self-tests and self-diagnosis in real situations and on feedback from others).
3. Self-perceived attitudes and values (based on actual encounters between self and the norms and values of the employing organization and work settings).

The career anchor concept emphasizes that until one has encountered a number of real-life situations, motives and values will interact with each other to fit the career options available. An individual may join an organization only to find that the security he or she thought "came with the job" is in fact nonexistent. Career anchors are intended to identify a growing area of stability within the person. It may well be that career anchors are the source of stability that permits growth and change in other areas. It should be recognized that the concept is designed to explain that part of your life which grows more stable as increased self-insight based on more life experiences is developed.

The concept of career anchors emerged directly from a longitudinal study of a representative group of 44 M.I.T. Management School male graduates who completed their graduate work in the early 1960s. The respondents in the study all returned to M.I.T. ten to twelve years later for in-depth individual interviews for the purpose of gathering comprehensive career histories.

Specifically, the 1974 interviews focused on the actual job history of each person and the reason for the choices or decisions that the graduate had made. When Schein examined the stated reasons for the decisions, there emerged in almost all cases a clear pattern of responses. The actual job histories of the 44 alumni differed, but the consistency in the reasons given for career decisions was great. The greater the job experiences, the more clear cut and articulate the alumni were in describing their career history.

Five career anchors emerged from the interviews:

Anchor 1   *Security*—Individuals with security as their anchor have tied their careers to a particular organization. The implications are that individuals who are security-oriented will accept, to a greater degree than the other career anchor types, an organizational definition of their careers. The security-anchored individuals would look for an organization that provided long-run stability, good benefits, and basic job security. The organization man as defined by Whyte (1956) would typify people who are security-oriented, because in order to remain in the organization, individuals must socialize themselves to its value and norms.

Anchor 2   *Technical/functional competence*—Technical/functional people
are motivated by the challenge of the actual work they do
(e.g., financial analysis, marketing, systems analysis, corporate
planning). Their anchor is the technical field, functional
area, or content of their work, not the managerial process
itself. The self-image of individuals in the technical/functional
competence group is tied up with their feelings of competence
in the particular area they are in.

Anchor 3   *Managerial competence*—The fundamental basis for the
managerial competence anchor is to be competent in the complex activities that comprise the idea of "management."
Managerial competence-oriented individuals perceive that
their competencies lie in the ability to analyze problems and
to remain emotionally stable and interpersonally competent.
Their career experiences would enable them to develop the
self-image that they had the skills and values necessary to rise
to general management levels.

Anchor 4   *Creativity*—Creative-anchored individuals have a need to create
something on their own. Creating is the fundamental need
operating, for example, in the entrepreneur. Creative-oriented
individuals keep getting into new ventures and trying their
hand at new kinds of projects. They are also very central and
visible while working on projects.

Anchor 5   *Autonomy*—The autonomy anchor encompasses those who
have found organizational life to be restrictive, irrational, and/
or intrusive into their lives. They are primarily concerned
about their own sense of freedom and autonomy. Autonomy-
oriented individuals are seeking work situations in which
they will be maximally free of constraint to pursue their professional or technical/functional competence.

Although other career anchors may exist, Schein has not been able to uncover them
in his research to date. Other plausible but perhaps less common career anchors that
might influence an individual's career development might be:

1. *Identity:* Individuals who are guided throughout their careers by the
    status and prestige of belonging to certain companies or organizations
    are identity-oriented. They want to be identified with a powerful or
    prestigious employer.
2. *Service:* Individuals who are service-oriented are concerned with seeing
    people change because of their efforts. They want to use their inter-
    personal and helping skills in the service of others.
3. *Variety:* Individuals who desire a large number of different types of
    challenges are variety-oriented. They want careers that provide a maxi-
    mum variety of assignments and work projects.

The following section of this paper describes the development of a self-report
instrument for measuring and analyzing career anchors.

METHOD

The population for this study was 1224 males who graduated between the years 1963 and 1973 from the School of Industrial Administration at Purdue University. From the 1224 alumni, an initial sample of 600 was randomly identified by going through an alphabetical listing of the alumni and selecting every other graduate from the list. Of the 600 questionnaires delivered, 320 were completed and returned (55% response rate). Thirty-nine states are represented in the sample.

Questionnaire Development

The questionnaire was originally designed through an iterative process by Schein and DeLong. The questionnaire used four-point Likert-type scale items to attempt to measure the five career anchors (security, technical/functional competence, managerial competence, creativity, and autonomy) and three other possible career drives (identity, service, and variety). Six items were created to collect data on each of the eight career variables. Sample items for each of the eight career variables are listed below:

1. *Managerial competence:* To rise to a position of management is important to me.
2. *Technical/functional expertise:* I will accept a management position only if it is in my area of expertise.
3. *Security:* Remaining in my present geographical location rather than moving because of a promotion is important to me.
4. *Autonomy:* A career that is free from organization restriction is important to me.
5. *Creativity:* The use of my skills in building a new business enterprise is important to me.
6. *Identity:* I want others to identify me by my organization and my job title.
7. *Variety:* I have been motivated throughout my career by using my talents in a variety of different areas of work.
8. *Service:* I have always sought a career in which I could be of service to others.

Three of the six items for each variable were written to assess the degree to which the conditions described in the statement were *important* to the respondents. The response "1" indicated "of no importance" and "4" indicated "centrally important."

The other three items for each variable were written to assess to what extent the conditions described in the statement were *true* for the respondents. In this case, the response "1" signified "not true" and "4" signified "completely true."

The items were assembled in two separate 24-item subinstruments according to the different response formats. The order of the anchor items in each section was determined on a random basis.

To estimate the reliability of the a priori dimensions within the questionnaire, a follow-up questionnaire was mailed to 100 randomly selected respondents from the 320 who completed the original questionnaire. The follow-up questionnaire contained all 48 career items from the first questionnaire, but excluded demographic data. Seventy-three of the 100 follow-up questionnaires were returned. Eight reliability coefficients were calculated, one for each career drive variable under study. A composite score for the career drive variables was computed by averaging the six items for each of the eight career variables for both the original and follow-up questionnaires. Pearson product-moment correlation coefficients were computed between the original and the follow-up scores. Table 4-1 shows the test-retest reliability coefficients.

Table 4-1   Reliability coefficients computed between subscale totals for the original questionnaire and follow-up questionnaire[a]

Career Variables	Test-Retest Reliability Coefficients
Technical competence	.71
Autonomy	.83
Service	.74
Identity	.74
Variety	.83
Managerial competence	.91
Security	.84
Creativity	.83

[a]$N = 73$.

Data Analysis

Two factor analyses were run. The first factor-analytic approach was employed as an internal validity check to determine whether the six items on the questionnaire measuring each career variable would cluster together from the full 48 $\times$ 48 correlation matrix. Since correlations between variables were of concern, R factoring was selected for the first factor analytic approach. In checking the internal validity of the instrument, the factor analysis produced nine factors. The nine factors reflect the eight original variables except that the security scale broke down into two separate scales.

Below are lists of each factor and the statements that clustered under each scale. Also included after each statement is the name of the career variable the statement attempted to describe and the factor loading for each statement.

Factor 1: *Technical competence*

1. Becoming highly specialized and highly competent in some specific functional or technical area is important to me. (Technical competence = .53)
2. Remaining in my specialized area as opposed to being promoted out of my area of expertise is important to me. (Technical competence = .67)
3. Remaining in my area of expertise rather than being promoted into general management is important to me. (Technical competence = .69)
4. I will accept a management position only if it is in my area of expertise. (Technical competence = .76)
5. My main concern in life is to be competent in my area of expertise. (Technical competence = .42)
6. I see myself more as a generalist as opposed to being committed to one specific area of expertise. (Managerial competence = −.45)
7. I would leave my company rather than be promoted out of my expertise. (Technical competence = .79)

Factor 2: *Autonomy*

1. The chance to pursue my own life-style and not be constrained by the rules of an organization is important to me. (Autonomy = .79)
2. A career that is free from organization restriction is important to me. (Autonomy = .75)
3. An endless variety of challenges in my career is important to me. (Variety = .60)
4. A career that permits a maximum of freedom and autonomy to choose my own work, hours, etc., is important to me. (Autonomy = .71)
5. I find life in most organizations to be restrictive and intrusive. (Autonomy = .45)
6. During my career I have been mainly concerned with my own sense of freedom and autonomy. (Autonomy = .73)
7. I do not want to be constrained by either an organization or the business world. (Autonomy = .74)

Factor 3: *Service*

1. The use of my interpersonal and helping skills in the service of others is important to me. (Service = .74)
2. The process of seeing others change because of my efforts is important to me. (Service = .54)
3. Being able to use my skills and talents in the service of an important cause is important to me. (Service = .57)
4. I have always sought a career in which I could be of service to others. (Service = .80)
5. I have sought a career that allows me to meet my basic needs through helping others. (Service = .81)
6. I like to see others change because of my efforts. (Service = .50)

Factor 4: *Identity*

1. Being identified with a powerful or prestigious employer is important to me. (Identity = .60)
2. To be recognized by my title and status is important to me. (Identity = .70)
3. I like to be identified with a particular organization and the prestige that accompanies that organization. (Identity = .70)
4. It is important for me to be identified by my occupation. (Identity = .63)
5. I want others to identify me by my organization and my job title. (Identity = .77)

Factor 5: *Variety*

1. A career that gives me a great deal of flexibility is important to me. (Variety = .60)
2. A career that provides a maximum variety of types of assignments and work projects is important to me. (Variety = .72)
3. The excitement of participating in many areas of work has been the underlying motivation behind my career. (Variety = .67)
4. An endless variety of challenges is what I really want from my career. (Variety = .74)
5. I have been motivated throughout my career by using my talents in a variety of different areas of work. (Variety = .70)

Factor 6: *Managerial Competence*

1. The process of supervising, influencing, leading, and controlling people at all levels is important to me. (Managerial competence = .74)
2. To be in a position of leadership and influence is important to me. (Managerial competence = .76)
3. To rise to a position in general management is important to me. (Managerial competence = .65)
4. I would like to reach a level of responsibility in an organization where my decisions really made a difference. (Managerial competence = .58)
5. I want to achieve a position that gives me the opportunity to combine analytical competence with supervision of people. (Managerial competence = .46)

Factor 7: *Security*

1. An organization that will provide security through guaranteed work, benefits, a good retirement, etc., is important to me. (Security = .82)
2. An organization that will give me long-run stability is important to me. (Security = .78)
3. I am willing to sacrifice some of my autonomy to stabilize my total life situation. (Security = .60)

Factor 8: *Security*

1. Remaining in my present geographical location rather than moving because of a promotion is important to me. (Security = .92)
2. It is important for me to remain in my present geographical location rather than move because of a promotion or new job assignment. (Security = .87)

Factor 9: *Creativity*

1. To be able to create or build something that is entirely my own product or idea is important to me. (Creativity = .64)
2. The use of my skills in building a new business enterprise is important to me. (Creativity = .54)
3. I have been motivated throughout my career by the number of products that I have been directly involved in creating. (Creativity = .65)
4. I would like to accumulate a personal fortune to prove to myself and others that I am competent. (Creativity = .38)

Of the 48 original statements describing the eight career variables, four statements did not cluster under any of the nine factors and have been discarded. More interestingly, under factor 1, six of the seven highest factor loadings were observed for items describing the career anchor "technical competence." In factor 2, five of the six highest coefficients were for "autonomy" items. Factor 3 had five of the six "service" items factoring together. Factor 4 indicated that five of the six "identity" items also factored together. The fifth factor correlated highly with five of the six "variety" items.

Factor 6 clustered around five of the six "managerial competence" items. Factors 7 and 8 both focused on the "security" anchor. Factor 7 had high coefficients corresponding to three items emphasizing job stability, benefits, and good retirement. Factor 8, on the other hand, clustered around the two items that focused on remaining in a certain geographical location as opposed to moving one's employment location. Factor 9 was comprised of four questions describing the career variable "creativity."

Although this factor analysis distinguished nine separate factors from the data, many of the original items from different factors were strongly intercorrelated. In addition, many of the latter factors were not accounting for reasonable amounts of additional variance from the original 48 X 48 correlation matrix. Thus, the factor analysis may have confirmed a conceptual distinction across nine factors, but empirically speaking, a more parsimonious model was required—at least based on our data collection instrument.

Toward this end, a second factor analysis was run to summarize the data. Items forming each of the eight factors were averaged (the two security factors were combined) and were subsequently factor-analyzed to yield Table 4-2.

Table 4-2 Breakdown of eight career variables into three major factors.

Career Variable	Factor 1	Factor 2	Factor 3
Technical competence	−.57	.33	.51
Autonomy	−.17	.84[a]	−.17
Service	.30	−.15	.57[a]
Identity	.18	.07	.75[a]
Variety	.73[a]	.16	.04
Managerial competence	.82[a]	−.06	.16
Security	−.33	−.12	.60[a]
Creativity	.24	.87[a]	.07

[a]Indicates factor loading coefficients that clearly cluster together.

These findings from Table 4-2 show that the eight career variables included in the analysis could be clustered into three main career orientations. As shown, factor 1 is primarily a combination of the "variety" and "managerial competence" career variables. Factor 2, on the other hand, is defined primarily by the loading of the "autonomy" and "creativity" variables. Finally, factor 3 is made up primarily by the combination of "service," "identity," and "security."

These results suggest that seven of the eight career anchor and career drive variables might be represented more clearly by only three separate dimensions—at least in terms of our self-report questionnaire data. Finally, the career anchor variable "technical competence" had a reasonably high loading with both factors 1 and 3. Interestingly enough, technical competence seems to have a strong inverse relationship with an orientation that is based on the career anchors of managerial competence and variety.

DISCUSSION

The original purpose of this study was to evaluate whether the five career anchors defined by Schein were independent and inclusive. Alumni from a management school were examined to determine their career orientations five to fifteen years out of graduate school. Using Schein's model as a theoretical framework, data were collected through the development of an instrument to determine whether the data would cluster around Schein's five career anchors. The results indicate that a rather strong conceptual typology emerged derived from Schein's longitudinal study.

Using factor analysis, three main career factors emerged from the data. One factor focused on a managerial orientation with technical competence displaying a strong negative association. The second factor centered around autonomy and creativity as a central career theme, while the final factor organized itself around the three career variables of service, identity, and security.

It is worth noting that two very different approaches in evaluating the career anchor model produced two different outcomes. Schein's development of the career anchor model was based on interview data. With the exception of Schein's biographical form, Schein's subsequent studies were also based on interview data. This study was the first to evaluate the career anchor model taking more of an empirical approach.

One hypothesis for the two very different results is that the multidimensional nature of the career anchor constructs makes measurement of the constructs very difficult. It may be that the questionnaire developed for this study is an inadequate measure of the complex constructs under investigation. More specifically, the instrument used to collect data measured values and needs of the various respondents. The questionnaire did not collect data centered around the respondents' self-perceived talents. Schein (1978) suggests that the individual undergoes a number of experiences that define for both the individual and the organization the employee's area of talents. Through more and more job experiences, both individual and organization gain new insights about each other. As more and more information is collected, the more accurate the perceptions are for the career occupant as he or she relates these perceptions to career decisions. Thus, the instrument used in this study may be a rather accurate measure of career orientations and values rather than Schein's career anchor model. In any event, the statistical results do indicate that the questionnaire identifies rather accurately specific career dimensions. Both factor analyses were surprisingly significant in factoring around a rather strong typology defining career orientations.

In regard to the three main career factors identified in this study, the high factor loading of the coefficients for "autonomy" and "creativity" under one factor, from a logical standpoint, was not surprising. Creative-oriented individuals, according to Schein, keep getting into new ventures and trying their hand at new kinds of projects.[3] Autonomy-oriented individuals are concerned with their own sense of freedom.

Both the autonomy- and creativity-anchored individuals may seek more individual freedom within and/or outside an organization than individuals oriented toward the other three career anchor variables.

It also seemed logical that "identity" (identifying with an organization or employer) and "security" (concerned about geographical location, benefits and long-term stability) would factor together because of an underlying assumption in both variables of an acceptance for organizational norms and values. However, both factor analyses hint at a strong separation in the definition of the career anchor security. In the first factor analysis, statements that defined security in relation to long-term stability factored under factor 7. Factor 8 had correlation coefficients that correlated with the "security" statements, focusing on geographical location as a dimension of security.

---

[3] It is also worth noting that throughout the creation of the instrument, creativity was the most difficult career variable for which to create descriptive statements.

The second factor analysis indicated that security had a relatively high inverse relationship (−.33) to managerial competence and variety. Security as a career variable clearly factored under factor 3 (.60). There is some indication that the statements describing geographical location as a part of security cluster closely with the statements describing technical competence.[4] Perhaps those with high scores in technical competence and security (committed to a geographical location) are unwilling to move and give up a certain geographical location, and also face the possibility of giving up technical competence for a promotion into general management.

One of the more revealing results from the final factor analysis is factor 1. Before the factor analysis was run, the investigator assumed that variety would cluster with creativity and autonomy. However, variety closely clustered with managerial competence.

Perhaps those who are interested in attaining an M.B.A. degree are actually pulled toward general management because management provides for job variety. Not only must the manager confront technical, financial, human, and analytical skills in integrating organizational needs, but the manager needs to manage a variety of skills.

The statistical results also indicate that one who indicates a high degree of interest in "managing" may give up his or her technical expertise. Not only must the person give up his or her technical expertise but the security of geographical location that may accompany technical competence. More specifically, on one end of a continuum there may be a technical orientation, while on the other end of the continuum there may be a managerial orientation.

As more and more literature focuses on various life-stage crises, perhaps one reason for a crises is that an individual is unwilling to make a decision along the managerial/technical dimension. The midlife crisis may be experienced because someone may perceive that his or her career orientation is managerially oriented and the organization perceives otherwise.

Hall and Thomas (1979) concluded that organizations need to begin to plan changes during the life span of not only an individual but of a particular program of development. Hall and Thomas also concluded that there is a high correlation between the program manager's career anchor and the phase or phases of a program in which the manager is most effective. Based on their research, Hall and Thomas suggest that individual career orientations be identified to enhance the productivity of both the individual and the organization. Frustration may exist whenever an improper match between an individual's career orientation and a particular phase of a program becomes apparent. It seems logical to assume that a mix of managers within an organization can bring about more long-term productivity and more human satisfaction between individual and organizational needs.

---

[4] Based on analyses from a separate factor analysis, the statements describing security in relation to "benefits" clearly factored with identity and service, whereas the statements describing security in relation to "geographical location" factored closely with technical competence.

Both individuals and organizations need greater insights into career orientations. This study may give additional information to organizations and whether the organizations' expectations fit the individuals' career needs.

The individual who experiences organizational pressures to accept a promotion yet wants to remain in his or her specialty may find the managerial/technical continuum useful in understanding his or her own career decisions.

The typology plays a more significant role as organizations begin to focus on human resources planning and development. Neither individual satisfaction nor organizational effectiveness can be achieved if a strategy does not exist to meet these needs. An organization that focuses on human resource planning must not only be concerned with organization effectiveness, but also with individual effectiveness (Schein, 1978).

In relation to career planning, Schein suggests the following:

> The dynamics of the matching process between individual and organization cannot be managed without more knowledge about: (a) individual life cycles and how self-, career, and family development interact throughout those cycles; (b) the nature of organizational career dynamics, career paths, career stages, and other aspects of how organizations recruit, utilize, and manage their human resources; (c) the reciprocal interaction of individual and organization, the process of organizational socialization, and the process of individual innovation. [P. 244]

One phase of individual innovation is understanding models of career development. The dynamics of finding one's career orientation and finding a sufficient range of job challenges to determine one's orientation is crucial. Without insight into one's own career orientation, the problems of mid and late career are much more likely to be severe. If human resource planning is to be viewed as a total system approach, both the organization and individual must be involved in the planning, implementation, and evaluation of the ongoing system.

Those involved with human resource planning may also want to know more about midlife and career orientations. Training and development functions within organizations need relevant models to guide and encourage their employees to make the time of career decision making a productive time for both the organization and the individual. This current study can be a means of determining career values and orientations. Since the organization is a complex system, one must consider how each subsystem can be managed toward optimum effectiveness. Greater understanding of the human element is only one facet of the organizational system, yet a most crucial one (DeLong, 1977). Schein's career anchor model and the rather new typology of career orientations (managerial/technical, autonomy and creativity, and security, identity, service) may add some structure in understanding that human component.

REFERENCES

Bailyn, L., and Schein, E.H. "Life/career considerations as indicators of quality of employment." In A.A. Biderman and T.F. Drury, eds., *Measuring Work Quality for Social Reporting*. New York: Sage Publications, 1976.

Bischof, L. *Adult Psychology*. New York: Harper & Row, 1976.

DeLong, T.J. "What do middle managers really want from firstline supervisors?" *Supervisory Management* (AMACOM), September 1977, *22,* no. 9.

Driver, M. "The career revolution in aerospace engineering." Unpublished paper delivered at Annual Conference of Allied Weight Engineers, Philadelphia, 1976.

Ginsberg, E., Ginsburg, S., Axelrad, S., and Herma, J. *Occupational Choice: An Approach to a General Theory*. New York: Columbia University Press, 1951.

Gould, R. *Transformations*. New York: Simon and Schuster, 1978.

Hall, D.T. *Careers in Organizations*. Pacific Palisades, Calif.: Goodyear Publishing Co., 1976.

Hall, G., and Thomas, F.J. "The impact of career anchors on the organizational development of program managers in the aerospace industry." Unpublished Master's thesis, Sloan School of Management, M.I.T., 1979.

Kalish, R.A. *Late Adulthood: Perspectives on Aging*. Monterey, Calif.: Brooks-Cole, 1975.

Kimnel, D.C. *Adulthood and Aging: An Introductory Development View*. New York: Wiley, 1974.

Levinson, D.J., Darrow, C.M., Klein, E.B., Levinson, M.H., and McKee, B. "The psycho-social development of men in early adulthood and the mid-life transition." In D.F. Ricks, A. Thomas, and M. Roof, eds., *Life History Research in Psychopathology,* Vol. 3. Minneapolis, Minn.: University of Minnesota Press, 1974.

McClelland, D.C., and Steele, R.S. "Defining motivation and growth motivation." In *Human Motivation: A Book of Readings*. Morristown, N.J.: General Learning Press, 1973a, pp. 233-48.

McClelland, D.C., and Steele, R.S. "Two faces of power." In *Human Motivation: A Book of Readings*. Morristown, N.J.: General Learning Press, 1973b, pp. 300-315.

Schein, E.H. *Career-Dynamics: Matching Individual and Organizational Needs*. Reading, Mass.: Addison-Wesley, 1978.

Scott, W.A. *Values in Organizations*. New York: Rand McNally, 1965.

Sheehy, G. *Passages*. New York: McGraw-Hill, 1976.

Super, D.E., and Bohn, M.J. *Occupational Psychology.* Belmont, Calif.: Wadsworth, 1970.

Thompson, P.H., Dalton, G.W., and Price, R. "Career stages: a model of professional careers in organization." *Organizational Dynamics,* Summer 1977.

Troll, L.E. *Early and Middle Adulthood.* Monterey, Calif.: Brooks-Cole, 1975.

Van Maanen, J., and Schein, E.H. "Career development." In J.R. Hackman and J.L. Suttle, eds., *Improving Life at Work.* Santa Monica, Calif.: Goodyear Publishing Co., 1977.

Whyte, W.H. *The Organization Man.* New York: Simon and Schuster, 1956.

Winer, B.J. *Statistical Principles in Experimental Design.* New York: McGraw-Hill, 1971.

5

Career Switching and Organizational Politics: The Case of Naval Officers

University of Utah

There exist multiple conceptual definitions of the term "career." Some classify the career as following and ascending over time a company's career path or accepting its definition of becoming successful. Others view the career as passing through a series of stages in order to become a full-fledged member of one's profession (irrespective of any particular organization). Some see the career as a life-long sequence of jobs or roles. There are even those who feel that the concept means one's total personal history through life, not just one's work history. In this volume, Driver's writing highlights various career concepts. Hall (1976) has also addressed this subject.

For this paper, *the career is viewed as a sequence of work-related experiences that comprise a work history and reflect a chosen work-related life theme.* Thus, the career is seen as long-term. It comprises more life space than a job but it is not all of life. And it demands individual choices in reference to a cognitive map about the dynamic interaction among work, self, family, and external social forces. This is so even if the person decides to do nothing.

This paper is concerned with career switching by those people who choose to change careers. Certainly, it is a difficult proposition for anyone to radically alter

65

one's work history as opposed to switching jobs; nevertheless, this is happening with increasing frequency (*Business Week*, 1977). The increase may be associated with recently documented adult life changes (Vaillant, 1977; Gould, 1972; Levinson, 1978). Another possibility is that career changes are congruent with social unrest and societal change. Perhaps uninteresting and stagnate organizations, inflexible job designs, and the employer's inability to attract and hold high-potential employees result in workers who drastically alter their career patterns. Finally, as Driver has suggested, some persons view career change as a means of attaining career success.

Some research on career changing is described below. This is followed by a discussion of career orientations in the military. There is something to be learned about how military careerists regularly plan and strategize for career change. The final section attempts to outline a theoretical framework for understanding career switching.

A LITERATURE REVIEW

Some argue that there is a trend, especially among professional and "successful" managers, toward early retirement (Walker, 1976). In the future, persons may cease their first occupations at about age 50 and begin actively pursuing a second career, especially if part-time or voluntary endeavors are included in the definition of a career (Kelleher, 1973).

Several major factors work against dropping the first career and taking up another: the lack of financial resources sufficient to risk a new career venture; personal insecurity associated with delving into the unknown, especially when one's family situation may require financial security and stability (i.e., older children may be requiring college educations, geographic stability, and regular parental involvement in their activities); age itself may mean low marketability as a result of age discrimination in hiring practices (Hughes, 1974). The decision to switch careers often focuses on one or more of these issues.

Most of the literature agrees that age is certainly one factor in opting for another career. Some associate career mobility with the two periods of restlessness in one's personal life development: the end of the identity period when one is still seeking one's niche (ages 28 to 32) and the midlife crisis (ages 40 to 48). The first corresponding age-career transition makes good sense because it takes some time to actually decide one's career (Hall, 1976), and the first few jobs may be viewed as learning experiences to that end.

The midlife-crisis career switch is a much more puzzling phenomenon. One study (Clopton, 1973) revealed that career shifters were acutely aware of their mortality and were otherwise experiencing a personal crisis. Miller (1976) discovered decreasing job satisfaction among those surveyed between ages 38 and 57. Most of the executives embarking on second careers are over age 45 (*Business Week*, 1977). Many recognize obsolescence as a critical managerial problem (Connor and Fielden,

1973; Thompson and Dalton, 1971, 1976). It is quite probable, therefore, that there will be more other-than-primary career activity either among those who are most aware of their midlife crisis and attempt the greatest effort to manage it (Schultz, 1974) or among those who are forced into early retirement because their companies view them as obsolete.

Indeed, Schultz (1974) believes that those who are most aware and growth-oriented switch to second careers. He explains:

> Recent studies have suggested that those who actively pursue a second career may be better adjusted and have a higher need to achieve and a greater sense of self-esteem and ambition than those who stay in their first careers. They seem to be people for whom personal challenge and fulfillment are highly important factors, even more so than salary.

These propositions must be qualified, however, because some research reveals that career stability also increases as persons grow older and have a greater need for security (McLaughlin and Tiedeman, 1974). Byrne's study (1975) also suggests that whereas about 9% of all professional, technical, and managerial employees changed occupations during 1972, only about 67% of those actually changed careers. In addition, over two-thirds of a very large sample of federal employees (300,000) had never switched organizations, geographic locations, or occupations—let alone their careers (Scism, 1974). There is evidence to suggest that many middle-aged employees who say they change careers actually switch over to management as part of a normal career transition up the hierarchy (Nigro and Meier, 1975; Byrne, 1975).

According to other studies, another reason for choosing a different career is the personality trait of the individual careerist. In Chapter 2, Driver describes how different employees conceptualize their career success. The Spiral pattern certainly provides for a second or even a third career. Laserson (1973) categorized four types of people who were career switchers: those who failed in their primary ventures, those who made major life-career changes based on psychological change, those who became bored and looked for new challenges, and those who possessed "in-reserve" resources and were secure enough to make a change.

A third reason for embarking on an alternative career (or not so embarking) is financial security. One study found that all sampled career changers had accumulated enough money to see them through a transitional period (Clopton, 1973). Case studies of second-careerists have also revealed that many tend to be financially secure and therefore able to act on their midlife fantasies. (Wheelock and Demroth, 1975). Early retirement provides a sense of "base" income that permits a more speculative career.

Finally, Schein's work (1978) uncovers basic values, motives, needs, and talents which keep a person pursuing a certain kind of career. These characteristics act as "career anchors" to influence a person's decision to change occupations, organizations, and objectives. The career anchor also influences career satisfaction according to how well a person's current career demands and opportunities match with his or her underlying needs, as prescribed by the career anchor.

The five primary anchors discovered by Schein are: (1) need for autonomy or independence at work, (2) need for job security, (3) need for technical-functional competence, (4) need for managerial experience, and (5) need for exercising creativity on the job. These values tend to hold constant during much of the work life regardless of a particular switch in actual work assignments or place of employment.

Although Schein has not argued this point, it is possible to postulate that at least two of the five anchors could be a basis for career switching. A creative profile could mean someone who gets bored once the person has achieved his or her original objective and then needs a new challenge (which may mean a new career). An autonomy-anchored individual would supposedly remain marginal to many endeavors and, if indeed he or she became involved in even the first career, may soon feel crowded and seek an opportunity for newfound independence—hence another career. A technical-functional competence person may be likely to look for a second job (and maybe a new career) at the point at which the organization requires that individual to switch over from a specialty to a managerial role. On the other hand, those persons with a managerial anchor would be most likely to stay and ascend the hierarchy—or be "linear" in Driver's terms. The security-minded would probably opt for stability.

CAREER SWITCHING: THE NAVY CASE

The military is a unique organization in that early retirement is the rule rather than the exception. A study currently in progress (Derr, 1977) indicates (tentatively) that up to 70% of career naval officers queried plan to remain in the service no more than twenty years. Someone of average rank and ability in the military may remain a maximum of twenty-five years. This means that most will retire at about age 40 to 45. Many nonmilitary career switchers do not face the prospect of a change deadline; they act more spontaneously, although some may indeed be just as oriented to changing at a given point in time as are those in the military. But as a group, military careerists can provide important information about how large numbers of those faced with major work changes plan to advance their next career venture. This report is based on results of lengthy individual interviews with some 70 officers and is tentative in that other sources of data (e.g., questionnaires) have not yet been analyzed. Those queried came from five different naval communities: aviation, surface, submarine, supply, civil engineering. Research instruments and methods are reported elsewhere (Derr, 1977).

Three different career orientations have become apparent. The first is labeled *current careerist* to connote the person's predisposition toward achieving success in the military or current career. The second orientation is that of the *balanced careerist,* someone who pursues simultaneously and with equal vigor his ongoing career and his next career. The *second-careerist,* a member of the third group, focuses mainly on his next work-life venture, often at the expense of his current career.

Current Careerists

An estimated 25% of those interviewed could be called current (military) careerists. They are motivated by aspirations for high rank, by patriotism, and by the search for adventure. They are most often unrestricted line officers in the surface warfare, aviation, and submarine communities. They have few second-career plans and desire to remain in the military, preferably in an action job, as long as possible.

How these current careerists plan to attain high rank as Naval officers is interesting. According to the perceptions of those interviewed, up to the rank of commander the military usually engages in a sort of preselection system whereby a person's assignments (billets) and his ratings determine his promotion. Thus, the system, in response to congressional pressure against favoritism, is quite rational and even automatic at the selection level. What every officer realizes, however, is that he must influence those who make assignments so that he has the right billet portfolio when he comes up for review. Thus, he spends endless hours on the telephone in contact with persons who assign billets, trying to influence these "detailers" in order to get the best next job. There is an awareness of which assignments are needed at what point in an officer's career and which ones not to take. The best billets are said to be visible, where influential others can see your work and come to know you. They may be jobs normally assigned to someone more senior or appear challenging or involve use of the latest equipment and technology. Once assigned, one must try to please the commanding officer (CO) in order to get high ratings.

Another tactic is to acquire a group of influential peers who will come to know one's value and consequently influence more senior officers who may be sitting on the selection boards. At the rank of captain and admiral, peers may indeed be members of the selection board. Those having attended the U.S. Naval Academy are seen to have a decided edge when it comes to having and using influential peers.

An important strategy is to select early a few "sponsors" (more senior officers). It is important to know how the system operates in order to judge whether these persons are themselves likely to be promoted. If these mentors adopt the mentee and go on to become influential, they can perform some very useful services. For example, they can intervene to influence which assignment a person gets. They can influence the selection boards for marginal cases. And at the more senior levels, where the procedures are more informal, they can politic among their peers for a given candidate.

Each officer community perceives its own "tickets" to be punched in order for members to advance up the hierarchy. Submariners must get nuclear training and good billets in nuclear submarines. Aviators should "stay in the cockpit" or remain flying as long as possible and should lead a squadron. Surface officers need to become the CO of a newer class destroyer or frigate. An officer's career in the Supply Corps is enhanced by Washington tours at headquarters as often and as long as possible. In the Civil Engineering Corps the careerist must rotate through a series of relevant experiences, such as public works, Seabees, and staff and professional certification as an engineer.

Finally, those interviewed saw luck or chance as an important variable that could enhance or hinder one's career. Being at the right/wrong place at the right/wrong time was seen as important. Many pointed to examples of otherwise good Naval officers whose careers were ruined because a ship was damaged for reasons beyond their control. If one got good billets, had influential peers, behaved competently, and was extremely lucky throughout his career, the interviewees thought one could, perhaps, make captain.

Balanced Careerists

Balanced careerists, about 50% of the sample population, saw themselves as potentially high-ranking navy officers, but they were equally concerned about preparing themselves for a second career, which, they believed, would begin after twenty years of service. They were attempting to pursue their navy careers and their postnavy careers simultaneously. Most officers in this category plan to make at least lieutenant commander. They pursue their navy careers as much to gain higher retirement benefits (half of base pay as of date of severance) as they do to succeed at their military occupations. Balanced careerists and their wives report a fear of Congress changing the retirement benefits on the twenty-year retirement option before they can get out.

Most officers in this category work hard at the strategies important to the current careerists. At the same time, however, they develop specific long-range plans for their life and work following retirement. One officer had purchased a farm in his hometown and was preparing to run it in eight more years. Another was pursuing courses to become an elementary school teacher. A third had become interested in computers during one tour of duty and wanted to find a niche in the computer technology industry. To this end, he was also trying to get all the experience and training possible in the military before severance (ten years away). He felt that he could accomplish this goal by influencing his shore billets and then using his sea billets to complete the navy career requisite.

A fourth example wanted to retire in a particular geographic area and attempted to influence his detailer to send him there whenever possible. His career plans were as yet unfixed, but he was considering various opportunities and making contacts in the region in order to decide his next venture and start to prepare for it.

A number of wives figured importantly in the balanced career pattern. Many mentioned a joint plan whereby they were willing to defer their own career agendas until their husbands' retirement, after which would come "their turn." From the wife's perspective the officer's second career plans required a job that gave him ample time for parenting and other support activities for her.

Balanced careerists, therefore, begin in earnest to plot out their second career as much as ten years prior to retirement and their planning becomes more intense as they get closer to the severance date. Many seek to get a specialized type of training (e.g., computer technician, operations research analyst, nuclear engineer) which will be a useful commodity in the civilian job market. Some invest in real estate and family businesses. Others cultivate contacts with civilian contractors or keep actively in touch with former officers who are now employed elsewhere.

For many, it will be indeed a career switch, since their primary activity as an officer is that of a general "commander" who rotates every two to three years between his military specialty (e.g., on a ship, in a squadron) and a more general management support position (e.g., project management, personnel, financial management). The military jobs that have the most second-career potential are frequently short-lived opportunities of perhaps two divided tours of duty in a whole military career. For example, an organization development specialist might spend three years as an internal consultant at a Human Resource Management Center, go back to sea duty, go to another shore billet, back to sea, and finally, go into a policy position in administering organization development (OD) programs. Moreover, one's specialty training (e.g., Naval Postgraduate School) normally takes place at midcareer and may be somewhat obsolete by the time the officer retires.

Balance is critical for this careerist. Although a number of billets are second-career-enhancing (e.g., graduate education, training as a technician), they may not enrich one's military experience portfolio. For line officers, the military tends to reward one for having served in combat, on ships, with the troops, or in some directly defense-related activity. The support activities are seen as necessary but not as critically important. Many of these activities could be accomplished by civil service. Becoming highly specialized, by becoming very knowledgeable in one's field or receiving a Ph.D., is somewhat suspect. Military officers are supposed to be general managers. It is, therefore, often difficult to pursue the current and secondary career simultaneously and sometimes, to the extent that one can influence the situation, one must seize on a second-career opportunity at the expense of his military career. The closer one is to retirement, the truer this is.

Second Careerists

The final group are the second careerists. At an early stage they choose to forgo a military career. Most of these persons are disenchanted with the Navy. They might dislike the nature of the work. Their wives and families may be dissatisfied. Perhaps career anchors have been violated (e.g., the pilot who is technically oriented and must get out of the airplane and switch over to administration). Or a combination of these factors may enter into their career malaise and cause them to withdraw their energy and become second-career-oriented.

Another segment of this group, unlike those who have become "turned off" to the navy, believe that their opportunities for a successful military career are limited. They perceive that it would be wiser to change their career direction. Some of the interviewees in this category had already been passed over once by a selection board and were expecting to be involuntarily retired in the near future.

It is important to understand the distinction between those who are second-career-oriented by choice and those who are not. The voluntary second-careerists and the balanced careerists are likely to both strive for some level of competence and advancement in their military careers. What differentiates them is that balanced careerists seem equally concerned about both careers (the navy and the next venture), whereas the voluntary second careerists clearly put their second career in first priority. This is manifest in how they use their time, energy, and planning moments and how they articulate their priorities.

For example, one officer at the Naval Postgraduate School was busy searching a new career because he had been denied promotion on the first round of the selection board. He was a Civil Engineering Corps officer and had not succeeded at demonstrating proficiency as an architect. Moreover, he had decided that he did not like and was not in fact particularly talented at it. Thus, he was busy exploring other career options and using his time and energy for that purpose.

Another submarine officer had joined initially to "see the world." He and his wife were at a point in the military career when they would have to choose between remaining in the navy, with very stringent requirements for family separation, or get out. They chose the latter course because they had already lived abroad once, their children were getting older, and they wanted to spend more time together as a family. This officer was busy pursuing a line of work broadly connected to some of his shore-duty experience and tied to several "contacts" he had made while in that job. He was quitting by choice.

A third second-careerist was an aviator whose goal was a Ph.D. in management. He worked hard to influence his detailer to give him billets that allowed him to be near university centers. He was preparing to teach at the junior college level. He also read extensively in his field and wrote about relevant aspects of his naval experience to demonstrate before retirement his academic competence by publishing several articles. He was to retire after twenty years as a lieutenant commander, having chosen jobs during the last seven years of his military service that were not career-enhancing for his navy occupation.

A distinction must be made between a second-career and a second-job orientation. One is basic to a change of life and work. The other is directed at a change of setting. Some naval officers who are second-career-oriented maneuver themselves into their second careers while still in the military. Upon retirement they simply change settings and pursue the same career in a new job. Following is an example of this phenomenon.

In one study in which the author participated (Giauque et al., 1977), over 2500 questionnaires were distributed to paramedical health care providers in the three branches of the armed forces. In-depth interviews were also conducted. Many physician assistants (PAs) entered the field, after having been medical corpsmen, to seek a second career. Seventy-five percent of the 242 respondents planned to remain no more than twenty years even if given the opportunity. Many had taken pay and status cuts (from master sergeant or master chief petty officer to warrant officer) to get into the PA program.

When queried, physician assistants seemed very much aware of the PA opportunities on the "outside," saw them as preferable to those in the military and hoped that the perceived job market would continue until they could retire. They spoke about the attractive PA positions on the Alaskan pipeline (at salaries rumored to be $30,000 per year), in insurance agencies, in private practice with former military physicians, and in teaching and administration. They seemed quite open about their intentions to use their current jobs as "bases" for launching activities related to their future jobs. Developing and maintaining skills, getting new educational experiences to enhance their credibility and competence, maintaining their credentials, building informal networks with current and former physicians and peers for future employment, and acquiring knowledge about future trends in the profession were all important strategies actively pursued.

Table 5-1 substantiates this point. It lists scores from a preference scale with several items supporting a nonmilitary physician assistant job. These items had considerably higher mean scores than those more oriented to the current military career.

Table 5-1   Second-Job Support Preferences
for Physician Assistants

Preference for:	Mean Score[a]
Autonomous working conditions (you can learn much on your own)	3.18
Technical competence (including training/experiences)	4.63
Creative/innovative opportunities (new learning opportunities)	4.10
Early retirement	3.60
Ample free time for self/family (to take extra courses, etc.)	4.20

[a]On a scale of 1 to 5, where a higher score means a greater preference.

One of the features distinguishing a second-career or second-job orientation, as compared to a balanced-career focus, is the extent to which time, energy, and attitudes are openly engaged in a future activity. This was the case with physician assistants, some of whom still had ten years of active duty remaining. Moreover, those in policy positions seemed to recognize the situation and responded by (1) refusing to recruit PAs prior to their having ten years' experience in the military so that they would remain for at least ten more years (until the twenty-year retirement date), (2) offering challenging job experiences and occasional skill-building workshops relevant to the next job, as opposed to increasing military benefits by allowing PAs to become regular officers (the highest rank they could attain was warrant officer III), and (3) allowing the job market myths to perpetuate without clarifying the "realities" so that the best medical corpsmen would be attracted to the PA program.

Thus, in the case of physician assistants, both the employer and the employee were second-career- and second-job-oriented. The Bureaus of Medicine seemed to realize that the PAs were highly motivated by second-career training leading to a second job. They appeared to take advantage of the PAs in terms of opportunities for them while in the military. The PAs, on the other hand, appreciated this second-career opportunity and worked hard at their professions in order to get the experience and skills needed for a second job. They took advantage of the military in preparing for their next PA jobs. Both the employee and employer seemed to benefit.

It is proposed that in some instances second-careerists do, in fact, match the short-term needs of the employing organization. In many cases, however, it appears to have been a bad career marriage early and leads only to a strategy whereby the careerist can separate from the organization having fulfilled some of his work/life goals.

Comparison of the Three Career Orientations

Table 5-2 summarizes the three categories of careerists that have been discussed.

It is important to stress here that the balanced careerist may be an excellent naval officer. If he is talented and energetic, he may well be able to manage two consuming activities at once. Indeed, he may be a more achievement-oriented, yet balanced individual who is a study prototype for career transitioning.

His strategy for pursuing two careers at once might be somewhat devious, however. He must keep his next career plans somewhat secretive because those who are rewarded most by the employer are current careerists. He must give off the image of being a current careerist and pursue his next career in a very unobtrusive manner.

Second-careerists, on the other hand, can be more overt in their strategies. Although they need to do the minimum to at least meet their own short-term objectives (e.g., get selected so they can have the twenty-year retirement benefits, get good military jobs which allow them to pursue their next career), they can also afford to be viewed as less than top-flight officer material. Sometimes second-careerists can pursue the current job with much enthusiasm and competence—especially when it is directly related to the second career.

One critical issue still to be determined is the extent to which the military setting is unique. Very few other organizations allow for or promote retirement at such an early age, thereby forcing some of their members to pursue second jobs at second careers. Moreover, few second-careerists embark on new ventures with such an income/benefit package. Finally, few enterprises promote major occupational change at an age corresponding to major life change (the midlife crisis), where the potential for both self-renewal and self-doubt are great.

Table 5-2 Characteristics of Naval Officer Retirees

Type	Approximate % of Sample	Extent of Second-Career Planning	Continued Commitment To Navy	Commitment To Next Career	Potential For Productivity
Current careerist	25	Very limited	High	Low	Excellent
Balanced careerist	50	Of equal importance to naval career	Mixed	Mixed	Good
Second careerist	25	Extensive	Low	High	Minimal (sometimes excellent if tied directly to next career)

THEORETICAL DISCUSSION

Career switching can be viewed as a person-organization power struggle. The organization traditionally rewards careerists who are talented, loyal, obedient, hardworking, and supported by a "wife" at home. Careerists respond to rewards and options offered by the organization and its self-interests in turn are served when they compete for its positions and rewards. But as has been shown in the case of the military and strongly implied if not substantiated in the literature reviewed, careerists themselves have multiple personal interests, which may or may not be served by the organization. Because their career interests can be fulfilled through the organization/occupation, current careerists employ strategies and ends compatible with organizational demands. Balanced careerists, on the other hand, find their interests sometimes congruent, sometimes incongruent with those of the organization/occupation. Second-careerists work in self-interest that is often at variance with that of the organization/occupation. Every careerist, to some degree, is aware of and participates in organizational politics.

In career politics at least two patterns are dominant: the politics of the current careerist and those of the career switcher. The ways in which current careerists in the military got billets and good reports, used sponsors and peer influence, and punched "tickets" is analogous to the competitive organizational politics frequently described in the literature (Crozier, 1964; French and Raven, 1959; Jay, 1967; Jennings, 1971; Korda, 1975; Kotter, 1977; Salancik and Pfeffer, 1977; Schein, 1976; Tushman, 1977). The politics are quite different in the instance of the career switcher, where self-interests are often basically incompatible with those of the organization/occupation. He must participate in somewhat more complicated political jousting.

It should be observed here that career switching is different from job hopping. The job hopper is more likely to be a current careerist whose self-interests are more congruent with those of the organization. This person usually works hard and renders service while he is in the enterprise, and he maintains the esteem of fellow workers, who probably view his change as "a better deal elsewhere." By contrast, a career changer is likely to be viewed by both the organization and fellow workers as threatening. His new interests are usually unrelated to the self-interests of either peers or the system and resources invested in him are not likely to have future payoffs for them.

Career switchers usually need a waiting period in which they use the current career to launch their next one. This period provides important time to search alternatives; to become informed about the "realities" and unintended problems in the new field; to investigate the external factors, such as societal changes, new laws, economic patterns, and other forces that might impinge on the new career; to gain more knowledge, new skills, and experiences relevant to launching the next work/life venture; and to exit from the current career at the right time, with the right financial backing, and the right reputation important to beginning anew.

A career switcher is likely to be secretive about his self-interests for fear of being treated as a traitor and/or losing the benefits that come from maximizing opportunities during this transition period. In fact, where possible and depending on the strength of his next career orientation, he will find ways to take advantage of the transition period by playing the current careerist political game. He presents himself as what the organization wants. In some way, perhaps some devious way, he matches attitudes and behaviors favorable to the organization while pursuing his own agendas. Gaining a more congruent career image allows him the favors and added opportunities necessary to develop his next career, and he maintains enough current influence to use the organization as a base from which to launch his next venture.

Some military officers who were balanced careerists discussed such a strategy. One told about coming to work very early in the morning, being conspicuous and appearing as if he were eager to get started and perform. He would then leave his door open, as if he were at a meeting, and spend from about 9 to 11 A.M. working on a second-career education program. Another officer described how he had manipulated the system to get second-career experience and training while making it appear as if he were doing this for a future navy billet.

Intentions such as career switching, which are incongruent with the organization, occupational norms, goals, and behavior patterns are, therefore, best either hidden or worked out within the context of more acceptable organizational activities. One must also use appropriate career strategies to match the career image one wishes to create. When possible it is advantageous to make one's career agendas seem congruent with organizational and occupational interests, to engage in the attitudes and activities for which current careerists are rewarded.

Maccoby (1976) discusses careerists in the technology industry. Those who seem to behave in ways most congruent with the industry needs and informal norms are most rewarded. Those least rewarded seem to have opted for strategies that blatantly promoted their "personal" agendas. This is precisely why the "gamesman" is so effective as a careerist. In Chapter 3, Bailyn addresses different career types. The high-potential employee who exemplifies "nonwork" (noncongruent) interests confuses his employer. One of the critical issues for the employee is how to use strategies that will create more congruent career images—or at least less noncongruent ones. This has proved to be important in the military, where balanced careerists, while actively pursuing their real interests, parade as warriors and, when necessary, go to sea or with the tropps to substantiate that image.

In some of Bailyn's other work (1977, 1978) "accommodators" are those who are willing to subordinate work needs for the sake of the family and self-report to be happier in their personal and marital lives. Yet they are not as rewarded by the organization as are those judged to be "careerists." One issue accommodators must probably face is how to give off more congruent career images while still accommodating. Because accommodation requires much time and energy at home, however, it imposes limitations on this strategy.

Evans and Bartolome (1978) found that most managers listed their families and personal lives as more important than their careers. Yet, at least between ages 25 and 35, they behaved in ways which demonstrated that they were more career-oriented. It is this author's proposition that not only do employees get great fulfillment through work during the "identity" adult life stage but also that they must behave so to establish the congruent career images that will gain them the equivalent of tenure, which probably comes for most at about age 35.

The two strategies most viable for influencing career imagery can be categorized as "overt" and "covert." One can behave openly when his real agenda matches or appears to match the organizational reward system. Such an *overt strategy* for career switchers might be manifest in the following situations, for example.

- Person A has decided to seek maximum organizational rewards for five years in order to attain the financial backing and reputation to launch his next career. He works hard at being a model employee and then, to the surprise of everyone, quits suddenly to do something else.
- Person B, while traveling on legitimate business for the corporation, makes the contacts he needs to start his new career.
- Person C, while attending professional meetings, searches out some new career options.
- Person D seeks out legitimate and needed training and experience partially to help the organization and partially to help him pursue his next career.

All of these cases presume that one appears to be performing adequately, even successfully, in his organizational career. In fact, he may be satisfying both current and future career interests simultaneously. He can use more overt political strategies.

When one feels he must pursue activities that may be viewed as noncongruent with organizational interests, he must use *covert strategies*. His objective may be to carefully mask his activities so that they seem congruent, are at least marginally related, or are not uncovered as being incongruent. Because pursuing a second career often requires a new work focus quite unrelated to the organization's interests, covert strategies, such as the following, are usually important in career switching:

- Person E seeks and gets a position in the enterprise which gives him lots of autonomy and he uses the free time and the organizational resources (e.g., telephone) to pursue his next venture.
- Person F is highly involved in out-of-work training and activities relevant to another career but is careful that those at work are unaware of the real purpose or the extent of his activities.
- Person G forms a secret coalition with others of the same mind and they cover for one another at work, thus freeing up the time and energy to advance their external interests.
- Person H gets the equivalent of tenure based on sterling past performance and uses this reputation to "coast"; while others perceive him as "getting retooled" for the next thrust, he works secretly on his new career.
- Person J does the minimum for remaining valued by the organization, with intermittent spurts of good performance so that he can be viewed as a "late bloomer," and uses the extra time and energy to achieve his own agenda.

The point here is to achieve some kind of favorable rating in the ongoing career, one must use strategies that project a favorable image. Sometimes a person can use overt means because they appear or are partially congruent. Sometimes it is necessary to employ covert strategies, masking activities that cannot be construed as congruent. Career switching allows for the use of both kinds of means, depending on the situation but stresses, given the nature of the change, more covert methods.

Career switching is basically political. One's real self-interests must often be kept secret or distorted. The information exchanged is strategic. Playing a kind of game, one tries to achieve personal interests, noncongruent perhaps with those of the organization, with as little personal cost as possible. How one manages the transition period between careers is indicative of one's political skill.

So far we have focused on the motives and strategies of the politics of career switching. How about the outcomes? What are the limits? Are there ethics in career politics such that it is the obligation of the careerist to be more loyal and the organization to facilitate better matching of interests (e.g., by offering multiple career paths and options)? This would be ideal, but the political forces naturally unleashed serve a similar function. Those who wish to pay the price of career success within organizations/occupations do what they can to advance up the hierarchy. This certainly serves the organization's interests as well. In the case of career switchers, some of them are more balanced careerists and often find creative ways to serve both the organization/occupation and their next careers. In the case of high-potential second careerists, they might in fact be very productive in those instances where they can do the organization's work while pursuing their next venture. In general, the organization/occupation clearly takes advantage of some careerists and gets more than it gives; through the politics of career switching some are able to get as much or more than they return.

REFERENCES

Bailyn, L. "Involvement and Accommodation in Technical Careers." In J. Van Maanen, ed., *Organizational Careers: Some New Perspectives.* New York: Wiley, 1977.

Bailyn, L. "Accommodation of Work to Family," In R. Rappoport, R.N. Rappoport, and J. Bumstead, eds., *Working Couples.* New York: Harper & Row, 1978.

Byrne, J.J. "Occupational Mobility of Workers." *Monthly Labor Review,* Vol. 98, February 1975, 53-59.

"Choosing a Second Career." *Business Week,* September 19, 1977.

Clopton, W. "Personality and Career Change." *Industrial Gerontology,* Vol. 17, Spring 1973, 9-17.

Connor, S.R., and Fielden, J.S. "Rx for Managerial Shelf-Sitters," *Harvard Business Review,* November-December 1973, 113-20.

Crozier, M. *The Bureaucratic Pheonomenon.* Chicago: University of Chicago Press, 1964.

Derr, C.B. "A Theory and Research Instrument for Studying U.S. Naval Officers." *Technical Report: The Naval Postgraduate School, No. 54-77-01,* August 1977.

Evans, P.A.L., and Bartolome, F. "Professional and Private Life: Three Stages in the Life of Managers." *Working Paper: The European Institute of Business* (INSEAD), March 1978.

French, J.R.P., and Raven, B. "The Bases of Social Power." In D. Cartwright, ed., *Studies in Social Power.* Ann Arbor, Mich.: Institute of Social Research, 1959.

Giauque, W.C., Derr, C.B., Eoyang, C., and Harris R. "Studies of the Effectiveness and Paramedical Usage in Medical Care Delivery." In A.M. Coblentz and J.R. Walter, eds., *Systems Science in Health Care.* London: Taylor & Francis, 1977.

Gould, R.L. "The Phases of Adult Life." *American Journal of Psychiatry,* Vol. 129, November 1972, 521-31.

Hall, D.T. *Careers in Organizations.* Palos Verdes, Calif.: Goodyear Publishing Co., 1976.

Hughes, C. "Special Report." *Harvard Business Review,* May-June 1974, 38-40.

Jay, A. *Management and Machiavelli.* New York: Holt, Rinehart and Winston, 1967.

Jennings, E.E. *Routes to the Executive Suite.* New York: McGraw-Hill, 1971.

Kelleher, C.H., "Second Careers: A Growing Trend," *Industrial Gerontology,* Vol. 17, Spring 1973, 1-8.

Korda, M. *Power: How to Get It, How to Use It.* New York: Random House, 1975.

Kotter, J.P. "Power, Dependence and Effective Management." *Harvard Business Review,* July-August, 1977, 125-36.

Laserson, N. "Profiles of Five Second Careerists." *Personnel,* Vol. 50, January-February 1973, 36-46.

Levinson, D.J. *The Seasons of a Man's Life.* New York: Knopf, 1978.

Maccoby, M. *The Gamesman: Winning and Losing The Career Game.* New York: Simon and Schuster, 1976.

McLaughlin, D.H., and Tiedeman, D.V. "Eleven-Year Career Stability and Change as Reflected in Project Talent Data through the Flanagan, Holland and Roe Occupational Classification Systems." *Journal of Vocational Behavior,* Vol. 5, October 1974, 177-96.

Miller, N. "Career Choice, Job Satisfaction and the Truth behind the Peter Principle," *Personnel,* Vol. 53, July-August 1976, 58-65.

Nigro, L.G., and Meier, K.J. "Executive Mobility in the Federal Service," *Public Administration Review,* Vol. 35, May-June, 1975, 291-95.

Salancik G., and Pfeffer, J. "Who Gets Power and How They Hold on to It." *Organizational Dynamics,* Vol. 5, No. 3, 1977, 2-21.

Schein, E.H. *Career Dynamics: Matching Individual and Organizational Needs.* Reading, Mass.: Addison-Wesley, 1978.

Schein, V. "Individual Power and Political Behaviors in Organizations." *Academy of Management Review,* Vol. 2, No. 1, 1976, 64-72.

Schultz, D. "Managing the Middle-Aged Manager." *Personnel,* Vol. 51, November-December 1974, 8-17.

Scism, T.E. "Employee Mobility in the Federal Service." *Public Administration Review,* Vol. 34, May-June 1974, 247-54.

Thompson, P.H., and Dalton, G.W. "Accelerating Obsolescence of Older Engineers." *Harvard Business Review,* September-October, 1971.

Thompson, P.H., and Dalton, G.W. "Are R&D Organizations Obsolete?" *Harvard Business Review,* November-December, 1976.

Tushman, M. "A Political Approach to Organizations," *Academy of Management Review,* Vol. 2, No. 2, 1977, 206-16.

Vaillant, G.E. *Adaptation To Life.* Boston: Little, Brown, 1977.

Walker, J.W. "Will Early Retirement Retire People?" *Personnel,* Vol. 53, January-February, 1976, 33-39.

Wheeelock, H., and Demroth, N. "Don't Call It Early Retirement." *Harvard Business Review,* September-October, 1975, 103-18.

ISSUES
IN MANAGING

INDIVIDUAL
DEVELOPMENT

6

Boundary Crossings: Major Strategies of Organizational Socialization and Their Consequences[*]

JOHN VAN MAANEN

Massachusetts Institute of Technology

From entry to exit, a person's career within an organization represents a series of transitions from one position or role to another (Van Maanen, 1976; Schein, 1971; Glaser, 1968). These boundary crossings may be few or many in number; entail upward, downward, or lateral mobility; and demand relatively mild to severe adjustments on the part of the individual. During such transitions, the individual must "learn the ropes" of his or her new position, status, and occupational role.[1] The intensity, importance, and visibility of this process varies, of course, by the type of organizational boundary crossed. It is probably most obvious (both to the individual and others) when a person first joins an organization—the outsider-to-insider

*This paper was first talked through at an M.I.T. Industrial Liason Program Symposium held in Los Angeles on January 21, 1977. A much abbreviated version of this paper appears in Van Maanen (1978). I would like to acknowledge the most helpful comments provided on an early draft of this paper by Professors Edgar H. Schein, Lotte Bailyn, Chris Argyris, and James Rosenbaum.

[1] Between- and within-role socialization are seen here as subcategories of organizational and occupational socialization which are both subsumed under the more general topic, "adult socialization." As I have argued elsewhere, the task and the group to which a person is assigned represent very key factors of influence in any role socialization process (Van Maanen, 1976).

passage. It is perhaps least obvious when a veteran member of an organization undergoes a simple change of assignment, shift, or job location. Nevertheless, a period of socialization accompanies every passage by an individual across organizational boundaries.[2]

The phrase "strategies of organizational socialization" refers to the ways in which the experiences of an individual in transition are structured for him or her by others in the organization. These tactics may be selected consciously by management, such as the requirement that all newcomers attend a training or orientation program of some kind. Or they may be selected unconsciously by management, representing merely precedents established in the dim past of an organization's history, such as the proverbial trial-and-error method of socialization by which the person learns how to perform a new task on his or her own. Regardless of the manner of choice, however, any given strategy represents a distinguishable set of events occurring to the individual in transition which make certain behavioral and attitudinal consequences more likely than others. It is possible, therefore, to denote the various strategies used by organizations and explore the differential results of their use upon the people to whom they are directed.

BACKGROUND

There are several assumptions that underlie this analysis. First, and perhaps of most importance, is the notion that individuals undergoing any transition are in a more or less anxiety-producing situation. They are motivated therefore to reduce this anxiety by learning the functional and social requirements of their new role as quickly as possible.[3] Second, the learning that takes place does not occur in a social vacuum strictly on the basis of the official and available versions of the new requirements. People crossing organizational boundaries are particularly vulnerable to clues on how to proceed that orginate in the interactional zone that immediately surrounds them. Thus, colleagues, superiors, subordinates, clients, and other work associates support and guide individuals who are learning new roles. They help interpret the events novices experience such that they can eventually take action in their altered situations and, ultimately, they provide individuals with a sense of

---

[2]What constitutes an organizational boundry is a question surrounded by controversy. Perhaps the best approach is that of Schein (1971), who suggests that there are three relatively distinct types: functional, hierarchical, and inclusionary boundaries (see also Van Maanen and Schein, 1979).

[3]There are essentially three general sources of anxiety associated with individual transitions. First, there are cultural anxieties created whenever a person is separated from an everyday social situation with which he or she has become intimately familiar. Second, psychological tensions are promoted by feelings of isolation and loneliness that may be associated intially with a new role as well as the performance anxieties a person may have when taking on new duties. Third, and perhaps of most importance to work organizations, sociological stress results when a person feels a lack of identification with the activities going on about him or her. Needless to say, different transitions will invoke different levels of these sources of personal anxiety. See Van Maanen (1977b) for a more extended view of these factors from the perspective of the individual undergoing socialization.

accomplishment and competence (or failure and incompetence). Finally, at a different level of abstraction, the stability and productivity of any organization depends in large measure upon the way in which newcomers to various organizational positions carry out their tasks. When the passing of positions from generation to generation of incumbants is accomplished smoothly, with a minimum of disruption, the continuity of the organization's mission is maintained, the predictability of the organization's performance is left intact, and in the short run at least, the survival of the organization is assured.

The view presented in this paper emphasizes the ways in which people adjust to novel circumstances. In some cases, the shift into a new work situation may result in a dramatically altered organization identity for the person such as often occurs when a factory worker becomes a foreman or a staff analyst becomes a line manager. In other cases, the shift may result in only minor and insignificant changes in a person's organizational identity, as is perhaps the situation when an administrator is shifted to a new location or a craftsman is rotated to a new department. Yet in any of these shifts, there is likely to be at least some surprise or what Hughes (1958) calls "reality shock" in store for the individual involved. When persons undergo a transition, regardless of the information they already possess about the new role, their a priori understandings of that role will undoubtedly change in either a subtle or dramatic fashion. As James (1892) observed long ago, "knowledge about" and "knowledge of" a phenomenon imply quite different levels of meaning. For example, becoming a member of an organization will upset the everyday order of even the most well-informed recruit.[4] Matters concerning friendship, time, purpose, preparation, demeanor, competence, and the person's future are suddenly made problematic. The individual must build a set of guidelines to explain and make meaningful the myriad of activities observed to be going on in the organization. To come to know an organizational situation and act within it implies that a person has developed some rules, principles, and understandings, or in shorthand notation, a perspective, for interpreting one's experiences associated with participating in a given sphere of the work world. This perspective provides the rules by which one can manage the unique and recurring strains of organizational life. It provides the person with an ordered view of the organization that runs ahead and directs experience, orders and shapes personal relationships in the work setting, and provides the ground rules under which everyday affairs are to be managed (Shibutani, 1962).

In short, socialization entails a great deal of social learning on the part of the individual. This learning consists of both normative and practical elements. Yet rarely, if ever, can such learning be complete until a newcomer has endured a period of initiation on the job. As Barnard (1938) remarked with characteristic clarity: "There is no instant replacement; there is always a period of adjustment."

The anaylsis presented here explores this period of adjustment primarily from a structural standpoint. The main focus is therefore upon externally-defined proper-

---

[4]There are a number of studies concerned with the nonmember-to-member transition. See, for example, Berlew and Hall (1966), Light (1980), Glaser (1964), Bell and Price (1975), Van Maanen (1973), Feldman (1976), Schein (1968), Dornbush (1955), and Lortie (1975).

ties peculiar to any given organizational setting in which socialization regularly occurs. These external properties are essentially process variables akin to, but more specific than, such general processes as education, training, apprenticeship, and indoctrination. This analysis follows the premise that people are differentially socialized not only because people are different, but also because organizational processes differ. And like a sculptor's mold, certain forms of socialization can be shown to produce remarkably similar outcomes.

STRATEGIES OF SOCIALIZATION

The following list of strategies are associated with any organizational socialization program. Each strategy operates in a way that uniquely organizes the learning experiences of a newcomer to a particular organizational role. Although much of the evidence presented below on the effects of a given strategy comes from studies conducted on the outsider-to-insider passage wherein a person first becomes a member of the organization, this study seeks to transcend these transitions by suggesting that each strategy is potentially, if not actually, available for use during any transition accompanying an individual's organizational career.

Critically, each listed strategy is not mutually exlcusive of the others. Indeed, they are typically combined in sundry and often inventive ways. The effects of the strategies upon people are consequently cumulative.[5] Although I discuss each tactic in relative isolation, the reader should be aware that a recruit to an organizational position often encounters all the listed strategies simultaneously. Furthermore, each strategy is given together with its counterpart or opposing strategy. In other words, each strategy can be thought of as existing on a continuum where there is a great deal of range between the two poles.

The term "strategy" is used here to describe each of the listed processes because the degree to which any one is used by an organization is not in any sense a natural or prerequisite condition necessary for socialization to occur. In other words, socialization itself always takes place upon a career transition. However, the form that it takes is a matter of organizational choice.[6] And whether this choice of strategies is made by design or accident, it is at least theoretically subject to rapid and complete change at the direction of the management of an organization. Thus, although any organizational socialization sequence can be described structurally

---

[5] Although I do not explore the typical ways in which the listed socialization tactics are clustered in practice, the reader should be aware that this is an area in which little empirical research has been conducted. It is, however, a vital concern. At the theoretical level, Wheeler's (1966) essay probably comes closest to examining the cumulative effects of various strategies.

[6] The inevitability of organizational socialization can be seen simply by the fact that organizations regularly transcend the lifetimes of their founders and somehow are able to sustain the involvement of new members on a rather predictable basis. Thus, if an organization is to survive, there must always be some way for newcomers functioning in any given role in the organization to learn how they are to behave, what they can expect of others, the limits of these rules, and the penalties for violation.

by the strategies investigated here, the relative use of a particular strategy is, by and large, a choice made by organizational decision makers on functional, technical, traditional, humanistic, economic, or perhaps arbitrary grounds. This is an important point, for it suggests that we can be far more self-conscious about employing certain people-processing techniques than we have in the past. In fact, a major purpose of this paper is to heighten and cultivate a broader awareness of what it is we do to people under the guise of "breaking" them in. Presumably, if we have a greater appreciation for the sometimes unintended consequences of a particular strategy, we can alter the strategy for the betterment of both the individual and the organization.

As denoted below, there are at least eight major strategic dimensions available to characterize the structural side of organizational socialization. These dimensons or processes were deduced logically from my own empirical observations and from accounts found in the social science literature. I do not assert that this list is exhaustive or that the processes are presented in any order of relevance to a particular organization or occupation. These are essential empirical questions that can only be answered by further research. I do assert and attempt to demonstrate, however, that these strategies are quite common and of consequence to the people passing through any organizational socialization sequence. By implication, then, these strategies have consequences upon the organizational system of which the individuals being processed are a part.

Finally, I should note that there is seemingly no logical end to a list of the processes that influence socialization outcomes. The list may well be infinite. At least at this juncture in the development of organization theory, questions concerning the use of the various strategies are just beginning to be answered by carefully designed study. My reasons for choosing these particular strategies are simply the visible presence (or omnipresence) of a strategy across what appears to be a wide variety of organizations and organizational boundaries as well as the seeming importance and power of that strategy upon the persons who are subjected to it.

Formal (Informal) Socialization Processes

The formality of a socialization process refers to the degree to which the setting in which it takes place is segregated from the ongoing work context and to the degree to which the individual's role as recruit is specified (Brim, 1966; Wheeler, 1966; Cogswell, 1967).[7] The more formal the process, the more the recruit's role is segregated and specified. Formal processes strictly differentiate the recruit from other organizational members. If the recruit is processed informally, much learning takes place via the social and task-related networks that surround the position he

---

[7]The term "recruit" is used here to denote the individual in transition. I include under this level all people within the organization who are new to their particular positions, tasks, or groups. The usage is therefore *not* restricted to those persons entering the organization from the outside. Similarly, the term "agent" is used to designate those individuals who have a hand in the recruit's socialization. They may be superiors, equals, or subordinates of the recruit.

or she assumes. Thus, informal socialization procedures are analytically similar to the familiar trial-and-error techniques by which one learns, it is said, through experience.

Generally, the more formal the process, the more stress there is upon influencing the newcomer's attitudes and values. The more the organization is concerned with the recruit's absorption of the appropriate demeanor and stance associated with the target role—that one begins to think and feel like a United States Marine, or an IBM executive, or a Catholic priest. In Bidwell's (1962) terms, formal processes emphasize status socialization (i.e., preparing the person to occupy a particular status in the organization) and informal processes emphasize role socialization (i.e., preparing the person to perform a specified task in the organization). The greater the separation of the recruit from the day-to-day reality of the organization, the less the newcomer will be able to carry over and generalize any abilities or skills learned in the socialization setting to the new position. Therefore, formal processes concentrate, implicitly, if not explicitly, more upon attitude than act.[8] For example, police recruits, sales trainees, and student nurses commonly denounce their formal learning experiences as irrelevant, abstract, and dull. Paradoxically, they are also expressing at the same time an attraction for certain components of the valued subcultural ethos, such as autonomy, pragmatism, and personal independence (Van Maanen, 1974; Shafer, 1975; Olsen and Whittiker, 1967).

Critically, formal processes almost always stress the "proper" or "right" way of behaving in lieu of the "practical" or "smart" way followed by the more experienced members in the organization. For example, many employees misrepresent their overtime statements or expense allowances; budget makers often pad their budgets with either fictitious expenses or exaggerated amounts for a given item; and supervisors almost invariably rate the performance of their subordinates as being far superior than is actually the case. All these are examples of how ideal organizational rules and policies are commonly broken.[9] Formal socialization processes convey primarily the ideal version of organizational procedures; rarely do they convey what, in practice, may be the case to most members of the organization. The padded budget, for example, is in many organizations a normal and expected tactic, almost a standard operating procedure. So standard is the practice that those responsible for providing funds have developed the counterstrategy of

---

[8] Of course, the length of the formal process is an important moderating factor in this regard. The longer the formal process, the more culture that is usually transmitted to the recruit—thus the greater the probability that a recruit will internalize the organizationally desired values, motives, and beliefs. I should also note that many organizations "farm out" this formal preparation phase to various educational institutions. Professional schools, for example, often handle much of the formal socialization demands of some types of organizations.

[9] Since these sorts of deviations are, by and large, expected in many organizations, it hardly seems reasonable to refer to the many rule breakers as "deviants" or, in terms coined elsewhere, "inefficaciously socialized" (Van Maanen, 1976). To the contrary, these examples illustrate a rather important principle: When "deviations" are frequently made by a large percentage of organizational members, they somehow become transformed into normal aspects of the system, aspects that a recruit is expected to learn. Thus, when many people do the wrong things (normatively speaking), this thing becomes right (practically speaking).

lopping off a certain percentage of a requested budget on the grounds that the lesser amount better mirrors the actual needs of the budget maker than the original budget. Moreover, the member who strictly adheres to the correct practice (the proper) rather than the currently acceptable social practices (the smart) is likely to be considered by others in the organization to be a "schlemeil" or "schmuck" (one who has not been socialized fully). Thus, the budget maker who presents a budget that modestly reflects the needs of his or her group or department is then a schmuck: his activities may harm his own group and, in the long run, may create havoc in the total system. The schmuck's budget—like those of other budget makers—gets cut by the regular percentage, and, as a result, his group cannot function in its accustomed fashion.

From this standpoint, formal socialization processes may be viewed tentatively as a "first wave" of socialization. The informal "second wave" occurs when the newcomer is actually placed in a designated organizational slot and must then learn the actual practices that go on there (Inkeles, 1966). Whereas the first wave stresses general skills and attitudes, the second wave emphasizes specified actions, situational applications of the rules, and the idiosyncratic nuances necessary to perform the role in the work setting. However, when the gap separating the two sorts of learning is large, disillusionment with the first wave may set in causing the individual to disregard virtually everything learned in the formal wave socialization.[10]

Looking to the individual in transition, formal strategies appear to produce stress in the form of a sort of Goffmanesque period of personal stigmatization. Whether or not this stigmatization takes the form of identifying garb (such as the peculiar uniform worn by police recruits), a special and usually somewhat demeaning title (such as "rookie," "trainee," or "junior"), or an insular position (such as an assignment to a classroom instead of an office or job), a person undergoing formal socialization is likely to feel isolated, cut off, and prohibited from assuming the everyday kinds of social relationships with more experienced organizational "betters." Furthermore, formal processes seldom use evaluations of an individual's performance in an advisory or diagnostic manner which would assist the person in discovering areas in need of improvement. Rather, they often use the results to make decisions bearing on the individual's future. Needless to say, if the performance evaluations have fateful consequences, people will orient their efforts solely toward getting good ones.

---

[10]There are several other consequences of the formal mode. Importantly, Becker (1972) points out that in most schools, students, since they do not know what is or is not relevant to the job they are preparing for, must learn all the curiculum that is presented. For example, in police training academies, recruits are taught fingerprinting, ballistics, and crime scene investigation, skills that are of peripheral, if not questionable merit for the patrolman. The result is that when recruits finally move to the street, a general disenchantment with the relevance of all their training sets in (Van Maanen, 1973). Even in the prestigous professional schools, the relevance of much training is doubted by practitioners and students alike (Abramson, 1967; Vollmer and Mills, 1966; Schein, 1972). Nor is this problem unknown in our high schools and colleges.

Informal socialization processes, wherein a recruit must negotiate within a far less structured situation than is promoted by formal processes, can induce personal anxiety as well. To wit, individuals may well have trouble discovering clues as to the where, what, when, and how of their assigned organizational roles. Under most circumstances, laissez-faire socialization increases the influence upon the individual of the immediate work group. There is no guarantee, though, that the direction provided by the informal approach will push the recruit in the direction desired and favored by those in authority within the organization (Roy, 1952).

Left to their own devices, recruits select their own agents. The success of the socialization process is then determined largely on the basis of mutual regard, the relevant knowledge possessed by an agent, and, of course, the agent's ability to transfer such knowledge. In most graduate schools, for example, students must seek out their own advisors. The advisor acts as a philosopher, friend, and guide for the student. And among professors—as is true of other organizations that train their members in similar ways—it is felt that the student who pushes the hardest by demanding more time, asking more questions, and so forth, learns the most. The freedom of choice afforded the recruit in the more informal processes consequently has a price. The person must force others in the setting to teach.

Finally, mistakes or errors made by recruits in an informal socialization process must be regarded as more costly and serious than mistakes occurring in formal processes which are often set up explicitly to allow for the occurrence of errors. Precisely because "real work" is interfered with, recruits may find themselves "bad reputations" that can follow them all their days in the organization. The rookie policeman who, for instance, "freezes" while he and his partner attempt to settle a tavern brawl on the street rather than in an academy role-playing exercise may well find himself ostrasized from the inner circle of patrolmen. The forgetful apprentice beautician who provokes a customer by dyeing her hair the wrong color may be forced to look elsewhere for an organization in which to complete the mandatory licensing requirement of the trade. Experienced organizational members know fully well that "mistakes happen," but the recruit is under a special pressure to perform well during an informal initiation period—or, to at least ask before acting. Learning on the job can be quite problematic to the novice. And where potential errors are relatively costly, veteran participants will ignore the recruit's need and desire for "real" experience on the grounds that they cannot "afford to take the chance."

Individual (Collective) Socialization Processes

The degree to which individuals are socialized singularly or as members of a group (collectively) is perhaps the most critical of the process variables. The difference is analogous to the batch versus unit modes of production. In the batch or mass-production case, recruits are bunched together at the outset and processed through an identical set of experiences, with the results being relatively uniform. In the unit or made-to-order case, recruits are processed individually through a more or less unique set of experiences, with the results being relatively different.

Becker (1964) argues persuasively that when a cohort group experiences a socialization program together, the outcomes almost always reflect an "in-the-same-boat" collective consciousness. Individual changes in perspective are built upon an understanding of the problems faced by all group participants. In Becker's words: "As the group shares problems, various members experiment with possible solutions and report back to the group. In the course of collective discussions, the members arrive at a definition of their situation and develop a consensus."

At the same time, however, the consensual character of the solutions worked out by the group allow the members to deviate more from the standards set by the agents than is possible under the individual mode of socialization. Collective processes, therefore, provide a potential base for recruit resistance.[11] In such cases, the congruence between managerial objectives and the actual practices and perspectives adopted by the group is always problematic—the recruit group being more likely than the individual to redefine or ignore agent demands. The dynamics of this phenomenon can be seen when students, for example, develop collective cribbing techniques to pass exams or when trainee groups invent consensual excuses to cover mistakes made by individual members. In these situations, the group solution is premised upon the tacit understanding among group members of the *quid pro quo:* "I'll scratch your back if you'll scratch mine."

Classic illustrations of the dilemma raised by the use of the collective strategy can be found in both educational and work environments. In educational settings, the faculty may beseech a student to study hard while the student's compatriots exhort him or her to relax-and-have-a-good-time. In many work settings, supervisors attempt to ensure that each employee works up to his level of competence while the worker's peers try to impress upon him that he must not be a "rate buster." To the degree that recruits are backed into the proverbial corner and cannot satisfy both demands at the same time, they will follow the dicta of those with whom they spend most of their time and who are most important to them (Shibutani, 1962).

The strength of group understandings depends of course upon the degree to which all members share the same fate. In highly competitive settings, group members know that their own success is increased through the failure of others; hence, the social support networks necessary to maintain cohesion in the group may break down. Consensual understandings will develop but they will buttress individual modes of adjustment. Junior faculty members in publication-minded universities, for instance, follow group standards, although such standards nearly always stress individual scholarship, the collective standard being, as it is, an individual one.

Critically, collective socialization processes often promote and intensify agent demands. Indeed, army recruits socialize each other in ways the army itself could never do, or, for that matter, would not be allowed to do. Graduate students are often said to learn more from one another than from the faculty. And although

---

[11] This is, of course, premised upon the requirement that members of the cohort group be allowed to interact with one another. Some socialization settings, such as monasteries and prisoner-of-war camps, go to great lengths to restrict and prohibit interaction among recruits. Thus, the collective process becomes an individual one and the power of the agents is increased considerably (see Schein, 1956).

agents may have the power to define the nature of the collective problem, recruits often have more resources available to them to define the solution—time, experience, motivation, expertise, and patience (or the lack thereof). In some cases, collective strategies result in the formation of an almost separate subworld within the organization comprised solely of recruits and complete with its own argot, areas of discourse, and unique understandings. A cultural perspective is developed that can be brought to bear upon common problems faced by the group. The "stick-togetherness" that grows in these situations depends on the open sharing of experience. Dornbush (1955) suggested that a "union of sympathy" developed among recruits in a Coast Guard Academy as a result of the enforced regimentation associated with the training program. Sharing similar difficulties and working out collective solutions clearly dramatizes to a recruit the worth and usefulness of colleagual relationships. Without the assistance and support of colleagues, individuals in transition would be lost.

Individual strategies also induce personal change. But the views adopted by people processed individually are likely to be far less homogeneous than the views of those processed collectively. Nor are the views adopted by the isolated recruits necessarily those most beneficial to them in their transitional positions since they have access to only the perspectives of their socialization agents. Certainly, a recruit may choose not to accept such views, although to reject them may well imply the severance of the individual from the organization. Furthermore, the rich, contextual perspectives that are available when individuals interact within a recruit group will not develop under individual strategies. In psychoanalysis, for example, the vocabulary of motives a recruit-patient develops to interpret his or her situation is quite personal and specific compared to the vocabulary that develops in group therapy (Laing, 1960). Of course, such socialization techniques can result in deep individual change—what Burke (1950) refers to as "secular conversion"—but they are lonely changes and are dependent solely upon the mutual regard and warmth that exists between agent and recruit.

Apprenticeship modes of work socialization are sometimes similar to therapist-patient relationships. If the responsibility for transforming an individual to a given status within the organization is delegated to only one person, an intense, value-oriented process is likely to follow. This practice is common whenever a role incumbant is viewed by others in the organization as being the only member capable of shaping the recruit. Caplow (1964) notes the prevalence of this practice in upper levels of bureaucratic organizations. Since the responsibility is given to only one organizational member, the person so designated often becomes a role model whose thoughts and actions the recruit emulates. Graduate schools, police departments, and craftlike trades all make extensive use of the individual socialization strategy. Outcomes in these one-on-one efforts are dependent primarily upon the affective relationships that may or may not develop between apprentice and master. In cases of high affect, the process works well and the new member is liable to quickly and fully internalize the values of the to be assumed role. However, when there are few affective bonds, the socialization process may break down and the hoped-for transition will not take place.

Although role skills may be transferred easily in the individual mode, a recruit's eventual confirmation or full acceptance in the new organizational role must await the judgment of the more experienced agent as to the recruit's conformity to agent demands. Ultimately, there is little middle ground. Either the person fails or succeeds. Becker and Strauss (1956) use the notion of sponsorship to discuss this tactic. Describing the interdependence of careers within an organization, they point out that during a new member's early career, he or she must be more concerned with satisfying the expectations of a sponsor than with satisfying the expectations of others on the scene. Additionally, the ability of the recruit to satisfy a sponsor influences the sponsor's status in the organizational world. If the recruit is doing well, the sponsor's role as an agent may be minor and distant. However, if the recruit is doing poorly, the sponsor's role as agent may be quite active and salient. Sponsorship is not without its dangers to the sponsor.

Overall, individual processes of socialization are expensive, both in time and money. Failures cannot be easily recylced or rescued. Nor are individual strategies particularly suitable for the demands of large organizations that must process many people across various boundaries each year. Hence, with growing bureaucratic structures, the use of mass socialization techniques have increased. Indeed, collective tactics, because of their ease, efficiency, and predictability, have tended to replace the traditional socialization mode of apprenticeship in the modern organization (Salaman, 1974; Perrow, 1972; Blau and Schoenherr, 1971).

Sequential (Discrete) Socialization Processes

Sequential socialization refers to those transitional processes that are marked by a series of identifiable stages through which an individual must pass to achieve a defined role and status within the organization. For example, persons being groomed for a particular managerial position may first be rotated across the various jobs that will comprise the range of managerial responsibility such as is the case in many banks. Similarly, police recruits in most departments must successively pass through such stages as academy classroom instruction, physical conditioning, firearm training, and on-the-street pupilage. Discrete processes are accomplished in only one transitional stage, as is the case when a factory worker becomes a shop supervisor without benefit of an intermediary training program or a department head in a municipal government becomes a city manager without first serving as an assistant in that role.[12] Presumably, any organizational position can be analyzed as to the immediate stages of preparation required of its incoming occupants.

When examining sequential strategies, it is crucial to note the degree to which each stage builds or expands upon the preceding stage. For example, the courses in most technical training programs are arranged in what is thought to be a simple-

---

[12] Perhaps the best example of a nonsequential strategy is cooptation of the dramatic and sudden variety rather than the more common slow and gradual types discussed by Selznick (1949). In the dramatic case, dissenting individuals are jerked clear of their adversary roles and dropped into the position to which they had formerly directed their fire.

to-complex progression. On the other hand, some sequential processes seem to follow no internal logic. Management training is, for instance, quite often disjoint with the curriculum, jumping from topic to topic with little or no integration across stages. In such cases, what is learned by a recruit in the program is dependent simply upon what is liked best in the sequence. If, however, the flow of topics or courses is harmonious and connected functionally in some fashion, the various minor alterations required of an individual at each stage will act cumulatively such that at the end, the person may find himself considerably different then he was when he started.

Relatedly, if several agents handle various portions of the socialization process, the degree to which the aims of the agents are common is very important to the eventual outcome. For example, in some officer's training schools of peacetime military organizations, the agents responsible for physical and weapon training tend to have very different perspectives on their jobs and of the recruits than those agents in charge of classroom instruction (Wamsley, 1972). Recruits quickly spot such conflicts when they exist and sometimes exploit them, playing agents off against one another. The result of such incongruities often lead to a more relaxed situation fo: the recruits, one in which they enjoy watching their instructors pay more attention to each other than they pay to the training program. A nearly identical situation has been reported in some police training programs (Van Maanen, 1974; McNamara, 1967).

In the sequential arrangement, agents may also be unknown to one another, separated spatially as well as having thoroughly different images of their respective tasks. Both Merton (1957) and Glaser (1964), for example, have remarked upon the difficulty many scientists apparently have when moving from a university to an industrial setting to practice their trade. The pattern is seemingly quite nonsequential, for many scientists discover that their academic training emphasized a far different set of skills and interests than is required in the corporate environment. As Avery (1968) observed, to become a "good" industrial scientist, the individual in transition has to learn the painful lesson that to be able to sell an idea is at least as important as having one in the first place. Consider, too, the range of views about a particular job an organizational newcomer may receive from persons in the personnel department, people in the training division, and colleagues on the job, all of whom have a hand (and a stake) in the recruit's transition. From this standpoint, empathy must certainly be extended to the so-called juvenile delinquent who receives "guidance" from the police, probation officers, judges, social workers, psychiatrists, and correctional officials. Such a sequence evocatively suggests that a person may well learn to be whatever the immediate situation demands. The person's resulting identity in these cases often has the stability of a pattern on an oscilloscope.

Besides the ambiguity that grows from the countervailing demands sometimes made upon individuals in sequential processes, there is also likely to be a strong bias in the presentation of each agent to make the next stage appear benign. Thus, recruits are told that if they will just "buckle down and apply themselves" while in stage A, stages B, C, D, and E will be easy. Agents usually mask, wittingly or unwittingly, the true nature of the stage to follow, for if recruits feel that their futures are bright, rewarding, and assured, they will be most cooperative at the stage they are in, not wishing to jeopardize the future which they think awaits them. To wit, the tactics of high school mathematics teachers who tell their students that if they will just work hard in algebra, geometry will be a "cinch" (Lortie, 1975). However, students sooner or later usually discover the truth. Consider also Goffman's (1961) observations of mental patients who, by the time they had moved through the elaborate sequence of "theraputic" stages in the hospital, had developed a large residue of mistrust toward their agents, the process itself akin to a "betrayal funnel." An extreme case of sequential betrayal occurs in state executions, where the condemned is usually told by his coaches on the scene that his demise will be quick and painless—"you won't feel a thing" (Levine, 1972; Eshelman, 1962).

When attempts are consistently made to make each step appear benign, the individual's best source of information on the sequential process is another person who has gone through it. And if organizational members who have been through the process can be located by recruits, they will have a great deal of influence toward shaping recruit perspectives. Thus, some organizations go a long way in attempting to isolate recruits from veteran members who represent perhaps wellsprings of factual data useful to recruits who are attempting to predict the outcome of the sequence they are being processed through. Certain profit-making trade schools apparently go to great lengths to make sure that their paying clientele do not learn of the limited job opportunities in, for example, the "glamorous and high-paying" worlds of radio and TV broadcasting, commercial art, or heavy equipment operation. Door-to-door sales trainees are continually assured that their success is guaranteeed, for the handy-dandy, one-of-a-kind product they are preparing to merchandise will "sell itself." Consequently, if recruits are to be allowed the privilege of interacting with more experienced organizational members, those controlling the process will invariably select a veteran member who will present a purified or laundered image of the end point in the sequence (Becker, 1972).

Finally, the degree to which an individual is required to continue through the entire sequence more or less on schedule is an important feature of this socialization strategy. A recruit may feel, for instance, that she is being pressured or pushed into certain positions or stages before she is ready. This is analytically similar to the business executive who does not want a promotion but feels that if he does not take it, his respective career will be damaged (Beckhard, 1977). Consider, too, the professor who feels that she cannot turn down the deanship without rupturing the respectful relationships she presently maintains with her faculty colleagues in the department (Cohen and March, 1973). Of course, it is also possible that a person may be so busy preparing for the next stage in the socialization sequence that his or her performance in the immediate stage so deteriorates that this next stage will never materialize. On the other hand, if the person does not slip or fail in any fashion, sequential socialization over a career may provide the individual with what Henry (1963) called a "permanent sense of the unobtained." Thus, the executive who, at 30 years of age, aims toward being the head of his department at age 40, will, at age 40, be attempting to make division head by age 50, and so on. The consumer sequence that stresses the accumulation of material goods has much the same character as does an artistic sequence that stresses the achievement of the perfect work. Sequential socialization of this sort has a Sisyphus-like nature, with the individual seeking perpetually to reach the unreachable.

Fixed (Variable) Socialization Processes

Organizational socialization processes differ in terms of the information and certainty possessed by an individual regarding the transition timetable. Fixed socialization processes provide a recruit with a precise knowledge of the time it will take to complete a given passage. The time of transition is standardized. Consider the probationary systems used on most civil service jobs. Such processes are fixed, for the individuals know in advance just how long their job status will remain probationary. Educational systems provide another good illustration of fixed processes. Schools begin and end at the same time for all pupils. Individuals move through the entire system roughly one step at a time. Fixed processes therefore provide a rather rigid conception of "normal" progress such that those who are not on schedule will be considered deviant.

Variable socialization processes provide no advance notice to those being processed of their transition timetable. What may be true for one is not true for another. Such processes require the recruit to search out clues to the future. To wit, prisoners serving what are called indeterminate sentences, such as the legendary and properly infamous "one-to-ten," must "dope out" timetable norms from the scarce materials available to them (Irwin, 1970; Taylor and Cohen, 1972). Apprenticeship programs often specify only the minimum number of years a person must remain in the apprentice role and leave open the precise time a person can expect to be advanced to the journeyman classification. Since the rates of passage across any organizational boundary are a matter of some concern to most participants, transition timetables may be developed on the basis of the most fragmentary and flimsy information. Rumors and innuendos about who is going where and when they are going characterize the variable strategy of socialization. Roth (1963) suggests that if a recruit has direct access to others who are presently in or have been through a very similar situation, a "sentimental order" will emerge among people as to when certain passages can be expected to take place. And regardless of whether or not these expectations are accurate, the individuals will measure their progress against them.

The vertically oriented business career is a good example of variable socialization. The would-be executive must push hard to discover the signs of a coming promotion (or demotion). Thus, the person listens closely to stories concerning the time it takes one to advance in the organization, observes as closely as possible the experiences of others, and, in general, develops an age consciousness delineating the range of appropriate ages for given positions (Roth, 1963). The process is judgmental and requires a good deal of time and effort on the person's part. However, in some very stable organizations, such as many governmental agencies, the expected rate of advancement can be evaluated quite precisely and correctly; thus, the process becomes, for all practical purposes, fixed.

In some cases, what is designed as a fixed socialization process more closely approximates a variable process described by the familar cliche "always a bridesmaid, never a bride." The transition timetable is clear enough, but for various reasons, the person cannot or does not wish to complete the journey. Colleges and universities have their "professional students" who never seem to graduate. Training programs have trainees who continually "miss the boat" and remain trainees indefinitely. Fixed processes differ therefore with regard to both the frequency and rate of the so-called role failure—those recruits who for one reason or another are not able to complete the process.

Relatedly, Roth (1963) suggests that a special category of "chronic sidetrack" may be created for certain types of role failures. He notes that in the fixed socialization processes of public schools, the retarded are shunted off to distinct classes where the notion of progress does not exist. Similarly, in some police agencies, recruits unable to meet certain agent demands often receive long-term assignments as city jailers or traffic controllers. Such assignments serve as a signal to the recruit and others in the organization that the individual has left the normal career path. To the extent that such organizational "Siberias" exist and can be identified by those in the setting, chronic sidetracking which serves remedial, custodial, or punitive functions is a distinct possibility when the fixed socialization strategy is utilized. On the other hand, sidetracking is quite subtle and problematic to the recruit operating in a variable socialization track. To wit, many people who are working in the upper and lower levels of management positions in large organizations are often unable to judge where they are going or how they are doing. Consequently, variable processes are likely to create much anxiety and perhaps frustration for individuals who are unable to construct reasonably valid timetables to inform them of the appropriateness of their movement or lack of movement in the organization.

When tests and evaluations make enigmatic what would otherwise be a fixed socialization process, an individual may also suffer much anxiety. As Mechanic (1962) notes, for example, tests often measure one's ability to cope or withstand stress and uncertainty more than they measure a person's skills or abilities. Needless to say, the more an individual's fate hangs in the balance of test or evaluation results, the more tension is created in the situation. Thus, recruits seek quickly to determine just how realistic a role failure is in the socialization setting. However, even in situations where testing is frequent, recruits may discover that "everybody gets through regardless." Safer (1975) reports that door-to-door sales trainees soon ascertain that classroom tests and exercises are of no importance compared to making sales when once on the job. Police recruits in most departments eventually learn that as long as they conform to the behavioral code of the police academy, there is little to no possibility of flunking out due to scholastic failure (Van Maanen, 1973). Students in various beauty colleges find that as long as they pay their fees on schedule, no one really cares whether or not they "butcher" a job—except perhaps the client (Notkin, 1972). In any case, appearances are sometimes deceiving, for the reality of the socialization process does not stalk about with a label. However, recruits will, under most conditions, be ingenious, deciphering organizational policy, and in their own minds at least, converting what is claimed to be a variable process into one that is relatively fixed.

It should be clear that to those in authority positions within an organization, time is an important resource by which control over others can be exercised. Variable socialization processes provide an administrator with a most powerful tool by which to influence behavior. But the administrator also risks creating an organizational situation that is marked by confusion and uncertainty among those concerned with their movement in the system. Fixed processes provide individuals with temporal reference points, allowing them to both ceremonially observe passages and hold together relationships forged during the socialization experiences. Such rituals then call to attention the common pursuit of organization members as well as solidifying the bonds linking recruits to one another. Variable processes may well initiate rites of passage, but the individual metamorphosis that is celebrated on these occasions will have very different meanings to those observing the ritual (Van Gennep, 1960). Variable processes are likely, therefore, to divide and drive apart those individuals who might otherwise show much cohesion were the process fixed.

Tournament (Contest) Socialization Processes

The practice of separating selected clusters of recruits into different socialization programs or tracks on the basis of presumed differences in ability, ambition, or backgrounds represents the essense of tournament processes (Cicourel and Kitsuse, 1963; Turner, 1960). Such tracking is often accomplished at the earliest possible date in a person's organizational career. Furthermore, the shifting of people between tracks in a tournament process occurs in only one direction: individuals are shifted downward and therefore eliminated from further consideration within the track they have left. The rule for the tournament socialization strategy is simple: "When you win, you win only the right to go on to the next round; when you lose, you lose forever" (Rosenbaum, 1976).

To the contrary, in contest socialization processes, a sharp distinction between superiors and inferiors is avoided. The channels of movement through the various socialization programs are kept open and dependent upon the observed abilities and stated interests of all those in the pool of organizational recruits. An example is useful here.

Consider the American public school system, where tracking decisions are sometimes made by school administrators and teachers as early as the ninth grade (Jencks et al., 1972). In schools where the tournament mode is practiced, only those students in a college-bound track are allowed to take certain courses. Those students in vocational tracks are discouraged and usually prohibited from taking courses geared for students in the college track. Mobility in the tournament mode occurs primarily in a down-and-out direction; relatively few persons move up and onward (Rosenbaum, 1976). In schools where tracking decisions are not made by administrators and teachers, the contest process is practiced, and there is considerable mobility both downward and upward within the system (Cicourel and Kitsuse, 1963). There is, furthermore, a sense of fairness implicit in contest processes by virtue of the freedom of choice allowed a student and the ever-present possibility that he or she might move up in the system. Movement is then premised upon the performance of individuals and not simply their placement in a particular track. Certainly, this is the stated ideal of American public education, although some observers suggest that the contest process exists in fewer than 25% of our high schools (Jencks et al., 1972; Katz, 1971; Karabel, 1972).

Although little empirical research along these lines has been conducted in work organizations, there are strong reasons to believe that some version of the tournament process exists in virtually all large organizations. Anecdoctal evidence suggests, for instance, to be passed over once for many management jobs is to be forever disqualified from that position. And accounts coming from the women strongly suggest that in most organizations, women are on very different tracks than men and have therefore been eliminated from the tournament even before they began. A similar situation is said to exist for most minority-group members. In a contest process, any individual could, in theory, rise to any level or compete for any position in the organization. Furthermore, individuals would have as much chance for a given job the second time around as they did the first time. Consider also the ubiquitous label "high-potential employee." Often the training for these high potentials is considerably different than for those persons not so labeled. The high-potential track is usually quite different than the track afforded the average or typical recruit. Of course, the tournament strategy dictates that even among the high potentials, to be dropped from the fast track means that reentry is forever prohibited. Certainly, as one moves through higher and higher levels in the organization, the tournament strategy becomes even more pervasive. Perhaps this is inevitable, but the point here is simply that the use of the tournament socialization process (particularly in the extreme and across all levels in an organization) can be expected to have a number of rather widespread consequences (see Rosenbaum, 1979).

First, the use of tournament processes suggests that the attainment of an individual within an organization is more likely to be explained by the tracking system existing within that organization than by the particular characteristics of the person (Jencks et al., 1972; Bowles and Gintis, 1973). Thus, the person who fails in organization X might well have succeeded in organization Y. Second, there is always something of Rosenthal's (1967) well-known self-fulfilling prophesy at work in tournament socialization wherein the individual who, for whatever reason, succeeds in getting himself labeled as, say, a "high potential" becomes seen in that light and can therefore do little wrong in the eyes of others in the organization. Third, those who fall out of the tournament at any stage are provided further socialization of only a custodial sort. They are expected to behave only in ways appropriate to their "plateaued" position. As Goffman's (1952) elegant quip denotes, they are "cooled out" and discouraged from making further efforts. The organization, in other words, has completed its work on them. Tournament socialization, more than the contest mode, can be seen then to shape and guide individual ambition in a very powerful way. Fourth, and relatedly, in tournament processes where a single failure has permanent consequences, those passing through tend to adopt the safest strategies of passage (Whyte, 1956; Argyris, 1964). This suggests that those who remain in the tournament for any length of time are socialized perhaps to be insecure, obsequious to authority, and differentiated, both socially and psychologically, from one another. On the other hand, those not remaining in the tournament tend perhaps to become fatalistic, homogeneous, and to varying degrees, alienated from the organization.[13]

The attractiveness and prevalence of tournament socialization strategies in work organizations appear to rest upon two major arguments. One reason given is that such processes promote the most efficient allocation of resources. Organizational resources, it is argued, should be allocated only to those most likely to profit from them. The other reason provided for tournament socialization is based primarily upon the faith that an early judgment on an individual's potential can be reliably and accurately made. Here the principles of selection psychology are utilized to separate the deserving from the undeserving members of the organization (Heritage, 1974). Various tracks are then legitimized by the testing and classification of people wherein each test and the resulting classification represents another level in the tournament process. The American Telephone and Telegraph Company represents perhaps the foremost proponent and user of this socialization process. Each transition from one hierarchical level to another is accompanied by the rigorous evaluation of an ever-declining cadre of those still remaining in the tournament (Langer, 1971).

Contest socialization, on the other hand, implies that preset norms for transition do not exist in a form other than demonstrated performance. Regardless of age, sex, race, or other background factors, each person starts out equal with all other participants. Like educational systems, this appears to be the stated policy of most American corporations. However, those who have looked most closely at these organizations have concluded that this Horatio Alger ideal is primarily a myth (Dalton, 1959; Glaser, 1968).

In summary, tournament socialization seems far more likely than contest socialization to drive a wedge between the individuals being processed. In tournament

---

[13] Turner (1960) argues that contest strategies encourage the individual to develop traits such as enterprise, initiative, perserverance, and craft. The tournament strategy, however, would seem to encourage traits such as low risk taking, short-run cycles of effort, and ever-changing spheres of interest based on the potential for personal gain. And it would seem that these traits become more pronounced the longer one remains in the tournament and as the stakes increase.

situations, it is each person out for himself, and rarely will they ever come together to act in unison either for or against the organization. Contest strategies, as the label implies, appear to produce a more cooperative spirit among recruits. Perhaps because one setback does not entail a permanent loss, people can afford to help one another over various hurdles and a more collegial atmosphere can be maintained.

Serial (Disjunctive) Socialization Processes

The serial socialization process, whereby experienced members groom newcomers about to assume similar roles in the organization, is perhaps the best guarantee that the organization will not change over long periods of time. In the police world, the serial feature of recruit socialization is virtually a taken-for-granted device and accounts in large measure for the remarkable intergenerational stability of patrolman behavior patterns (Westley, 1970; Rubenstein, 1973; Manning and Van Maanen, 1978). Innovation in serial modes is unlikely, but continuity and a sense of history will be maintained even in the face of a turbulent and changing environment.

If, however, the newcomer is not following in the footsteps of his or her predecessors, the socialization pattern can be labeled disjunctive. Whereas the serial process risks stagnation and contamination, the disjunctive process risks complication and confusion. Recruits who are left to their own devices may rely on definitions for their tasks that are gleaned from inappropriate others. But the disjunctive pattern also creates the opportunity for recruits to be inventive and original. Without an old guard about to hamper the development of a fresh perspective, the conformity and lockstep pressures created by the serial mode are absent. Some entrepreneurs automatically fall into a disjunctive process of socialization, as do those who fill newly created positions in an organization. In both cases, there are few people, if any, available to the individual who have had similar experiences and could therefore coach the newcomer in light of the lessons they have learned.

Similarly, what may be a serial process to most people may be disjunctive to others. Consider black patrolmen entering a previously all-white department or the Navy's recent attempts to train women to become jet pilots. In these cases, the demographically deviant newcomers do not have access to another who has shared their set of unique problems. Certainly, such situations make passage considerably more difficult for the person, particularly if they are going it alone, as is most often the case.

Sometimes, what appears to be serial is actually disjunctive. To illustrate, recruits may be prepared inadequately for spots in one department by agents coming from another department. Often, this is the situation when the personnel department handles all aspects of training. It is only later, after the newcomers have access to others who have been through the same process, that they discover the worthlessness and banality of their training (Van Maanen, 1976). Agent familiarity with the target position is a crucial factor in the serial strategy.

Occasionally, what could be called "gapping" presents a serious problem in serial strategies. Gapping refers to the historical or temporal distance between recruit and agent. For example, a recruit has the greatest opportunity to learn about his future from those with whom he works. But the past experiences of those with whom he works that are passed on to him with good intentions may be quite removed from his own circumstance. When a newcomer hears others tell of being promoted within a month or two after starting, he may well begin to wonder what is wrong with him if he is still working the same job six or seven months after starting. He may believe this is a reflection on his own competence. And needless to say, it is important to consider what the more experienced employees think of their junior counterpart who has not yet been promoted. Roth (1963) notes that if this were simply a matter of contrast between the twenty-year veteran and the green recruit, the differences could be readily reconciled. However, in many organizations, pathways and opportunities are constantly changing, thus creating major to minor gaps in the knowledge separating a recruit and his agents. Such experiential and informational gaps—arising from economic fluctuations, policy shifts, or different recruiting and promoting tactics—may make it difficult for newcomers to see whether or not the particular pathways they are on are leading in desired directions.

It is generally true that recruits representing the first class will set the tone for the classes to follow (Merton, 1957). It is not suggested that those following are paginated seriatim, but simply that for those to come, it is easier to learn from others already on hand than it is to learn on their own as originators. As long as there are others available in the socialization setting whom the recruits consider to be "like them," these others will act as guides, passing on the consensual solutions to the typical problems faced by the newcomer. Mental patients, for example, often report that they were only able to survive and gain their release because other, more experienced patients "set them wise" as to what the psychiatric staff deemed appropriate behavior and indicative of improvement (Stanton and Schwartz, 1954; Goffman, 1961).

Serial modes create something analogous to Mead's (1956) notion of a postfigurative culture. Just as children in stable societies are able to gain a sure sense of the future that awaits them by seeing in their parents and grandparents an image of themselves grown older, employees in organizations can gain a sense of the future by seeing in their more experienced elders an image of themselves further along in the organization. A danger exists, of course, that the image itself will be undesirable from the standpoint of the recruit, and the person will leave the organization rather than face what seems to be an agonizing future. In industrial settings where worker morale is low and turnover is high, a serial pattern of initiating newcomers into the organization is to maintain and perhaps amplify the already poor situation.

An interesting case of the disjunctive pattern is provided by Klineberg and Cottle (1973). They note that first generation rural-to-city migrants suffer a serious break between their past and present experiences. So serious is this break that migrants' images of a better future usually lie unconnected to any concrete activities toward which migrants could direct their efforts. The bridge between means and ends is apparently destroyed in these disjunctive transitions. Without a set of sufficiently similar others who have progressed through the transition, newcomers will have no one to look toward as role models in their situation. Indeed, the sociologist who claims, for example, that veteran patrolmen serve as role models for rookie patrolmen is simply saying that the rookies typically classify the behavior of the veterans as relevant to themselves because the veterans have been over the same ground the rookies are presently traversing. The rookies can learn the appropriate modes of behaving, then, simply by listening, watching, and emulating the behavior of their more experienced colleagues.

The analytic distinction between serial and disjunctive socialization processes is sometimes brought into sharp focus when an organization undertakes a "housecleaning" whereby old members are swept out and new members brought in to replace them. In extreme cases, an entire organization can be thrown into a disjunctive mode of socialization, with the result that the organization no longer will resemble its former self. It is also true that occasionally the persons presumably being socialized have more experience and knowledge of the situation than do those who are to socialize them. For example, in colleges where faculty members are constantly entering and exiting, long-term students exert much control over the institution. Certainly, in organizations such as prisons and mental hospitals, recruit turnover is often much smaller than the staff turnover. In these organizations, it is not surprising that they are often literally run by the inmates. Similarly, in many work organizations, a person who must be exceptionally good to be, say, a project director at age 25, must be exceptionally mediocre to be in that same position at age 50 or 55. Because of such circumstances, the age-graded stereotype of the youthful, naive, and passive junior member who is coached wisely by a mature, informed, and still-active mentor is frequently false. The process may have been designed as a serial one, but to the recruit the process is disjunctive, for he is unwilling to take the agents of his socialization seriously.

Open (Closed) Socialization Processes

During or upon a transition, an individual is frequently a part of a larger group that can be described as relatively open or closed (Ziller, 1965). In open socialization processes, the assignment of a recruit is made to a group that is in a continual state of membership flux. Individuals quickly recognize the transitory nature of their membership and can be expected then to act in self-oriented ways. In such circumstances, they will be concerned primarily with acquiring transferable information and maintaining their own self-esteem rather than the status of the group (Goffman, 1959). To the contrary, closed socialization processes involve a newcomer within a relatively long-standing and permanent group. Transfer rates in and out of the group are low and an extended time perspective prevails. As such, the group usually has developed (or is developing) elaborate rituals and tests through which the newcomers must pass if they are to become integrated within that group. Closed socialization strategies then involve the individual with the common life and purpose of a distinct and long-standing group within the organization.

Both psychologically and sociologically, the differences in behavior between temporary and permanent groups are often striking. For example, the helping relationships that unfold to assist a recruit are likely to be much more pronounced if the socialization process is closed than if it is open. In closed socialization processes, a recruit is more likely as well to encounter group goals that are only vaguely formulated, since specific goals may well threaten a permanent group's reason for existence (Parsons, 1960). Furthermore, the newcomer's attachment to the group, rather than the organization, must be demonstrated. In closed processes, questions concerning the newcomer's commitment to the group, his involvement in matters peripheral to the group's concern, and, critically, his loyalty to other group members are sure to be raised (Ziller, 1976). For example, police recruits, upon entering a squad in the patrol division, undergo a most closed process of socialization. They are tested repeatedly and closely as to their prudence, their trustworthiness, and their willingness to share the risks of police work (Van Maanen, 1974). Officers from other squads are told explicitly not to interfere, and even supervisors maintain something of a hands-off approach toward the new recruit. For the newcomer it is a very demanding and critical period. If he passes the acid tests and demonstrates his concern for other squad members, he is accepted as part of the team. If he does not pass, he may well be eliminated from the organization altogether. Closed socialization processes are therefore analytically akin to Bakke's (1950) fusion process, in which an individual's self-concept becomes inextricably tied to the self-concepts of others.

Open socialization processes produce very different results. Loyalty is presumably less an issue to group members than is competence. Juries, project teams, ad hoc committees, and so forth represent typical open socialization settings. Social relationships among colleagues may be somewhat strained, since the necessity to maintain good ones is lessened by virtue of the short-run nature of the group. There are some advantages to this mode, however. An interesting study is reported by Torrance (1955), who examined the decision-making abilities of individuals undergoing both open and closed socialization. He investigated aircrews who had trained together. After training, some crews were scrambled (open socialization), whereas other crews remained intact (closed socialization). To Torrance's surprise, the scrambled crews were far superior on the performance of various task-related problems than were the intact crews. Interpreting these results, he concluded that the relative lack of power differentials and social status among the scrambled groups allowed for a more open and honest consideration of alternative solutions to the problems facing the group than would be possible when power and status were established and relatively fixed, as was the case for the intact crews. Janis (1972) has reported very similar findings more recently.

Different techniques of handling conflict might also be expected to develop between individuals undergoing either closed or open socialization. In the open case, aggression and withdrawal may well be more popular tactics, since they are relatively easy to apply, reliable in their effects, and since the group is in constant flux, unlikely to have any long-range consequences for the individual. In the closed case, negotiation, mediation, and perhaps subtle dissimulation tactics are more

religious cults, elite law schools, self-realization groups, drug rehabilitation programs, professional athletic teams, and so on. All of these organizations require a recruit to pass through a series of robust tests in order to gain privileged access to the organization.

In general, simply the endurance of the ordeal itself promotes a strong fellowship among those who have followed the same path to membership. Lortie (1968) observed that entrance into some occupations, such as college teaching, professional crime, dentistry, and the priesthood, require a person to experience a "shared ordeal." Enduring the ordeal than provides the newcomer with a set of colleagues who have been through the same process as well as symbolizing to others on the scene that the newcomer is committed fully to the organization. For those who pass completely through the ordeal, the gap separating recruits from members narrows appreciably while the gap separating members from nonmembers grows.

Clearly, divestiture rather than investiture strategies are more likely to produce similar results among recruits. And it should be kept in mind that the ordeal aspects of a divestiture process represent an identity-bestowing as well as an identity-destroying process. Coercion is not necessarily an assault on the person. Indeed, it can also be a device for stimulating many personal changes that are evaluated positively by the individual. What has always been problematic with coercion is the possibility for perversion that its use involves.

SUMMARY AND CONCLUSIONS

I have attempted to provide in this essay a partial framework for analyzing some of the more pervasive strategies used by organizations for controlling and directing the behavior of their members. Obviously, there are other strategies that could have been discussed. For instance, the tightness or looseness of day-to-day supervision could be depicted as a socialization strategy (Argyris, 1964). So, too, could the degree of demographic and attitudinal homogeneity or heterogeneity displayed by incoming recruits be considered a socialization strategy affecting the probability that a single perspective will come to dominate the group of newcomers (Newcomb, 1958; Cartwright and Zander, 1960). What I have tried to do here, however, is to describe those processes that are both ignored by organizational researchers and taken for granted by organizational decision makers.

It is true, of course, that an individual undergoing a transition does not represent a human version of the *tabula rasa,* merely waiting patiently for the organization to do its work. Indeed, some people play very active roles in their own socialization (Light, 1980). Each strategy discussed here contains only the possibility, not the actuality of effect. For example, individuals undergoing collective socialization may withdraw from the situation, abstaining from the group life that surrounds other recruits. Or a person may undergo a brutal divestiture process with a calculated indifference and stoic nonchalance. A few exceptions are probably the rule in even the most tyrannical of settings.

However, the preponderance of evidence suggests that the eight strategies presented above play a very powerful role influencing any individual's conception of his or her work role. By teasing out the structural elements which, by and large, define an organization boundary passage, it is apparent that for most persons a given set of experiences in the organization will lead to rather predictable ends. For instance, if we are interested in strategies that seem to promote a relatively high degree of similarity in the thoughts and actions of recruits and their agents, a combination of the informal, closed, divestiture, and serial processes would probably be quite effective. If dissimilarity were desired, collective, open, investiture, and disjunctive strategies would be preferred. Or if a relatively passive group of undifferentiated recruits were to be produced, we might expect that the combination of formal, collective, sequential, tournament, and divestiture strategies would be required. Other combinations could be expected to manufacture other sorts of recruits with, I suspect, few exceptions. At any rate, there are far too many potential hypotheses that could be suggested by combining various strategies to be presented in this brief conclusion. The point I wish to emphasize here is simply that much control over individual behavior in organizations is a direct result of the manner in which people are processed through the organization. By directing attention to the breakpoints or transitions in a person's work career, much is to be gained in terms of understanding how organizations shape the performances and ambitions of their members. And most critically, the strategies by which these transitions are managed organizationally are clearly subject to both empirical and practical manipulation.

To researchers, therefore, I would hope that this paper stimulates more interest in the strategies of people processing than has heretofore been the case. Indeed, this may be a matter of some urgency, for as Blau and Schoenher (1971) and Perrow (1972) have argued recently, the trend in modern organizations is apparently one of decreasing control through traditional means such as direct supervision or the immediate application of rewards or punishments and increasing the control over organizational members by using such indirect means as recruitment, selection, training, and career-path manipulation. To these remote-control mechanisms we might well add the eight strategies described in this paper while continuing our search for others. Let me suggest here that if we are to ever begin to understand how organizations can be said to behave, we must first understand how the people that run them behave. Thus, it is mandatory that we examine the ways in which people in positions of organizational authority got there. By so doing, we will no doubt learn considerably more about the strategies and consequences of organizational socialization.

To practicing managers, I would hope that this paper suggests certain features of their own organizations that promote various types of behavioral styles among their subordinates, peers, and superiors. Since many of the strategies for "breaking in" employees to various roles lie beneath the surface of organizational life, they are rarely discussed or considered to be matters of choice in managerial decision-making circles. Those strategies that do get considered often are left unchanged

simply because their effects are not widely understood. Other strategies are frequently justified on the traditional illogic of "I had to do it that way and so are the people who follow me." Yet as I have attempted to show, socialization processes are not products of a fixed, evolutionary pattern; they can be changed. However, the unfortunate situation seems to be that certain strategies are institutionalized out of inertia, not considered choice and action. In sum, this is hardly the most rational practice to be followed by members of a profession that is marked by its apparent concern for the effective utilization of resources—be those resources material or human.

REFERENCES

Abramson, M. *The Professional in the Organization.* Chicago: Rand McNally, 1967.

Argyris, C. *Integrating the Individual and the Organization.* New York: Wiley, 1964.

Avery, R.W. Enculturation in industrial research. In B.G. Glaser, ed., *Organizational Careers: A Sourcebook for Theory.* Chicago: Aldine, 1968, pp. 175-81.

Bakke, E.W. *Bonds of Organization.* New York: Harper, 1950.

Barnard, C. *The Functions of the Executive.* Cambridge, Mass.: Harvard University Press, 1938.

Becker, H.S. *Outsiders: Studies in the Sociology of Deviance.* New York: Free Press, 1963.

Becker, H.S. Personal change in adult life. *Sociometry, 27,* 1964, 40-53.

Becker, H.S. A school is a lousy place to learn anything in. In B. Greer, ed., *Learning to Work.* Beverly Hills, Calif.: Sage, 1972.

Becker, H.S., and Strauss, A. Careers, personality, and adult socialization. *American Journal of Sociology, 62,* 1956, 253-63.

Becker, H.S., Greer, B., Hughes, E.C., and Strauss, A. *Boys in White.* Chicago: University of Chicago Press, 1961.

Beckhard, R. Managerial careers in transition. In J. Van Maanen, ed., *Organizational Careers: Some New Perspectives.* New York: Wiley, 1977, pp. 153-65.

Bell, C.G. and Price, C.M. *The First Term: A Study of Legislative Socialization.* Beverly Hills, Calif.: Sage, 1975.

Berlew, D.E., and Hall, D.T. The socialization of managers: effects of expectations on performance. *Administrative Science Quarterly, 11,* 1966, 207-23.

Bidwell, C.E. Pre-adult socialization. Paper read at the Social Science Research Council Conference on Socialization and Social Structure. May 1962.

Blau, P.N., and Schoenherr, R.A. *The Structure of Organizations.* New York: Basic Books, 1971.

Brim, O.G. Socialization through the life cycle. In O.G. Prim and S. Wheeler, eds., *Socialization after Childhood.* New York: Wiley, 1966.

Bowles, S., and Gintis, H. I.Q. in the U.S. class structure. *Social Policy,* 3, 1973, 1-27.

Burke, K. *A Rhetoric of Motives.* Englewood Cliffs, N.J.: Prentice-Hall, 1950.

Caplow, T. *Principles of Organization.* New York: Harcourt, Brace, 1964.

Cartwright, D., and Zander, A., eds. *Group dynamics: Research and theory.* Evanston, Ill.: Row, Peterson, 1960.

Cicourel, A.V., and Kitsuse, J. *The Educational Decision Makers.* Indianapolis, Ind.: Bobbs-Merrill, 1963.

Cogswell, B. Some structural properties influencing socialization. *Administrative Science Quarterly,* 14, 1967.

Cohen, M.D., and March, J.G. *The American College President.* New York: McGraw-Hill, 1973.

Dalton, M. *Men Who Manage.* New York: Wiley, 1959.

Dornbush, S. The military academy as an assimilating institution. *Social Forces,* 33, 1955, 316-21.

Eshelman, B. *Death Row Chaplain.* Englewood Cliffs, N.J.: Prentice-Hall, 1962.

Faulkner, R.R. Coming of age in organizations: a comparative study of career contingencies and adult socialization. *Sociology of Work and Occupations,* 1, 1974, 173-91.

Feldman, D.C. A contingency theory of socialization. *Administrative Science Quarterly,* 21, 1976, 433-52.

Glaser, B.G. *Organizational Scientists: Their Professional Careers.* Indianapolis, Ind.: Bobbs-Merrill, 1964.

Glaser, B.G., ed. *Organizational Careers: A Sourcebook for Theory.* Chicago: Aldine, 1968.

Goffman, E. On cooling the mark out. *Psychiatry,* 15, 1952, 451-63.

Goffman, E. *The Presentation of Self in Everday Life.* New York: Doubleday, 1959.

Goffman, E. *Asylums.* New York: Anchor Books, 1961.

Goode, W.J. The theoretical limits of professionalization. In A. Etzioni, ed., *The Semi-Professions and Their Organization,* New York: Free Press, 1969.

Henry, J. *Culture against Man.* New York: Random House, 1963.

Heritage, T. Assessing people. In N. Armistead, ed., *Reconstructing Social Psychology.* London: Penguin, 1974.

Hughes, E.C. *Men and Their Work.* New York: Free Press, 1958.

Inkeles, A. Society, social structure, and child socialization. In J.A. Clausen, ed., *Socialization and Society.* Boston: Little, Brown, 1966.

Irwin, J. *The Felon.* Englewood Cliffs, N.J.: Prentice-Hall, 1970.

James, W. *Psychology.* New York: Holt, 1892.

Janis, I. *Victims of Groupthink.* Boston: Houghton Mifflin, 1972.

Jencks, C., et al. *Inequality: A Reassessment of the Effect of Family and Schooling in America.* New York: Basic Books, 1972.

Kanter, R.M. Commitment and social organization: a study of commitment mechanisms in utopian communities. *American Sociological Review,* 33, 1968, 409-17.

Karabel, J. Community colleges and social stratification. *Harvard Education Review,* 42, 1972, 521-62.

Katz, M. *Class, Bureaucracy, and Schools.* New York: Praeger, 1971.

Klineberg, S., and Cottle, T.J. *The Present of Things Past.* Boston: Little, Brown, 1973.

Laing, R.D. *The Divided Self.* London: Tavistock, 1960.

Langer, E. The women of the telephone company. *New York Review of Books,* 1971.

Levine, S., ed. *Death Row.* San Francisco: Glide, 1972.

Light, D. *Becoming Psychiatrists.* New York: Norton, 1980.

Lipset, S.M., Trow, M., and Coleman, J.S. *Union Democracy.* New York: Free Press, 1956.

Lofland, J. *Doomsday Cult.* Englewood Cliffs, N.J.: Prentice-Hall, 1966.

Lortie, D.C. Shared ordeal and induction to work. In H.S. Becker, B. Greer, D. Reisman, and R.S. Weiss, eds., *Institutions and the Person.* Chicago: Aldine, 1968.

Lortie, D.C. *Schoolteacher.* Chicago: University of Chicago Press, 1975.

McNamara, J. Uncertainties in police work: the relevance of police recruits' background and training. In D.J. Bordua, ed., *The Police: Six Sociological Essays.* New York: Wiley, 1967.

Manning, P. and Van Maanen, J., eds. *Policing.* Los Angeles: Goodyear Press, 1978.

Mead, M. *New Lives for the Old.* New York: Morrow, 1956.

Mechanic, D. *Students under Stress.* New York: Free Press, 1962.

Merton, R.K. *Social Theory and Social Structure.* New York: Free Press, 1957.

Newcomb, T.M. Attitude development as a function of reference groups: the Bennington study. In E.E. Maccoby, T.M. Newcomb, and E.L. Hartley, eds.,

Readings in Social Psychology, 3rd ed. New York: Holt, Rinehart and Winston, 1958.

Notkin, M.S. Situational learning in a school with clients. In B. Greer, ed., *Learning to Work.* Beverly Hills, Calif.: Sage, 1972, pp. 49-58.

Olsen, V., and Whittiker, E.M. *The Silent Dialogue.* San Francisco: Joses Bass, 1968.

Parsons, T. *Structure and Process in Modern Society.* New York: Free Press, 1960.

Perrow, C. *Complex Organizations: A Critical Essay.* New York: Scott, Foresman, 1972.

Rose, A. Incomplete socialization. *Sociology and Research,* 44, 1960, 238-47.

Rosenbaum, J. *Educational Inequality.* New York: Wiley, 1976.

Rosenbaum, J.E. Tournament mobility: Career patterns in a corporation. *Administrative Science Quarterly,* 24, 1979, 220-41.

Rosenthal, R. *Experimenter Effects in Behavioral Research.* New York: Appleton-Century-Crofts, 1967.

Roth, J.A. *Timetables.* Indianapolis, Ind.: Bobbs-Merrill, 1963.

Roy, D. Quota restriction and gold bricking in a machine shop. *American Journal of Sociology,* 57, 1952, 426-42.

Rubenstein, J. *City Police.* New York: Farrar, Straus, & Giroux, 1973.

Salaman, G. *Community and Occupation.* London: Cambridge University Press, 1974.

Schein, E.H. The Chinese Indoctrination program for prisoners of war. *Psychiatry,* 19, 1956, 149-72.

Schein, E.H. Organizational socialization. *Industrial Management Review,* 2, 1968, 37-45.

Schein, E.H. The individual, the organization, and the career: a conceptual scheme. *Journal of Applied Behavioral Science,* 7, 1971, 401-26.

Schein, E.H. *Professional Education: Some New Directions.* New York: McGraw-Hill, 1972.

Selznick, P. *The T.V.A. and the Grass Roots.* Berkeley: University of California Press, 1949.

Shafer, M. Selling "selling." Unpublished Master's thesis. M.I.T., 1975.

Shibutani, T. Reference groups and social control. In A. Rose, ed., *Human Behavior and Social Processes.* Boston: Houghton Mifflin, 1962, pp. 128-47.

Stanton, A.H., and Schwartz, M.S. *The Mental Hospital.* New York: Basic Books, 1954.

Taylor, D., and Cohen, S. *Psychological Survival.* London: Penguin, 1972.

Torrance, E.P. Some consequences of power differences on decision making in permanent and temporary groups. In A.P. Hare, E.F. Borgatta, and R.F. Bales, eds., *Small Groups.* New York: Knopf, 1955.

Turner, R. Modes of social ascent through education: sponsored and contest mobility. *American Sociological Review,* 41, 1980, 855-67.

Van Gennep. A. *The Rites of Passage.* Chicago: Univeristy of Chicago Press, 1960.

Van Maanen, J. Observations on the making of policemen. *Human Organizations,* 32, 1973, 407-18.

Van Maanen, J. Working the street: A developmental view of police behavior. In H. Jacob, ed., *The Potential for the Reform of Criminal Justice.* Beverly Hills, Calif.: Sage, 1974, pp. 83-140.

Van Maanen, J. Breaking-in: a consideration of organizational socialization. In R. Dubin, ed., *Handbook of Work, Organization, and Society.* Chicago: Rand-McNally, 1976.

Van Maanen, J. Experiencing organizations. In J. Van Maanen, ed., *Organizational Careers: Some New Directions.* New York: Wiley, 1977, 17-73.

Van Maanen, J. People processing. *Organizaional Dynamics,* 7, 1978, 18-36.

Van Maanen, J, and Schein, E. Toward a theory of organizational socialization. In B. Staw, ed., *Research in Organizational Behavior,* 2, 1979, 209-69.

Vollmer, H.M, and Mills, D.J, eds. *Professionalization.* Englewood Cliffs, N.J.: Prentice-Hall, 1966.

Wamsley, G.L. Constrasting institutions of Air Force socialization: happenstance or bellweather? *American Journal of Sociology,* 78, 1972, 399-417.

Westley, W. *Violence and the Police.* Cambridge, Mass.: M.I.T. Press, 1970.

Wheeler, S. The structure of formally organized socialization settings. In O.G. Brim and S. Wheeler, eds., *Socialization after Childhood.* New York: Wiley, 1966.

Whyte, W.H. *The Organization Man.* New York: Simon and Schuster, 1956.

Ziller, R.C. Toward a theory of open and closed groups. *Psychological Bulletin,* 65, 1965, 164-82.

Ziller, R.C. Group dynamics over time. Paper presented at the American Psychological Association National Convention, Washington, D.C., September 1976.

7

Successful Management and Organizational Mugging

J. PETER GRAVES

California State College, San Bernardino

Recent research on professional careers has more strongly than ever implicated the manager as a key figure in the growth and development of subordinates. But the results of the study reported here suggest that organizations, far from supporting managerial action that helps subordinates' careers, are promoting the opposite. It was found that the behaviors that bring tangible organizational rewards—pay increases—are not the same as the ones that get the job done effectively. Subordinate career development is enhanced by effective management. The managerial approach that brings organizational rewards, termed *successful management,* is a major cause of "organizational mugging." Individuals may attempt to fight back against an organization that takes unfair advantage of their talents, but it is the organization that must act to ensure meaningful career growth of its members.

THE MANAGER AND CAREERS

A careful analysis of a long-prevalent pattern of career development has recently been reported by Thompson and Dalton (1976). The result of their research, based upon 1500 scientists and engineers in five R&D organizations, permits a meaningful discussion of the ways in which managers can positively affect the career growth of those they supervise.

Career Stages

The pattern observed by these researchers described career development in terms of stages. Each stage differs from the others in activities, relationships, and psychological adjustments. Moreover, successful performance at each stage is a prerequisite for moving on to the next. Individuals who continue to move through these stages retain their high performance ratings; those who do not move tend to be less valued by the organization.

Stage 1:   Four stages are identified, with stage 1 noted as the apprenticeship period. Here an individual works under relatively close supervision and direction. In addition, most highly successful professionals have an informal "mentor" at this time. Surprisingly, some people stay in this stage most of their careers and are never able to assume independent responsibility for their own work. However, that group represents a small minority. The majority of professionals make a successful transition into the next stage.

Stage 2:   The second stage is one of independence and specialization. A majority of professionals look forward to having their own project or area of responsibility. Earning this opportunity and taking advantage of it moves a person into stage 2. Most of the solid professional work in the organization is done by individuals in this category. About 40% of the professionals in the organizations surveyed are in stage 2. However, from an individual point of view, it is risky to remain in this stage because managers have rising expectations as a person's age and salary level increase. As a result, those who remain in this stage after age 40 tend to receive lower performance ratings. Professionals who move into stages 3 and 4 are quite successful in avoiding that fate.

Stage 3:   The role of the professional in stage 3 changes from one of being concerned with one's own development and progress to one in which a substantial effort is expended in behalf of others. Not all individuals do this in the same way or in identical roles. Some may become mentors to other younger professionals. Others, by the power of their technical contributions, become valued consultants to groups in and out of the organization. Still others move into the administrative structure of the organization and away from the technical aspects of the work.

Stage 4:   The professionals who move into this stage do so because they (a) begin to exercise a significant influence over the future direction of the organization, (b) are engaged in wide and varied interactions both in and out of the organization, and (c) are involved in the sponsoring and development of promising people within the organization. Stage 4 people are heavily involved in external relationships. This outside contact is critical because it not only brings information into the organization, but it gives the organization the visibility it needs to market its goods and services.

It has been suggested that the stages are just another way of looking at the same old levels of organizational hierarchy, giving the pyramid but another name. It is true that there are many managers in stages 3 and 4, but the researchers found many nonmanagers there also. In stage 3, for example, 65% of the professionals were not in supervisory positions; in stage 4, 26% were not. In the organizations surveyed, a significant proportion of the professionals were able to remain contributors in their technical specialties and still be highly valued by the organization.

The Need for a Flexible Approach

But to arrive at the point of valued contribution as either a manager or a non-manager takes more than an awareness of the direction of necessary growth. Although an individual can and should have a significant impact on the development of his or her career, managerial actions sometimes exert tremendous, if not the dominant, influence on the subordinate's work life.

The model of career stages carries with it clear implications of the kinds of managerial actions and attitudes that help the development of subordinates' careers. Since it is not likely that all subordinates will be at the same point in their careers, it is necessary for the managerial behavior to be appropriate to the career stage of the subordinate. As individuals may be viewed to be developing through stages, so also must the nature of supervision adapt to the career growth of those supervised.

For example, it is important that the person in stage 1 have a meaningful relationship with a mentor. Whether this mentor is the manager or another senior professional, the supervisor can greatly assist the establishment of the relationship. The supervisor must tolerate the individual's need for greater detail and clarity in the assignments received. The need for frequent and realistic feedback on performance is greater in this stage. Professionals at this stage in their careers should be encouraged to complete all training or education in the basic knowledge of their occupations, perhaps earning advanced degrees. The manager's encouragement, approval, and in some cases tolerance of the special conditions in this stage is essential for the subordinate's success.

In contrast to stage 1, the professional in stage 2 requires an entirely different set of circumstances. The individual should begin to devote significant time and effort to a specific project area or specialty. This work should be more challenging and of longer duration than stage 1 assignments. Individuals should begin to make important project or job decisions themselves, should receive and accept greater responsibility in determining what to do and how to do it. Continuing education activities should be directed toward sharpening technical skills in their specialties. It is very important to develop a specialty in this stage, but the manager should carefully monitor the status and future of the project or specialty these individuals are working on. The stage 2 person is highly vulnerable to shifts in priority and funding of his or her work area.

In the same manner, the nature of supervision that is required for continued growth through stages 3 and 4 must be appropriate to the individual, and his or her work history, talents, and aspirations. This places a tremendous burden on the individual manager to be aware of and sensitive to the needs of each subordinate.

Even without the model of career stages, a manager who is honest with subordinates and keeps them informed on job-related matters, involves them in meaningful goal setting, and delegates challenging work will have a positive effect on their careers. This is an underlying philosophy in the many programs of managerial assessment and training in organizations today. It is one such assessment center, sponsored by Syntex Corporation, called the Career Development Center (CDC), which provided the basis for the study reported here.

THE PRESENT INVESTIGATION

Subjects

The subjects for this study were 90 managers from 20 large organizations in technology-based industry, public utilities, manufacturing, and municipal government. All subjects had been participants in the Career Development Center. The time since participation ranged from 12 to 48 months, averaging about 30 months. The subjects occupied first-level and middle-management positions in their organizations, with an average salary of $23,410 in late 1976. Their average in 1976 was 36.4 years. Most had bachelors degrees, a third had completed master's degrees, and a few the doctorate.

Data Gathering

The study was an attempt to better understand the relationship between managerial behavior and job performance. Thus, a variety of measures of behavior and attitudes were obtained and then compared with indices of job performance.

Predictors of Performance: Some of the measures of behavior and attitudes were obtained at the assessment center. These data included test scores on instruments such as FIRO-B, Gordon Personal Inventory and Profile, Verbal and Abstract Reasoning, and reading skills. Measures of managerial behavior commonly stressed by assessment centers were also obtained. All of these data, for the purposes of this study, were considered predictors of managerial performance, and were to be compared with current indices of performance for their predictive validity.

Present Behaviors: Data concerning another set of behaviors were gathered at the same time as current performance data by means of the Objective Judgment Quotient (OJQ), a highly reliable assessment instrument developed by Wyvern Research Associates. This instrument was completed by the subject himself, his superior, and two colleagues (subordinates or peers). The results provided a measure of each of 14 behaviors for every subject.

Job Performance: Two measures of job performance were obtained. One measure used was a reflection of salary growth rate over the recent past. The specific index used was "percent salary increase per month" since CDC participation. The second measure of job performance was obtained at the same time as the OJQ instrument was completed. The subject himself, his superior, and two colleagues rated the subject on a six-point scale according to the degree of perceived similarity to "the most effective manager you have ever known." The subject was rated high if he were seen as very similar in behavior to effective managers, low if seen as not comparable at all. The persons rating were cautioned not to compare the subject to the highest paid or most upwardly mobile, but the most effective. It was thus hoped to obtain two performance indices which reflected (1) organizational recognition of on-the-job performance and (2) similarity to effective managers.

Results

The examination of primary interest was to determine if assessment center measures of behaviors and attitudes are good predictors of managerial performance. The results were surprising for two reasons.

The first surprise was that very few of the measurements from the assessment center were good predictors of future managerial performance. Of eleven skill areas observed and assessed at CDC, only two—conflict resolution and delegation—were significantly related to future performance.

Even more surprising, however, was that, although the two performance measures were related to each other, they did not bear uniform relationships to all the variables. There were some behaviors, for example, which were positively related to one performance measure but negatively related to the other. Only three variables were positively related to both performance indices; for 15 others their correlations with the two performance scores were significantly different from each other. It thus became apparent that it was more meaningful to distinguish *between* salary growth rate and managerial effectiveness when discussing the relationship between behavior and performance.

Success and Effectiveness: Success is the term applied to the performance measure of salary growth rate. This is likely to be a fairly sensitive indicator of organizational recognition. Effectiveness is the term applied to the evaluation provided by superiors and colleagues regarding the subjects' actual job performance.

It should not be surprising that success and effectiveness are related positively to each other. But the relationship is more complicated than a single correlation coefficient would indicate. The two indices are not simply different ways of measuring the same phenomenon. This is seen by the manner in which behavioral, biographical, and test data relate to both success and effectiveness.

Figure 7-1 attempts to visually represent the direction and strength of each variable of interest on the two dimensions of success and effectiveness. The dashed lines indicate levels of statistical confidence beyond which the correlation coefficients for a variable are significantly different. The variables beyond the dashed lines do not relate in the same way to success as they do to effectiveness.

The variables in Figure 7-1 can generally be classified into three categories: (1) those behaviors that are positively related to *both* success and effectiveness, (2) those that are negative on effectiveness and positive on success, and (3) those that are positive on effectiveness and negative on success. Of primary interest to the present discussion are the last two categories. It appears as though a number of qualities or skills important to "climbing the ladder" are negatively related to

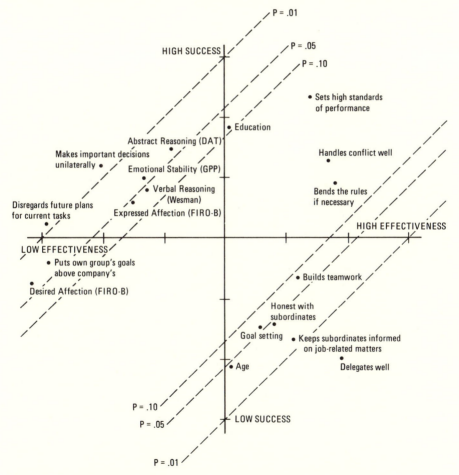

FIGURE 7-1 Eighteen variables of importance and their relationship to success and effectiveness. Each dot represents the pair of correlation coefficients for that variable.

effective performance in the managerial role. The obverse of this appears also to be the case: that some behaviors strongly related to effectiveness are negatively related to organizational ascendancy.

Successful and Effective Management

For purposes of further discussion, successful management will be defined by those variables to the upper left of the dashed lines in Figure 7-1. This managerial approach stresses individual, unilateral action by the manager toward short-term goals of his or her own work unit: verbal and reasoning abilities, as well as a controlled public image, not given to much emotion or excitability.

Effective management embodies the behaviors to the lower right in Figure 7-1. Delegation, team building, goal setting, honesty with subordinates, and keeping them informed on job-related matters are the central behaviors in this approach.

WE'VE GOT A PROBLEM HERE

The point must not be overlooked that there are definite short-run benefits of successful management as opposed to effective management. It takes time, hence costs money, to involve subordinates in goal setting, information sharing, delegation, and so on. It is easy to say in nearly any situation, "If we don't solve the short-run aspects of this problem, there might not be a long run to worry about." In situations of rapid change and economic constraint, the pressures to deal with problems from a short-run perspective are enormous.

Indeed, organizations seldom even view the issue of career development to be a concern of management at all. Rather, the personnel department, employee development division, or other staff groups are charged with providing career planning and development programs. Some of these are excellent; most are not. But a watchword of advice common to nearly all of them is the admonition to "take charge of your own career!"

A significant degree of responsibility for career growth certainly rests with the individual. But the tremendous impact of managerial decision making and organizational policy is often either ignored or treated as a benign force readily amenable to any individual's career "plan." The effect of line management is so pervasive that it may be considered a well-established and ongoing system for the development of careers. For every time a person is promoted, assigned a new job, given additional responsibilities, and so on, a career development decision has been made. And it is likely to be a decision with greater impact than the individual action alone could effect.

"Organizational Mugging"

An organization that rewards managerial behavior that has adverse impact on subordinates' careers may wittingly or unwittingly be guilty of "organizational mugging." The choice of this rather unpleasant term derives from the similarities between street mugging and taking advantage of a person career-wise.

Let us examine the elements of the analogy further. The individual unlucky enough to be mugged on the street at first finds himself in a singularly helpless situation. Although the choice of alternative routes probably existed earlier, avenues of escape are no longer apparent. He is confronted by an individual or group promising a certain "incentive." Whether this incentive is visible or not, employed or not, is unimportant. The belief in its existence is sufficient to command compliance. Then he must turn over everything of value he possesses. The insistence upon total "commitment" is significant. Only the more sophisticated forms of crime extract less than 100% payment over longer periods of time. Once the commodity of value has been secured and no more appears forthcoming, the victim is released on his own again. It is the contention of this paper that successful management is a chief cause of "organizational mugging."

Personal Defenses Against Mugging

Don't Go That Way: One of the most common personal defenses against street mugging is to use alternative routes to reach the same destination. This, of course, does nothing to reduce the incidence of the crime, but is a means for one individual to avoid it. In the same sense, an individual who changes organizations or even occupations because of the high risk of mugging may solve his or her own dilemma but this does nothing to change the factors that caused it. He may even contribute to the recurrence of such practices in the organization he leaves. When those who cannot tolerate a certain state of affairs leave the organization, the only ones left will be those who can. A similar situation occurs in the various processes of government when honest and upright citizens refuse to participate because of the dishonesty of the incumbents. The incidents of dishonest practices is thereby likely to increase, not decrease. When pedestrains avoid a particular street or neighborhood because of the danger of mugging, that area becomes more sparsely traveled and isolated, increasing the danger for those who must walk there.

Striking Back: A second personal defense is to strike back at the mugger. This, of course, is not a recommended course of action in the presence of a real criminal, nor is it advisable from an organizational point of view. Nonetheless, a commonly observed behavior pattern by individuals frustrated and helpless to improve their situation is retaliation. Regardless of its precise form—simple resistance to direction or even larceny and sabotage—such behavior illustrates the vast creative potential that can be turned against the organization. There may be some uncomfortable with the choice of the term "creative potential," preferring to reserve it for appropriate contributions to organizational goals. But anyone familiar with such resistance must agree that many and varied are the forms of antiorganizational behavior. Of course, these activities contribute little, if anything, to the improvement of the organization and nothing to career development.

Safety in Numbers: A third predictable means of self-protection from organizational disregard for careers is simply phrased: "safety in numbers." It works on the street to a remarkable degree, and professionals in greater numbers are considering various forms of unions, associations, and collective bargaining as means of self-protection and to effect organizational change. It is a peculiarity of professionals, as a category of personnel, that neither of these objectives is meaningfully achievable through unionization. It has been observed that an individual who turns to a union for protection from management is merely switching from being subject to the whims of one group to the whims of another. That the situation is so simple is doubtful, but the success of the union is in large measure dependent on its ability to organize its members into a uniform, homogeneous power block. And this has precisely the same effect upon career development as when management treats subordinates as a homogeneous, monolithic block, desirous of the same things, motivated by similar opportunities, possessing common aspirations. In either instance, the individual's career goals must fit the structures deemed "appropriate" by the leaders, be they union or company. On the other hand, the kind of supervision implied by the model of career stages is highly individualized, attempting to make important personnel decisions on the basis of the career growth of the subordinate.

That unions have changed organizations is perhaps an understatement. But change meaningful to subordinate career growth has not occurred as a result of unionization. Unions have succeeded in effecting important improvements in areas that affect human physiological and security needs, but not the higher needs, of which career satisfaction is an example. Furthermore, the polarization between management and nonmanagement that tends to occur with unionization would seriously impair, if not destroy, the mentor/apprentice relationship as well as the relationships between management and nonmanagement in stages 3 and 4.

What the Organization Can Do

In contrast to the steps taken by individuals against the effects of successful management, which have little substantive impact on the situation, there are practical steps that the organization can take to improve the prospects for meaningful career development.

Turn On the Lights: One positive step is analogous to installing better street lighting in high-risk crime areas. It is important that attention be drawn to the impact of decisions affecting job assignments, promotions, and the like. When such decisions are made without involving others, and with an eye to short-run as opposed to long-range concerns, there is great risk of negative effects on careers. This is not to recommend in any form that the process by which such decisions are made be open to public view; rather, that the decision simply involve more persons than the manager acting alone. Other managers, the individuals affected by the issue, interested third parties—all may be considered for involvement in such decisions.

The Career Ombudsman: The use of a "career ombudsman" has been suggested as a means of providing organizational support for the airing of problems associated with careers. Presumably, this would be an individual with some influence and respect in the organization, such as a manager, former manager, or even a number of such individuals who each take their turn in this role. It would be this person's responsibility to mediate complaints that arise from personnel decisions and act as an interested third party on important considerations.

Reward the Right Behaviors: Ultimately, however, for any of these suggestions to have positive effect, they must be backed by genuine organizational improvement toward effective management and away from successful management. In the simplest terms, this means the organization must reward effective management. Managers will persist in a behavior or pattern of behaviors as long as there is incentive to do so. The most effective deterrent to street crime is to enable youth to obtain meaningful employment, thus reducing the incentive for criminal behavior. A knowledge of effective management alone is insufficient incentive to change; individuals must believe that it is to their personal as well as the organization's benefit to be concerned with career development.

AND FINALLY . . .

One need not be a great fan of career development to find value in this last suggestion. Good career development is but one of many benefits that can come from effective management. Effective management is, after all, exactly that—effective. And when this kind of supervision is also rewarded, the distinction between effectiveness and success will become meaningless, and among other things, the streets will be a little safer for those who travel them.

REFERENCES

Thompson, P.H. and Dalton, G.W. Are R&D organizations obsolete? *Harvard Business Review,* November-December, 1976, pp. 105-16.

ISSUES IN PROFESSIONAL

IV

AND ORGANIZATIONAL ROLES

8

The Four Stages
of Professional Careers:
A New Look
at Performance
by Professionals *

GENE W. DALTON, Brigham Young University

PAUL H. THOMPSON, Brigham Young University

RAYMOND L. PRICE, Hewlett-Packard Corporation

A person has to be able to change or he'll stagnate, but it is so hard to change in this organization. I'd like to move up or pursue a related career, but I'm cast in the role of radiochemist and I don't know how to move out of it. I have to go outside of work to get my rewards. [40-year-old engineer]

I really wonder what to do. I like technical work, but when I look at the specialists 15 years my senior still in those little cubbyholes, it scares me. I think I'll get a chance to try management, but if you let yourself get too far from your field, you're out on a limb with no way back if it doesn't work out. [28-year-old scientist]

I manage nearly three hundred professionals; and by all practical standards, I'm very successful. But I'm not satisfied. I feel it is time to make a change and try doing something new. However, it might mean that I wouldn't directly manage anyone anymore. I wonder what would happen to my career and my influence around here. [52-year-old manager]

*Reprinted by permission of the publisher, from *Organizational Dynamics,* Summer 1977.
© 1977 by AMACOM, a division of American Management Association. All rights reserved.

These are some of the concerns we've heard expressed as we have talked with several hundred professionally trained employees over the past three years. These are the knowledge workers, the fastest growing part of our workforce, who at present constitute 32 percent of the workforce. (Blue collar workers are 33 percent of the workforce.) Their initial training was as engineers, scientists, accountants, MBAs, and so on, and they have spent their working lives as employees of large, complex organizations dependent in large part on their professional skills. Having done well in college and graduate school, they entered these organizations with high career expectations. They brought with them scarce and valued skills, but few had any clear understanding of what forging a career in an organization is like. Few came with any understanding of the constantly changing activities, relationships, and emotional adjustments they would have to learn to manage if they were to remain highly valued contributors throughout their careers.

Perhaps it should come as no surprise, therefore, that we so often perceived a sense of frustration, bewilderment, even betrayal, as these people spoke about their careers. Any career guidance they may have received in college or graduate school was usually limited to helping them choose courses or majors. No one had given them an accurate preview of what life in a complex organization would be like.

Nor did many of them feel they had received much more help in career planning after they entered organizational life. A few talked about getting some valuable training or advice from a supervisor or a friend. But a large number expressed feelings that are captured best by a comment from a young financial analyst in a bank: "Nobody has helped me do any real career planning. I suspect it's because they're not sure of where they are going themselves."

We have in fact encountered uncertainty among managers of professional employees about how to guide the careers of their subordinates. From these managers we constantly heard comments such as these:

> We bring in about a dozen of the best young people we can each year. Two years later, about eight are contributing. The rest are floundering and usually leave. I wish I could understand it. Those who floundered came with records as good as the others. [Laboratory Director]

> We have some men in their 40s or 50s who are among our lowest performers. Their salaries are out of line with what we get from them, but they have been here so long we aren't likely to bring ourselves to fire them. We've told them to take courses to get current, but I can't see it's had any effect. What will we do with them for the next 15 or 20 years? [Chief Engineer]

CAREER MODELS

Those of us who study careers in organizations have found ourselves perplexed by these same questions. Several years ago we began examining the relationship between age and performance among engineers. In a study of 2,500 engineers in seven large organizations, we found a negative correlation after age 35 between age and performance rating. The older the engineer after the mid-30s, the lower his performance rating was likely to be.

But the message seemingly implied by these statistics was brought sharply into question when we examined our data more closely. Not all older engineers had low ratings. In fact, the top third of the engineers over 50 were almost as highly valued as the top third in any age group. Many engineers had remained highly valued contributors for the duration of their careers. But more of those in their 40s and 50s had lower ratings than did younger engineers.

Why have some professionals remained high performers over the years while others have not? What have they done differently?

Existing Career Models

We have concluded that part of the confusion about careers has grown out of the career models we have all used, explicitly or implicitly. The first and most influential of these is of course the pyramidal model of organizations (and of careers), so graphically illustrated by most organizational charts. Authority, status, and pay all increase as the individual moves up the chart.

Implicit in this model is the concept that career development consists of moving as rapidly and as far up the pyramid as possible. As professionals first moved into industrial and governmental organizations, this was the sole career model they encountered. Many professionals with advanced degrees became prime candidates for management positions.

But there were also many who were dismayed to find that the ability and willingness to manage seemed almost the sole criteria for advancement, recognition, or reward in their organizations.

Similarly many organizations found that the pyramidal model failed to take important realities into account. Too often, they found themselves promoting a key technical specialist to a management position because it was the only way to reward him. More and more firms began to set up special new pay and promotion schemes such as the dual ladder for their professional employees in order to recognize the critical contributions they could make as individuals. In almost all those organizations, however, professionals began griping about the realities of the dual ladder:

> Ours isn't a real dual ladder; it's been bastardized. It's been filled with ex-managers.
>
> The men in the upper technical slots don't do real technical work. They prepare proposals and brochures.
>
> The real rewards don't go to those on the technical ladder.

These criticisms have not subsided. Instead they have persisted and indeed increased in recent years.

The Obsolescence Model

As the number of professionals with 20 and 25 years' experience grew, a new problem and a new model of professional careers began to emerge. The low performance ratings of many of these senior employees led to use of the metaphor of obsolescence. The picture projected by the metaphor was that of a rapidly changing technology in which the skills of the older professionals were rapidly outdated and in which recent graduates who had mastered the latest tools and techniques were at a premium.

Interestingly, the model carries with it an implied solution to the problem. When it is assumed that professionals become obsolete like machines, when we begin to talk as if a professional education has a half-life of so many years, like a uranium sample, the obvious solution is to update or reeducate professionals and to restore them to the state they were in when they came out of school—on top of the newest and most sophisticated techniques.

Millions of dollars have been spent on continuing education programs in companies and in universities. In addition, professional groups have pressed for legislation that requires continuing education as the price of continuing professional practice. For example, lawyers in Minnesota are required to take the equivalent of 15 course hours a year to avoid being placed on a restricted status. The Engineering Foundation of Ohio recently suggested a law requiring almost the same qualification of engineers. Accountants in several states face the possibility of having to return to the classroom in order to retain their professional status.

All this money and effort rests on a questionable model. It has not been demonstrated that courses improve performance. Our studies have in fact shown repeatedly that the high performers are no more likely to have taken continuing education courses than the low performers.

A NEW MODEL

If the high performers are not taking more courses than their peers, how *are* they different? What, if anything, are they doing differently? In what respects have their careers been different?

To answer these questions, we interviewed 550 professionally trained employees: 155 scientists in four laboratories, 268 engineers in four organizations, 52 accountants in three firms, and 75 professors in three universities. We selected our subjects to give us representative samples of high- and low-rated performers. We began by simply asking them to describe their own careers and those of their fellow professionals. What, we asked them, characterized the high performers they knew? We coded their responses carefully and compared them with the way the high-rated and the low-rated performers described their own careers.

Our early analysis yielded only frustration. Each promising uniformity exhibited too many contradictions. Each new hypothesis failed to find support in the data. It was only when we began to look at the effects of time that a clear pattern began to emerge. High performers early in their careers were performing different functions from high performers at mid-career. And both these groups were different from high performers in late-career.

As we investigated further, it became increasingly clear that there are four distinct stages in a professionally trained employee's career. Each stage differs from the others in the tasks an individual is expected to perform well in that stage, in the types of relationships he engages in, and in the psychological adjustments he must make.

It was the individuals who were moving successfully through these stages who had received the high performance ratings. Conversely, individuals who had remained in the early stages were likely to be low-rated.

In Stage I, an individual works under the direction of others as an apprentice, helping and learning from one or more mentors.[1] In Stage II, he demonstrates his competence as an individual contributor. In Stage III, he broadens and acts as a mentor for others. Those in Stage IV provide direction for the organization. Table 8-1 shows some of the central features of each stage. It is important to realize that while the stages can be thought of as distinct, there are elements in each stage that are present in each of the other stages, although in a different form. Our description of each stage focuses on the issues that clearly differentiate one stage from the next.

STAGE I

When a young professional joins an organization, he is immediately confronted with several challenges. He must learn to perform at least some of the organization's tasks competently. He needs to learn which elements of the work are critical and which activities require the greatest attention. He must learn how to get things done, using both formal and informal channels of communication. Finally, he must do this while he is being closely observed for indications of competence and future potential.

Because he lacks experience, and because others do not yet know how much they can rely on his judgment, he works under the fairly close supervision of a more experienced person. In other words, he must usually begin by helping someone else do the work for which no supervisor is responsible.

Activities

Much of the work in Stage I may involve fairly routine duties. One manager observed:

[1] We would like to acknowledge the helpfulness of the ideas of Daniel Levinson and his associates at Yale University. Their concept of the mentor helped us understand much of the phenomena we observed in this stage.

Table 8-1 Four Career Stages

	Stage I	Stage II	Stage III	Stage IV
Central activity	Helping Learning Following directions	Independent contributor	Training Interfacing	Shaping the direction of the organization
Primary relationship	Apprentice	Colleague	Mentor	Sponsor
Major psychological issues	Dependence	Independence	Assuming responsibility for others	Exercising power

There is a lot of detailed work to be done between the time a project is conceived and its actual implementation. A new person is often stuck with many of these detailed tasks. I like a subordinate who recognizes that someone has to do the routine work and therefore doesn't complain about it all the time.

However, it is important for the person in this stage not to become completely bogged down in this detail work. He is also expected to show some initiative and be innovative in finding solutions to problems. So another manager commented:

I like a subordinate who has an aggressive attitude. He has to show initiative, be innovative, and be willing to take some risks. With an aggressive attitude, I can normally guide him in the direction in which he needs to go.

The differing views expressed by these managers illustrate the fact that it is often difficult to achieve the optimum balance in Stage I between willing acceptance of routine assignments and aggressive searching out of new and more challenging tasks.

Another characteristic of the work in this stage is that the individual customarily gets assignments that are part of a larger project or activity directed by a senior professional or a supervisor. Many young professionals find such a relationship frustrating. They are eager to have their own project or their own clients.

Such an attitude is understandable, but a person who tries to escape the subordinate relationship too quickly will miss out on an important aspect of career development. He will fail to learn what others have gained by experience. More important, if he undertakes sole responsibility for work he's not prepared to do, he may soon acquire a reputation for mediocre performance, which will be hard to overcome.

Relationships

As we have just indicated, the primary relationship in Stage I is that of being a subordinate. Our interviews suggest that the individual's skill in managing that relationship may be a critical factor in building an effective career. Ideally, in this stage he will work with a mentor who knows how to design a study, structure an audit, or analyze the critical risks involved in a loan. He works closely with the mentor, learning from observation and from trial and correction the approaches, the organizational savvy, and the judgment that no one has yet been able to incorporate into textbooks. He follows instructions and carries out detailed and sometimes boring work in exchange for the things he learns and the sponsorship of his mentor.

If he learns quickly and well at this stage, he will be given increasing responsibility. If he fails to do so, however, he may continue to do the routine work under close supervision as long as he remains with the organization. Tom Johnson's experience in a large research organization illustrates this point:

In my first two years in the company I was unhappy with my job. I worked for a man that I disliked and did not respect. He provided very little assistance or guidance. As a result, I made little or no progress. Then I began to work with another engineer who could get things done; he protected me from the flack coming down from above. He provided a climate that I enjoyed and he was willing to go to bat for me. When he became a formal group leader, I insisted on being transferred into his group, where I became the informal leader. Later, he recommended me for a supervisory position.

Tom's experience points out some of the benefits of having a good mentor in the early stages of a career as well as some of the problems of having a poor one. The mentor knew the right people and could show Tom how the system worked—how to lay out a job, how to get computer funds, how to requisition necessary equipment and travel funds, how to negotiate faster delivery from suppliers, and so on. A mentor is also extremely helpful when anyone is learning the ropes in a complex organization.

A good mentor often becomes a model that the Stage I person can follow whenever he is unsure how to approach a problem. He instructs and provides the subordinate with a chance to try his hand, while making sure that he doesn't make important errors. These and other benefits suggest that finding a good mentor should be a key agenda item for any professional entering an organization. Providing him with the opportunity to find such a mentor is an equally important responsibility of higher-ups in the organization.

Psychological Issues

The psychological adjustments a person makes in Stage I are as critical as the way the activities are performed or the relationships that are developed. One of the major problems is adjusting to the dependence inherent in the role of subordinate. The people we interviewed said that in this stage a person "is expected to willingly accept supervision and direction. . ." and "is expected to exercise *directed* creativity and initiative."

Many professionals looked forward to completing their education so they could be free of the demands of their professors and find the independence they believed their profession provides. It is easy to understand their irritation when they find themselves forced once again into a dependent relationship. A physicist in a highly respected applied research laboratory described his feelings during his first year:

My first year here was frustrating. I had a good record in graduate school. I was ready to go to work and make a contribution. But for a year, no one paid much attention to my suggestions. I almost left. It took me a year to realize that I didn't yet understand the complexity of the problems we were working on. Now I try to take enough time with new people to help them understand the dilemma of that first year.

Another difficult adjustment is learning to live with the never-ending routine work. A recent MBA described his frustrations in this area as follows:

My job is very boring. All I'm doing is routine financial analysis. This work could be done by a high school graduate with a calculator. They didn't tell me in the MBA program that I'd be doing this routine work. We spent our time in the program discussing cases with important problems to be solved.

Many young professionals find themselves in a similar position, and it is a risky one. If they lose interest in the job and do sloppy work or lay down on the job, they may acquire a reputation that will compromise their future career development.

STAGE II

The primary theme in Stage II is independence. The individual who makes the transition into Stage II successfully does so by developing a reputation as a technically competent professional who can work independently to produce significant results. John, a young financial analyst, describes his transition into this stage:

After about a year and a half with the company, I was capable of working on my own and therefore was placed in charge of monitoring the procurement accounts. Before this time, whenever a person from another department came in to ask a question, I had to consult with my supervisor before making a decision. When I was in charge of the accounts, this was no longer necessary.

Activities

Most professionals look forward to having their own project or area of responsibility. This does not mean that they are allowed to work completely on their own, because most projects must be coordinated with other projects and activities, but they are no longer closely supervised on the specific methods or getting the job done.

In this stage, a person is expected to hone his professional skills to a high level. One way to achieve this competence is to develop an area of specialization. The major career dilemma in this stage is how much to specialize. There is a great deal of discussion and dissension on this issue—with most people taking a strong stand in favor of their particular point of view. An article in *Business Week* (October 12, 1974) offers this advice to aspiring managers:

Get experience in several fields—engineering, sales, manufacturing—right off, and be sure to get your ticket punched in finance early. If you're heading for the president's office, become a generalist fast. . . . Get out of your specialty fast, unless you decide that's all you ever want to do. This means rapid rejection of the notion that you are a professional engineer, lawyer, scientist, or anything but a manager.

Our data suggest that this advice could be misleading if a young professional interprets it to mean that he need never develop and demonstrate solid competence in some critical task of the organization. For in doing so, he will fail to establish a major building block to his career.

The environment in which most professionals operate is changing so rapidly that it is nearly impossible for any one individual to develop expertise in all areas of his field or profession. Therefore, it is often advisable to become a specialist, at least temporarily, and gain a reputation for competence within that specialty.

Using this strategy of focusing his energies in one area enables the individual to develop a sense of competence. In addition to increasing his self-esteem, the individual also tends to enhance his visibility in the organization. A person who has done outstanding work in one area is more likely than a jack-of-all-trades to gain visibility in a large organization.

There are two primary approaches to selecting an area of specialization. One strategy is to choose a content area in which to specialize, such as a CPA who is an expert on tax problems for banks, or a scientist who focuses on nondestructive testing, or a banker who concentrates on loans to utilities. The other is to develop a set of specialized skills and apply those skills in solving a variety of problems. People who are skillful in computer applications, statisticians, and those who are particularly effective in dealing with clients all fall into this category.

There are risks of specializing, of course, such as becoming pigeonholed in one area, or ending up in a specialty that's being phased out. But our research suggests that a carefully selected specialty in Stage II has usually formed the base for a productive and successful career. Failure to establish such a base is a risk few professionals can afford to take.

Relationships

In Stage II, peer relationships take on greater importance. A person at this stage continues to be someone's subordinate. But he comes to rely less on his supervisor or mentor for direction. This transition is not easy, involving as it does a change in attitude and behavior on the part of the supervisor as well as the individual himself.

Some supervisors are unable to make this switch, and the subordinate may need a transfer to accomplish the transition. Ray's experience as an electrical engineer with two supervisors illustrates this point.

> My first project engineer taught me a lot about basic engineering, but after a while I didn't need all the handholding and direction. So I was happy to be transferred to a new project. The new project engineer was a better manager. He helped me to expand my sphere of influence. He encouraged me to develop contacts with people in my field, both inside and outside the company. He showed me how to interact with these people as well as how to make presentations to management and customers. I also learned how to write papers while I worked with him, and several of my papers were published during that period.

Psychological Issues

It seems logical that everyone would want to move from dependence to independence; the transition should be easy. Far from it. By age 25 we have usually had a great deal of experience and indoctrination in being dependent, but little preparation for real independence. From the first grade to graduate school, to ensure a good grade the student has to find out what the teacher wants him to do and then do it. Similarly, on the first job the task is to find out what the boss wants done and then do it.

To move into Stage II, a professional needs to go beyond that dependence and begin to develop his own ideas on what is required in a given situation. He needs his own standards of performance. Some help in developing those standards is available from peers and from professional standards, such as generally accepted accounting principles or engineering safety standards. Still, judgment is necessary in applying any professional standards.

Developing confidence in one's own judgment is a difficult but necessary process. One scientist's experience with this process may illustrate the point:

> I had been working with my mentor on research projects for three years before I developed the necessary confidence to submit a proposal on my own. But I found that my confidence was short-lived. I had been used to making decisions, but I had always checked them with my mentor; and he made the final decision, wrote the final draft, and so on. Now that I had my own project I lacked the confidence to make any of the important decisions. He was unavailable for about six months, and I was almost paralyzed during that period. I made very little progress on the project. Eventually I discovered that I could get the opinions of other people in the department and then make a decision using their input. It was a major discovery for me to find I didn't need a boss to approve my decisions.

This quotation came from a scientist, viewed by others as a very promising young man, who later became a successful professional.

Some people find Stage II uncomfortable and spend too little time in it to develop the skills that have to be acquired in this stage. This often happens when an individual takes on a supervisory position before he has had a chance to establish himself as a competent professional. Often the organization and the individual conspire in moving the person into a management position too soon.

The opportunity may be enticing, but it involves a high degree of risk. Time after time in our study, we encountered first-level managers who were not effective in their positions because they did not understand the technical aspects of the work they were supervising. This tended to undermine the manager's self-confidence as well as the confidence of his subordinates.

Our research indicates that doing well in Stage II is extremely important in the process of career development. Moreover, many people remain in Stage II throughout their careers, making substantial contributions to the organization and experiencing a high degree of professional satisfaction. However, the probability that they will continue to receive above-average ratings diminishes over time, if they do not move beyond this stage.

STAGE III

We have sometimes called Stage III the mentor stage because of the increased responsibility individuals in this stage begin to take for influencing, guiding, directing, and developing other people. It is usually persons in this stage who play the critical role in helping others move through Stage I.

A second characteristic of persons in Stage III is that they have broadened their interests and capabilities. The tendency to broaden comes about quite naturally for many professionals as part of the work process. One researcher who had been very specialized described his experience this way:

> When you are very close to the data, you are able to see the small differences. If you are observant and in a fruitful area, you soon have more ideas than you can possibly pursue by yourself. You run the risk of eliminating some potentially good ideas unless you get others to help you.

From dealing with two or three clients, a bank lending officer or a public accountant may develop knowledge and skills that have applications throughout an entire industry. We have seen engineers learn or develop a new type of computer technique to solve a particular problem, for example, only to find that the approach has wide application to a range of problems facing the organization.

The third characteristic we observed of individuals in Stage III is that they deal with people outside the organization (or organization subunit) for the benefit of others inside. They obtain contracts, get budgets approved, secure critical and/or scarce resources or project funds, help others get salary increases, and so on. The reputation an individual has developed for results and solid achievement in Stage II is initially the keystone to this part of Stage III work.

Activities

We identified three roles played by those in Stage III: informal mentor, idea man, and manager. These are not mutually exclusive; one individual may play all three roles. The point that deserves emphasis here is that a person can carry out Stage III activities from more than one role base.

Informal Mentor.   Often an individual begins to play the role of informal mentor as an outgrowth of his success in Stage II. He is asked to do more work because of his increased capabilities and contacts, which means that he needs more assistance. He begins to find others who can help do the detail work and develop his initial ideas. In doing this, he becomes a mentor for the people who assist him.

One informal technical mentor described his role in these words:

Right now I find the sponsors for our work. I do the conceptual thinking, develop the project, and then get someone to support it. After I get the job, then I must supervise and collaborate with others who do most of the actual work.

He remained the force behind the project and also worked closely with those doing the detail work.

Idea Man.   Some professionals are exceptionally innovative. Often this kind of individual becomes an idea man or consultant for a small group. Others come to him for suggestions on how to solve current problems. Sometimes he originates an idea and then discusses it with others, who may pursue it independent of his supervision. Either way, he is involved with and influences more than his own individual work. John Jensen, a 59-year-old scientist, described his work in this way:

I sell ideas. I would describe myself as an innovative scientist. When I work on a problem, it starts to bug me. At some time, I will read something and apply it back to solve the original problem. Others often come to me with problems they cannot solve. Generally I can pull some information from my experience or reading and give them a direction to follow in solving the problems.

Manager.   The most common role in Stage III and the one most easily understood is the formal role of manager or supervisor. Usually the management role for a Stage III person is not more than one or two levels in the organizational structure away from the work itself.

Professional competence usually continues to have some importance in the performance of the manager's work. Often the formal management role is given to a mentor who already has been informally performing many of the functions expected of a manager.

Transition to the formal role of manager is not dramatic. Bob Smith, a 37-year-old manager, described a fairly typical pattern of a professional moving into a Stage III management role:

I gained knowledge of other programs and began to develop outside contacts. Finally, I discovered I could sell programs. With more programs coming in, I managed several long-term projects under time and money constraints. The business was expanding, and I was directing more and more technical people. Soon I became acting section manager and, after three months, the section manager.

Relationships

Probably the most central shift that occurs as a person moves into Stage III is the nature of his relationships. In Stage II he had to learn to take care of himself. In Stage III he has to learn to take care of others, to assume some form of responsibility for their work. When the mentor receives an assignment on which he needs the collaboration of others, he quickly learns the importance of tapping additional skills. To get even a small group of professionals working together effectively requires more than technical skills and an interesting problem. A scientist who had been doing a lot of independent work described the process:

> I wrote a successful proposal for basic research in energy. Now there are three other people working on the project. We are going full blast and having a ball. But there are new questions. I have always asked my boss to give me independence, and I gave him loyalty in return. Now I have to learn to do that with the people under me.

He finds that he needs interpersonal skills in setting objectives, delegating, supervising, and coordinating.

At this point he also has begun to accept the fact that he has to satisfy a number of people—multiple bosses. He experiences a shift in the relationship with those above him in the hierarchy. He now has responsibilities downward as well as upward, and he feels some of the tugs of the proverbial man in the middle. He must learn to cope with divided loyalties. If he is seen as only looking upward, he will find it hard to retain the loyalties of those working for him. At the same time, unless he has strong influence—and is perceived as having such influence—he will be ineffective at influencing the people he directs.

Psychological Issues

Moving into Stage III requires a number of internal changes as well. The individual must develop a sense of confidence in his own ability to produce results and to help others do the same. He needs to be able to build the confidence of junior people, not tear it down. If he is threatened by the success of his apprentices, he will not be able to provide them the guidance and freedom they need if they are to progress. There must be a delicate balance between directing them and providing them with the freedom to explore and to test their skills.

Second, he must be psychologically able and willing to take responsibility for someone else's output. As a mentor he assumes an obligation to both the apprentice and the customer. Implicitly he promises both parties that the output will be satisfactory.

Some competent people experience formal supervisory responsibility for others as confining and uncomfortable. Whenever this occurs, the question for the individual and his superiors is whether he can find a role in which he can still exert a broad influence without supervising others or whether he should move back into Stage II work.

Those in Stage III also often find themselves pulling away from technical work. The question is: How far? Some move fairly far away from it without ambivalence. Others, like Bill Rivers, make a great effort to stay close to their field. He describes both the feeling and the effort as follows:

I assumed when I came here that being a good scientist was all that was necessary. Later I found that science was more than just research. You have to conceive, sell, and direct a program. I began to do all those things and found myself in management mainly because I didn't want to work for the other guys they were considering. I want to stay close to technical work and maybe move back into it. Because I know it is difficult to move out of management into technical work, I have stayed close to my field, written papers, and still consider myself to be a scientist.

Some, like Rivers, are able to meet these combined demands better than others, but the tension of keeping a foot in each camp is a problem for almost every professional at this stage of his career.

One further adjustment a person in this stage must make is learning to derive satisfaction out of seeing his apprentices move away from him, become independent, or take on new mentors. This can be a major source of gratification or of difficulty. Even though the mentor expects and looks forward to such eventual movement, differences in expectation about timing and methods may constitute a potential source of conflict and disappointment.

Not surprisingly, this adjustment seems to be harder for the Stage III individual without a formal supervisory position. The formal supervisory position carries certain psychological supports and a role clarity unavailable to those in less traditional roles. Counseling and dealing with the outside on behalf of others inside are part of the role definition of the supervisor. For the informal mentor, it is often less clear that these things are part of his job. On the other hand, the lack of an official boss-subordinate role often allows the nonsupervisor to enter into richer, more comfortable counseling relationships.

Along with conflicts, Stage III also brings long-term satisfactions. Challenges come from broadening the individual's thinking, increasing his knowledge by moving into new areas, or applying his skills to new problems. There is adequate social involvement, recognition from peers, and the satisfaction of helping junior professionals further their careers. Generally, the organizational rewards—both money and status—have reached a fairly satisfactory level. Some people find Stage III, with its combination of counseling, technical proximity, and recognition and rewards, viable and satisfying until retirement. Some find that they are stagnating and are hard-pressed to keep up with younger competitors. Others move on to a new stage.

STAGE IV

Finally, as our study progressed it became clear that the careers of some individuals contain a definable fourth stage. The key characteristic that identified people in this stage was the influence they had in defining the direction of the organization or some major segment of it. Many of these Stage IV people occupied line management positions; others did not. But each had come, in his own way, to be a force in shaping the future of the organization.

A stereotype of organizations pictures this influence as being exercised by only one person—the chief executive officer. But this influence is in fact more widely distributed among key people than is commonly thought. They exercise this influence in a number of ways: negotiating and interfacing with the key parts of the environment; developing the new ideas, products, markets, or services that lead the organization into new areas of activity; or directing the resources of the organization toward specific goals.

Because these functions are so critical to the growth and survival of the organization, those who fulfill them are highly valued, and only those persons whose judgment and skill have been proved in the past are trusted to play these roles. Stage IV people have gained credibility by their demonstrated ability to read the environment accurately and respond appropriately.

Activities

The Stage IV people we encountered usually played at least one of three roles: manager, internal entrepreneur, idea innovator.

Upper-level managers are usually but not always in Stage IV of their careers, while a number of middle-level managers are making the transition to this stage. Unlike the Stage III supervisors, they are usually not involved in guiding Stage I people or even supervising people in Stage II. They are not close enough to the details of the daily work to perform in these roles. Instead, they formulate policy and initiate and approve broad programs.

One Stage IV manager described how he had changed his activities in order to work on directing his part of the organization as follows: "I have tried to develop my staff so that I could concentrate on where we are going instead of where we are at the moment. Consequently, things are running more smoothly, and I have more time to myself."

By no means are we implying that Stage IV managers spend all their time doing long-range planning. But the work they do and the decisions they make shape the direction of the organization, or at least a significant part of it.

There are others who, through their entrepreneurial activities within the organization, exercise an important influence on the direction of the firm. They are people with new ideas and a strong sense of the direction in which the organization should go. They bring resources, money, and people together in the furtherance of their ideas. One professional who seemed clearly in Stage IV described his work this way:

> I had an idea for a new product area and was getting very little support through the formal channels. So I talked to a couple of people on my level and convinced them it was a good idea. We went ahead and did it. Today it is bringing in a significant part of our sales. Luckily, it worked out all right.

Entrepreneurs like this are often considered mavericks in their organizations. As long as they are successful at it, however, it is legitimate to be a maverick.

The third type, the idea innovator, seems distantly removed from the manager and the entrepreneur, but he has one thing in common with them—innovative ideas. The biggest opportunities, the most significant breakthroughs, probably most often originate with an individual contributor. He may puzzle over a problem or an idea for years before the solution finally presents itself. Such individuals may work quite closely with a manager or someone else to sell their ideas. Don Jones is an example of the technical or individual contributor. His department manager described him as follows:

> Don is one of the brightest people I know, but he doesn't like to talk. His knowledge of the field, however, is outstanding. He is talented, hardworking, and disciplined. He sets goals for himself on a technical project and achieves them. Every two or three years he has a new direction he wants the company to follow, and he is almost always right. He is not a salesman; he gets people like me to sell his ideas.

Often, the Stage IV individual contributor has also established a reputation outside the organization by his professional achievements and/or publications. This enhances his credibility inside the organization and may enable him to play a key role in recruiting and business development.

Relationships

One of the major ways in which those in Stage IV influence the direction of the organization is through the selection and development of key people. One of the managers we interviewed described this part of his work as follows:

> Since I first moved into management I have consistently tried to develop my staff. Just as others have sponsored me and made it possible for me to take their positions when they moved up, I have done the same.

There is of course a similarity between Stage III and IV in this respect. But there is also a difference. The individual in Stage IV is not concerned with getting new people started. Instead, he selects those who show promise of performing Stage IV activities in the future and grooms them. The focus is on opening up opportunities, assessing, and providing feedback rather than on teaching and instruction. He watches these people, notes their strengths and weaknesses, counsels them, and tries to guide each one into areas where he is most likely to be effective.

The development of key people is not restricted to Stage IV people in management roles but also forms a significant part of the work of Stage IV nonmanagers. The entrepreneurs and the idea men also tend to spend a considerable amount of time and energy in the development of key people and, interestingly, often not into their own mold. In one of the large laboratories we studied, the director and two of the associates had been mentored by one senior scientist. He noted that he had suggested they move toward management because their greatest strengths seemed to be in that area. We frequently found that these nonmanagerial Stage IV people had played a major role in developing many of the most able managers.

Another characteristic of Stage IV people is that they are heavily involved in key relationships outside the organization. One of our Stage IV interviewees described himself as multiorganizational because he worked on so many external boards, committees, and associations. These outside contacts are critical not only because they bring into the organization current information about events and trends in the environment but also because they give the organization the visibility it needs to market its goods, services, and people. Senior partners in CPA firms, for example, are expected to be involved in professional associations and to have developed extensive relationships in the banking and legal communities.

We often found, particularly among nonmanagement Stage IV people, that writing and publication had been and continued to be a means of achieving visibility and contact. But extensive publication or extensive contact of any kind with the outside is no guarantee of Stage IV status inside the organization. Unless the publications or the outside relationships are structured and focused in areas of major concern to the organization, such activities are not likely to be viewed positively by others in the organization.

Psychological Issues

The psychological shifts a person must make to move successfully into Stage IV are even greater than the changes he must make in his activities and relationships. As we indicated, managers in Stage IV removes themselves from day-to-day operations and transactions. Even as a Stage III mentor it is possible to stay close enough to the operations to retain a sense of personal control. But that must be relinquished by managers moving into Stage IV. Nonmanager Stage IV people often stay closer to some aspects of operations, but they are also relentlessly pulled away. One of the essential psychological shifts in moving to Stage IV is to learn not to second-guess subordinates on operating decisions. It is necessary to learn to influence by means other than the direct supervision of ongoing work—through ideas, through personnel selection, through reviews, through resource allocation, and through changes in organizational design. The need for this mode of influence is even greater for non-managerial Stage IV people.

Another critical shift for those moving into Stage IV is a broadening of perspective and a lengthening of time horizons. These individuals must learn to think about the organization as a whole and act in terms of that framework. They must learn to think about the needs of the organization beyond the time period during which they will personally be affected, to think not about next month or next year but about the next five to ten years—or beyond.

Last, because the issues are critical, because they affect the lives of so many people, and because the decisions must be made on the basis of personal judgments, people in Stage IV must also become accustomed to use power. Even if the individual himself is not initially comfortable in the exercise of power, he will find himself forced to exercise power because so many others depend on him to fight for their programs. He also needs to be able to form alliances and to take strong positions without feeling permanent enmity toward those who differ with him.

QUESTIONS RAISED BY THE MODEL

Whenever we discuss this model with professionals and managers, a number of questions arise. One, for example, is whether our data predict that a person who skips a stage will be a failure. We can only answer that we have interviewed a number of successful people who said they did not experience Stage I and a few who said they did not go through Stage II. Some people replied that they did not have a mentor but learned "how the system works" and so on from their peers. In some cases a group of new people joined the organization at the same time, and they helped each other learn what they needed to know.

The preponderance of our interviews suggest, however, that this alternative strategy is usually not as effective as working with a competent mentor. The mentor is better equipped to help the new employee make the transition from the academic setting into a professional career.

Some people say the model implies that the only successful people are those who have progressed to Stage IV. That is not our position. People in all four stages make an important contribution to the organization. A number of people in each stage will be a failure. We can only answer that we have interviewed a number of that as people grow older they are less likely to be highly valued if they don't move beyond the early stages.

The data in Figure 8-1 provide an illustration of that point. We asked managers in two research and development organizations to classify the people in their departments in one or another of the four stages. Figure 8-1 contrasts stage and performance for all individuals over age 40. This figure suggests that only a small proportion of the people still in Stage II are rated as above-average performers. The implication is clear: To maintain a high performance rating throughout his career, an individual should seek to move at least to Stage III.

Another frequent question is, do people only move forward in these stages? If they do revert to an earlier stage, what is the likelihood of their being able to make the eventual transition to one of the later stages? That seems to depend on the climate of the organization. In some organizations, there seemed to be enough flexibility in both the formal and the informal systems to allow people to do some moving back and forth between stages. Even in these organizations, however, the thought of moving from Stage IV implied demotion, and people were reluctant to make such a transition. An example will illustrate the point.

At age 50, George Dunlop found himself in an uncomfortable position. He had been department manager of a group of 300 employees for eight years, and he realized the job was losing the challenge it had once had for him. He thought it unlikely that he would be promoted to the next step in the management hierarchy,

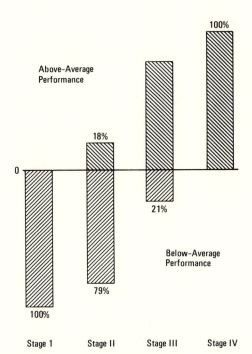

100%

Above-Average
Performance

18%

0

21%

Below-Average
Performance

79%

100%

Stage 1   Stage II   Stage III   Stage IV

FIGURE 8-1 Relationship between stage and performance level for people over age 40

and he felt that he might end up holding that position for the next 15 years. About that time he was given an opportunity to make a shift, which he describes as follows:

I was asked to do a major study for the president that would require my full-time effort. I was reluctant to accept the assignment if it meant giving up my position as department manager because I didn't know where it would lead. I agreed that I would work on it full time for six months, but I would only take a temporary leave from my position as department manager. In order to do the study I had to go back and learn a lot about surveys, interviews, analyzing questionnaire data, and so on. After I finished the study, the president asked if I would take a position in which some of the things proposed in the report might be implemented. He invited me to become his assistant and work out of the office of the president. It sounded interesting, but I still had a lot of questions. There was the question of status. When I was head of a large department, I had secure status. I expected it to be difficult to assume a staff position with no one but a secretary reporting to me. It took time to adjust to the idea.

After some extensive soul-searching, I decided to take the new position, and it has worked out very well. I enjoy my work, and I believe I'm having a major impact on the whole organization.

George accepted a position which, in our terms, temporarily moved him from Stage IV to a variety of Stage II activity in which he specializes in a new area of research. However, he made the transition successfully. He learned to exert considerable influence in his new role and clearly moved back into Stage IV, but in a different kind of work. This was done in a large laboratory where a precedent had been established by a former laboratory director who had made a similar move. In other organizations, we found less movement of this sort.

Some people have asked if the stages are merely another way to describe the management hierarchy. Stages III and IV are not limited to people in formal management positions in most organizations. Table 8-2 shows the percentage of managers and individual contributors in each stage in five organizations. Table 8-3 indicates the proportion of professionals and managers who were described by their superiors as being in each stage.

Upper-level managers described many nonmanagers as doing Stage III and IV work. We believe that any effective professional organization will have many nonmanagers in Stages III and IV. Professional organizations that are so rigidly structured that they provide no opportunities for Stages III and IV among nonmanagers are the poorer for it.

CONCLUSION

What is the value of this way of conceptualizing professional careers in organizations? What implications does it have for managing professional employees?

Edgar Schein pointed out in 1971 that "we do not have readily available concepts for describing the multitude of separate experiences that the individual encounters during the life of his organizational career." We experienced the need for such concepts in trying to wrestle with the problems of obsolescence and performance among professionally trained employees. To explain the differences we found in performance ratings, we especially needed a clearer picture of what Schein calls the organizational definition of a career—"the set of expectations held by individuals inside the organization which guide their decisions about who to move, when, how, and at what speed."

Table 8-2   Percentage of people in each stage holding management and nonmanagement positions in five R&D organizations

stage	individual contributors (%)	managers (%)	total (%)
I	100.0	0.0	100
II	98.7	1.3	100
III	65.2	34.8	100
IV	25.9	74.1	100

Table 8-3 Proportionate distribution of professionals and managers in each stage reported by five R&D organizations

stage	proportionate distribution of professionals in each stage (%)
I	13.4
II	46.2
III	29.3
IV	11.1
	100.0

The concept of career stages has provided us with a way of describing that set of expectations. But it is important to note that these expectations were not necessarily a part of the formal organization. In fact, in the organizations we studied it was the informal and often unstated expectations about the critical activities and relationships a person should engage in at each stage that determined both formal and informal rewards. In our view, the study of an organization as a setting in which careers are lived provides both a fruitful lead and a new perspective for understanding organizations.

But our model of career stages has both pragmatic and theoretical implications for those who live in organizations as well as for those who manage them. Individuals need a longitudinal framework within which to form their own career decisions. Managers need a framework for predicting some of the long-term consequences of short-term career decisions. Managers in several organizations have found it useful to examine the stages of career development in their own organizations as a way of identifying the factors that block or facilitate movement between stages.

Performance Appraisal and Career Development

Too often performance appraisal interviews focus only on the past year or, at best, on plans for the forthcoming year. Rarely do a manager and a subordinate discuss careers, in the main because neither the manager nor the subordinate has a way to talk about career development in terms other than the prospects for promotion. The career stages model can be helpful in guiding such a discussion. A number of managers have found that just discussing the model with individuals helps them to think more clearly about their careers and begin to identify alternatives and strategies for development that they hadn't previously considered.

The concept of stages can help a person think more clearly not only about what he should be doing and learning in his present job but also about what he should do if he wants to advance to another stage. A person who has learned what he needs to do in Stage I can begin to demonstrate his ability to work independently, develop an expertise that others recognize, and begin to apply that expertise. A person in Stage II may begin to take a new employee under his wing, show him how the system works, teach him some of the finer technical points, and so on. The Stage I person who wants to progress in the organization could ask himself: "Am I reluctant to make decisions on my own?" A person aiming for Stage IV could ask himself whether he is able to think about the needs of the organization as a whole and not just about his own group.

Timing

We aren't saying that anyone can promote himself to Stage IV. We do say that people can begin to do the work of the next stage and thus facilitate the transition to that stage. However, timing is a significant issue. There is a fine line between trying to move too quickly into the next stage and staying in the present stage long enough to obtain a learning base sufficient for subsequent growth. Too many people are so intent on getting into management that they don't establish the technical base they will need when they are called on to direct others.

Finally, and this is important, the individual must be responsible for deciding whether to stay in that organization. Sometimes an individual is capable of moving into Stage III or Stage IV activities and willing to do so, but the opportunities in the present organization are limited. On the other hand, failure to develop the skills and attitudes needed at the next stage could negate the effect of a change of organizations.

Manpower Planning

Although the primary responsibility for career management lies with the individual, the organization can do some things to facilitate career development. To become aware of the problem is the indispensable first step. Many managers are insensitive to the changing level of opportunities in their organizations. One company was having serious problems with turnover in its sales force. The company had grown rapidly for ten years, doubling sales every three years. Then growth leveled off to 5 percent a year. However, the district sales managers continued to recruit new salesmen with promises of promotion into management within 18 months and so on. When the promised promotions didn't materialize, the disillusioned salesmen left to go to work for the competition, usually within two or two and one-half years.

An awareness of this problem can come from an analysis of the demographic data. How many employees, engineers, accountants, and managers, for example, does the organization have in each stage? What are the prospects for expansion and for having new positions open up? What is the turnover in each group?

It is also important for managers to share data with their people. Recently 60 upper-level managers in a large organization were asked whether they thought they would be promoted at least one more time before retirement. Fully 80 percent said no, not because they felt they lacked ability but because they felt there were no opportunities. In fact, the organization was planning on having most of them assume higher-level responsibilities.

Dual Ladders

The concept of career stages could help to explain some of the confusion and disillusionment that have arisen around the dual ladder. In attempting to recognize the contributions a nonmanagerial professional can make to an organization, most dual ladder programs have dichotomized the technical and the managerial roles. Often the roles in the technical ladder are described in terms of the lone individual contributor—a super Stage II person.

As we noted earlier, organizations have other roles for their experienced and competent senior people to fill. Stage III people, whether or not they are in management, tend to deal with the outside, train and develop others, and provide direction for important projects or activities. A recognition of the similarities between the activities and relationships of Stage III managers and Stage III nonmanagers could help professionals to recognize that some experience in a management position may be a legitimate form of preparation for a senior technical role, just as a Stage III or IV nonmanager may make the best candidate for a formal management slot.

Job Assignments

All our research indicates that the job assignment is the single most important variable in career development. There are many ways in which this variable can be manipulated. A person who is seen as too narrow can be moved to a new project that forces him to apply his existing skills to new problems. Someone who is finding it difficult to become independent of his mentor can be transferred to a job that facilitates such a transition. A change of job assignment is no panacea, but it can be pivotal in helping people develop their careers.

Finally, organizations need to find ways of loosening their structures, rules, and procedures to make it possible for more people to move through the stages. In most organizations more people combine the ability and desire to do Stage III and IV work than are allowed to do so. Often there are policies or traditions that permit only certain people to deal with customers, suppliers, and so on or that make it difficult for individual contributors to serve as mentors. Some managers are unwilling, for example, to let senior employees serve as mentors to the newcomers in the organization. Sometimes their fear is justified, but more often it prevents the formation of a very productive relationship.

Most organizations and most managers are both unsuccessful and uncreative in managing senior professionals. Organizations that learn to perform that task well will have a considerable competitive advantage.

Organizations need to be more creative in making it possible for people to move both ways through the stages without the fear of a clear or permanent loss of status or prestige. Often the individual and the organization are locked into motivating an unrewarding relationship. It needs to become much easier for people like George Dunlop to make the transition that he made. As more senior managers set the example of this type of transition, hopefully it will become a more acceptable career alternative.

Consciously or unconsciously we all carry in our heads models to help us think about careers in organizations. We have concluded that many of the models being used to make decisions that affect careers are misleading. In our view, the longitudinal concept of career stages can be helpful to both professionals and managers as they make decisions about their careers.

9

Managing Careers: The Influence of Job and Group Longevities

RALPH KATZ, Massachusetts Institute of Technology

Any serious consideration of organizational careers must eventually explore the dynamics through which the concerns, abilities, and experiences of individual employees combine and mesh with the demands and requirements of their employing work environments. How do employees' needs for security, equitable rewards, and opportunities for advancement and self-development, for example, interact with the needs of organizations for ensured profitability, flexibility, and innovativeness? More important, how should they interact so that both prescription sets are filled satisfactorily?

Further complexity is added to this "matching" process with the realization that interactions between individuals and organizations are not temporally invariant but can shift significantly throughout workers' jobs, careers, and life cycles. As employees pass from one phase in their work lives to the next, different concerns and issues are emphasized; and the particular perspectives that result produce different behavioral and attitudinal combinations within their job settings. Over time, therefore, employees are continuously revising and adjusting their perspectives toward their organizations and their roles in them. And it is the perspective that one has formulated at a particular point in time that gives meaning and direction to one's work and to one's career.

Because the effectiveness of a given organizational unit ultimately depends on the combined actions and performances of its membership, we must begin to examine more systematically the impact of such varying perspectives on the predilections of unit members for particular kinds of activities, interactions, and collective judgments. Clearly, a better understanding of the substantive nature of such dispositions and behavioral tendencies will help clarify accommodation processes between organizations and individuals so that eventual problems can be dealt with to their mutual benefits. To accomplish such objectives, however, we need to develop more process-oriented frameworks for analyzing the diverse kinds of concerns and associated behaviors that tend to preoccupy and characterize employees as they proceed through their respective jobs, project groups, and organizational careers.

A MODEL OF JOB LONGEVITY

Based on some recent findings in the areas of job satisfaction and task redesign, Katz (1980) has been working to develop a more general theory for describing how employees' perspectives unfold and change as they journey through their own discrete sequences of job situations. In particular, a three-transitional stage model of job longevity has been proposed to illustrate how certain kinds of concerns might change in importance according to the actual length of time an employee has been working in a given job position. Generally speaking, each time an employee is assigned to a new job position within an organization, either as a recent recruit or through transfer or promotion, the individual enters a relatively brief but nevertheless important "socialization" period. With increasing familiarity about his or her new job environment, however, the employee soon passes from socialization into the "innovation" stage, which, in turn, slowly shifts into a "stabilization" state as the individual gradually adapts to extensive job longevity, (i.e., as the employee continues to work in the same overall job for an extended period of time). Table 9-1 summarizes the sequential nature of these three stages by comparing some of the different kinds of issues affecting employees as they cycle through their various job positions.[1]

Socialization

As outlined under the initial socialization stage, employees entering new job positions are concerned primarily with reality construction, building more realistic understandings of their unfamiliar social and task environments. In formulating

---

[1] For a more extensive discussion of the job-longevity model, see Katz (1980). In the current presentation, the term "stabilization" is used in place of "adaptation" since individuals are in effect adapting to their job situations in all three stages, albeit in systematically different ways.

Table 9-1   A Model of Job Longevity

Job Longevity Stages	Primary Areas of Concern

Stage 1. SOCIALIZATION: Reality Construction[a]

a) To build one's situational identity
b) To decipher situational norms and identify acceptable, rewarded behaviors
c) To build social relationships and become accepted by others
d) To learn supervisory, peer, and subordinate expectations
e) To prove oneself as an important, contributing member

Stage 2. INNOVATION: Influence, Achievement, and Participation

a) To be assigned challenging work
b) To enhance one's visibility and promotional potential
c) To improve one's special skills and abilities
d) To enlarge the scope of one's participation and contribution
e) To influence one's organizational surroundings

Stage 3. STABILIZATION: Maintenance, Consolidation, and Protection

a) To routinize one's task activities
b) To preserve and safeguard one's task procedures and resources
c) To protect one's autonomy
d) To minimize one's vulnerability
e) To cultivate and solidify one's social environment

[a]The listed items are not meant to be exhaustive; rather they are intended to illustrate both the domain and the range of issues within each stage.

their new perspectives, they are busily absorbed with problems of establishing and clarifying their own situational roles and identities and with learning all the attitudes and behaviors that are appropriate and expected within their new job settings. Estranged from their previous work environments and supporting relationships, newcomers must construct situational definitions that allow them to understand and interpret the myriad of experiences associated with their new organizational memberships. They need, for example, to learn the customary norms of behavior, decipher how reward systems actually operate, discover supervisory expectations, and more generally learn how to function meaningfully within their multiple group contexts (Schein, 1978). Through information communicated by their new "significant others," newcomers learn to develop perceptions of their own roles and skills that are both supported within their new surroundings and which permit them to organize their activities and interactions in a meaningful fashion. As pointed out by Hughes (1958) in his discussion of "reality shock," when new employees suddenly discover that their somewhat "overglorified" work-related expectations are neither realistic nor mutually shared by their boss or co-workers, they are likely to feel disenchanted and will experience considerable pressure to either redefine more compatible expectations or terminate from their work settings.

The importance of such a "breaking-in" period has long been recognized in discussions of how social processes affect recent organizational hires trying to make sense out of their newfound work experiences. What is also important to recognize is that veteran employees must also relocate or "resocialize" themselves following their displacements into new job positions within their same organizations (Wheeler, 1966). Just as organizational newcomers have to define and interpret their new territorial domains, veteran employees must also restructure and reformulate perceptions regarding their new social and task realities.[2] As they assume new organizational positions and enter important new relationships, veterans must learn to integrate their new perceptions and experiences with prior organizational knowledge in order to develop fresh situational perspectives, including perceptions about their own self-images and their images of other organizational members.

Such perceptual revisions are typically necessary simply because work groups and other organizational subunits are often highly differentiated with respect to their idiosyncratic sets of norms, beliefs, perceptions, time perspectives, shared language schemes, goal orientations, and so on (Lawrence and Lorsch, 1967). As communications and interactions within an organizational subunit continue to take place or intensify, it is likely that a more common set of understandings about the subunit and its environment will develop through informational social influence. Such shared meanings and awarenesses not only provide the subunit's members with a sense of belonging and identity but will also demarcate the subunit from other organizational entities (Pfeffer, 1981). Consequently, as one shifts job positions and moves within the organization, one is likely to encounter and become part of a new set of groups with their correspondingly different belief systems and perspectives about themselves, their operations, and their operating environments. It is in this initial socialization period, therefore, that organizational employees, and newcomers in particular, learn not only the technical requirements of their new job assignments but also the interpersonal behaviors and social attitudes that are acceptable and necessary for becoming a true contributing member.

Since employees in the midst of socialization are strongly motivated to reduce ambiguity by creating order out of their somewhat vague and unfamiliar surroundings, it becomes clear why a number of researchers have discovered organizational newcomers being especially concerned with psychological safety and security and

---

[2]The extent to which a veteran employee actually undergoes socialization depends on how displaced the veteran becomes in undertaking his or her new job assignment. Generally speaking, the more displaced veterans are from their previously familiar task requirements and interpersonal associations, the more intense the socialization experience.

with clarifying their new situational identities (Kahn et al., 1964; Hall and Nougaim, 1968). In a similar vein, Schein (1971) suggests that to become accepted and to prove one's competence represent two major problems that newcomers and veterans must face before they can function comfortably within their new job positions. It is these kinds of concerns that help to explain why Katz (1978a) discovered that during the initial months of their new job positions, employees are not completely ready to respond positively to all the challenging charactertistics of their new task assignments. Instead, they appear most responsive to job features that provide a sense of personal acceptance and importance as well as a sense of proficiency through feedback and individual guidance.[3] Van Maanen's (1975) study of urban police socialization also demonstrated that for about tne first three or four months of their initial job assignments, police recruits are busily absorbed in the process of changing and solidifying their own self- and job-related perceptions as they finally come to know the actual attitudes and behaviors of their veteran counterparts.

How long this initial socialization period lasts, therefore, probably depends on how long it takes employees to feel accepted and competent within their new work environments. Not only is the length of such a time period greatly influenced by the abilities, needs, and prior experiences of individual workers and influenced as well by the clarity and usefulness of the interpersonal interactions that take place, but it also probably differs significantly across occupations. Based on the retrospective answers of his hospital employee sample, for example, Feldman (1977) reports that on the average, accounting clerks, registered nurses, and engineering tradesmen reporting feeling accepted after one, two, and four months, respectively although they did not feel completely competent until after three, six, and eight months, respectively. Generally speaking, one might posit that the length of one's initial socialization period varies postively with the level of complexity within one's job and occupational requirements, ranging perhaps from as little as a month or two on very routine, programmed-type jobs to as much as a year or more on very skilled, unprogrammed-type jobs, as in the engineering and scientific professions. With respect to engineering, for example, it is generally recognized that a substantial socialization period is often required before engineers can fully contribute within their new organizational settings, using their particular knowledge and technical specialties. Thus, even though one might have received an excellent education in mechanical engineering principles at a university or college, one must still figure out from working and interacting with others in the setting how to be an effective mechanical engineer at Westinghouse, DuPont, or Procter and Gamble.[4]

---

[3]After comparing the socializaton reactions of veterans and newcomers, Katz (1978a) suggests that newcomers may be especially responsive to interactional issues involving personal acceptance and "getting on board," whereas veterans may be particularly concerned with re-establishing their sense of competency in their newly acquired task assignments.

[4]One of the factors contributing to the importance of this socialization period lies in the realization that engineering strategies and solutions within organizations are often not defined in very generalizeable terms but are peculiar to their specific settings (Allen, 1977; Katz and Tushman, 1979). As a result, R&D project groups in different organizations may face similar problems yet may define their solution approaches and parameters very differently. And it is precisely because technical problems are typically expressed in such "localized" terms that engineers must learn how to contribute effectively within their new project groups.

Innovation

With time, interaction, and increasing familiarity, employees soon discover how to function appropriately in their jobs and to feel sufficiently secure in their perceptions of their workplace. Individual energies can now be devoted more toward task performance and accomplishment instead of being expended on learning the previously unfamiliar social knowledge and skills necessary to makes sense out of one's work-related activities and interactions. As a result, employees become increasingly capable of acting in a more responsive, innovative, and undistracted manner.

The movement from socialization to the innovation stage of job longevity implies that employees no longer require much assistance in deciphering their new job and organizational surroundings. Having adequately constructed their own situational definitions during the socialization period, employees are now freer to participate within their own conceptions of organizational reality. They are now able to divert their attention from an initial emphasis on psychological safety and acceptance to concerns for achievement and influence. Thus, what becomes progressively more pertinent to employees as they proceed from socialization to the innovation stage are the opportunities to participate and grow within their job settings in a very meaningful and responsible manner.

The idea of having to achieve some reasonable level of psychological safety and security in order to be fully responsive to challenges in the work setting is very consistent with Kuhn's (1963) concept of "creative tensions." According to Kuhn, it is likely that only when conditions of *both* stability and challenge are present can the creative tensions between them generate considerable innovative behavior. Growth theorists such as Maslow (1962) and Rogers (1961) have similarly argued that the presence of psychological safety is one of the chief prerequisites for self-direction and individual responsiveness. For psychological safety to occur, however, individuals must be able to understand and attach sufficient meaning to the vast array of events, interactions, and information flows involving them throughout their workdays. Of particular importance to growth theorists is the idea that employees must be able to expect positive results to flow from their individual actions. Such a precondition implies that employees must have developed sufficient knowledge about their new job situations in order for there to be enough predictability for them to take appropriate kinds of actions.[5]

A similar point of view is taken by Staw (1977) when he argues that if employees truly expect to improve their overall job situations, they must first learn to predict their most relevant set of behavioral-outcome contingencies before they try to influence or increase their control over them. One must first construct a reasonably valid perspective about such contingencies before one can sensibly strive to manage them for increasingly more favorable outcomes. In short, there must be sufficient awareness of one's environment, sufficient acceptance and competence

---

[5] It is also interesting to note that in discussing his career-anchor framework, Schein (1978) points out that career anchors seem to represent a stable concept around which individuals are able to organize experiences and direct activities. Furthermore, it appears from Schein's research that it is within this area of stability that individuals are most likely to self-develop and grow.

within one's setting, and sufficient openness to new ideas and experiences in order for employees to be fully responsive to the "richness" of their job demands.

Stabilization

As employees continue to work in their same overall job settings for a considerable length of time, without any serious disruption or displacement, they may gradually proceed from innovation to stabilization in the sense of shifting from being highly involved in and receptive to their job demands to becoming progressively unresponsive. For the most part, responsive individuals prefer to work at jobs they find stimulating and challenging and in which they can self-develop and grow. With such kinds of activities, they are likely to inject greater effort and involvement into their tasks which, in turn, will be reflected in their performances (Hackman and Oldham, 1975; Katz, 1978b). It seems reasonable to assume, however, that in time even the most challenging job assignments and responsibilities can appear less exciting and more habitual to jobholders who have successfully mastered and become increasingly accustomed to their everyday task requirements. With prolonged job longevity and stability, therefore, it is likely that employees' perceptions of their present conditions and of their future possibilities will become increasingly impoverished. They may begin essentially to question the value of what they are doing and where it may lead. If employees cannot maintain, redefine, or expand their jobs for continual challenge and growth, the substance and meaning of their work begins to deteriorate. Enthusiasm wanes, for what was once challenging and exciting may no longer hold much interest at all.

At the same time, it is also important to mention that if an individual is able to increase or even maintain his or her own sense of task challenge and excitement on a given job for an extended period of time, then instead of moving toward stabilization, the process might be the reverse (i.e., continued growth and innovation). As before, the extent to which an individual can maintain his or her responsiveness on a particular job strongly depends on the complexity of the underlying tasks as well as on the individual's own capabilities, needs, and prior experiences. With respect to individual differences, for example, Katz's (1978b) findings suggest that employees with high growth needs are able to respond to the challenging aspects of their new jobs sooner than employees with low growth needs. At the same time, however, high-order-need employees might not retain their responsiveness for as long a job period as employees with low-growth-need strength.

It should also be emphasized that in addition to job longevity, many other contextual factors can affect a person's situational perspective strongly enough to influence the level of job interest as one continues to work in a given job position over a long period of time. New technological developments, rapid growth and expansion, the sudden appearance of external threats, or strong competitive pressures could all help sustain or even enhance an individual's involvement in his or her job-related activities. On the other hand, having to work closely with a group of unresponsive peers might shorten an individual's responsive period on that particular job rather dramatically. Clearly, the reactions of individuals are not only influenced by psychological predispositions and personality characteristics but also by individuals' definitions of and interactions with their overall situational settings (Homans, 1961; Salancik and Pfeffer, 1978).

Generally speaking, however, as tasks become progressively less stimulating to employees with extended job longevity, they can either leave the setting or remain and adapt to their present job situations (Argyris, 1957). In moving from innovation to stabilization, it is suggested that employees who continue to work in their same overall job situations for long periods of time gradually succeed in adapting to such steadfast employment by becoming increasingly indifferent and unresponsive to the challenging task features of their job assignments (Katz, 1978a). In the process of adaptation, they may also redefine what they consider to be important, most likely by placing relatively less value on intrinsic kinds of work issues. The findings of Kopelman (1977) and Hall and Schneider (1973) suggest, for example, that when individuals perceive their opportunities for intrinsic-type satisfactions and challenges to be diminishing, they begin to match such developments by placing less value on such types of expectations. And as employees come to care less about the intrinsic nature of the actual work they do, the greater their relative concern for certain contextual features, such as salary, benefits, vacations, friendly co-workers, and compatible supervision.

The passage from innovation to stabilization is not meant to suggest that job satisfaction necessarily declines with long-term job longevity. On the contrary, it is likely that in the process of adaptation, employees' expectations have become adequately satisfied as they continue to perform their familiar duties in their normally acceptable fashions. If aspirations are defined as a function of the disparity between desired and expected (Kiesler, 1978), then as long as what individuals desire is reasonably greater than what they can presently expect to attain, there will be energy for change and achievement. On the other hand, when employees arrive at a stage where their chances for future growth and challenges in their jobs are perceived to be remote, then as they adapt, it is likely that existing situations will become accepted as the desired and aspirations for growth and change will have been reduced. As a result, the more employees come to accept their present circumstances, the stronger the tendency to keep the existing work environment fairly stable. Career interests and aspirations may become markedly constricted, for in a sense, adapted employees may simply prefer to enjoy rather than try to add to their present job accomplishments.

Underpinning the descriptive changes represented by the stabilization stage is the basic idea that over time individuals try to organize their work lives in a manner that reduces the amount of stress they must face and which is also low in uncertainty (Pfeffer, 1980; Staw, 1977). Weick (1969) also relies on this perspective when he contends that employees seek to "enact" their environments by directing their activities toward the establishment of a workable level of certainty and clarity.

In general, one might argue that employees strive to bring their work activities into a state of equilibrium where they are more capable of predicting events and of avoiding potential conflicts.[6]

Given such developmental trends, it seems reasonable that with considerable job longevity, most employees have been able to build a work pattern that is familiar and comfortable, a pattern in which routine and precedent play a relatively large part. According to Weick (1969), as employees establish certain structures of interlocked behaviors and relationships, these patterns will in time become relatively stable simply because they provide certainty and predictability to these interlinked employees. It is further argued here that as individuals adapt to their long-term job tenure and become progressively less responsive to their actual task demands, they will come to rely more on these established modes of conduct to complete their everyday job requirements. Most likely, adapted employees feel safe and comfortable in such stability, for its keeps them feeling secure and confident in what they do, yet requires little additional vigilance or effort. In adapting to extended job longevity, therefore, employees become increasingly content and ensconced in their customary ways of doing things, in their comfortable routines and interactions, and in their familiar sets of task demands and responsibilities.

If change or uncertainty is seen by individuals in the stabilization period as particularly disruptive, then the preservation of familiar routines and patterns of behavior is likely to be of prime concern. Given such a disposition, adapted employees are probably less receptive toward any change or toward any information that might threaten to disturb their developing sense of complacency. Rather than striving to enlarge the scope of their job demands, they may be more concerned with maintaining their comfortable work environments by protecting themselves from sources of possible interference, from activities requiring new kinds of attention, or form situations that might reveal their shortcomings. Adapted employees, for example, might seek to reduce uncertainty in their day-to-day supervisory dealings perhaps by solidifying their attractiveness through ingratiating kinds of behavior (Wortman and Linsenmeier, 1977) or perhaps by isolating themselves from such supervisory contacts (Pelz and Andrews, 1966). Or they might seek to reduce uncertainty by trying to safeguard their personal allocations of resources and rewards through the use of standardized practices and policies. Whatever the specific behaviors that eventually emerge in a given setting, it is likely that employees who have become unresponsive to the challenging features of their assigned tasks will strongly resist events threatening to introduce uncertainty into their work environments.

One of the best examples of the effects of such long-term stability can still be found in Chinoy's (1955) classic interviews of automobile factory workers. Chinoy discovered that although almost 80% of the workers had wanted to leave their

---

[6]There are, of course, alternative arguments, such as in activation theory (Scott, 1966), suggesting that people do in fact seek uncertainty, novelty, or change. The argument here, however, is that as individuals adapt and become increasingly indifferent to the task challenges of their jobs, it is considerably more likely that they will strive to reduce uncertainty and maintain predictability rather than the reverse.

present jobs at one time or another, very few could actually bring themselves to leave. Most of the workers were simply unwilling to give up the predictability and comfortableness of their presently familiar routines and cultivated relationships for the uncertainties of a new job position.

SITUATIONAL VERSUS INDIVIDUAL CONTROL

In presenting this three-stage model of job longevity, I have tried to describe some of the major concerns affecting employees as they enter and adapt to their particular job positions. Of course, the extent to which any specific individual is affected by these issues depends on the particular perceptual outlook that has been developed over time through job-related activities and through role-making processes with other individuals, including supervisors, subordinates, and peers (Weick, 1969; Graen, 1976). Employees, as a result, learn to cope with their particular job and organizational environments through their interpretations of relevant work experiences as well as their expectations and hopes of the future. To varying degrees, then, situational perspectives are derivatives of both retrospective and prospective processes, in that they are built and shaped through knowledge of past events and future anticipations.

One of the more important aspects of the socialization process, however, is that the information and knowledge previously gathered by employees from their former settings are no longer sufficient or necessarily appropriate for interpreting or understanding their new organizational domains. Newcomers, for instance, have had only limited contact within their new institutional surroundings from which to construct their perceptual views. Similarly, the extent to which veterans who are assuming new job positions can rely on their past organizational experiences and perspectives to function effectively within their new work settings can also be rather limited, depending of course on their degrees of displacement.

Essentially, individuals in the midst of socialization are trying to navigate their way through new and unfamiliar territories without the aid of adequate or even accurate perceptual maps. During this initial period, therefore, they are typically more malleable and more susceptible to change (Schein, 1968). In a sense, they are working under conditions of high "situational control" in that they must depend on other individuals within their new situations to help them define and interpret the numerous activities taking place around them. The greater their unfamiliarity or displacement within their new organizational areas, the more they must rely on their situations to provide the necessary information and interactions by which they can eventually construct their own perspectives and reestablish new situational identities. And it is precisely this external need or "situational dependency" that enables these individuals to be more easily influenced during their socialization processes through social interactions (Salancik and Pfeffer, 1978; Katz, 1980).

As employees become increasingly cognizant of their overall job surroundings, however, they also become increasingly capable of relying on their own perceptions for interpreting events and executing their everyday task requirements. In moving from socialization into the innovation or stabilization stage, employees have succeeded in building a sufficiently robust situational perspective, thereby freeing themselves to operate more self-sufficiently within their familiar work settings. They are now working under conditions of less "situational" but more "individual" control, in the sense that they are now better equipped to determine for themselves the importance and meaning of the various events and information flows surrounding them. Having established their own social and task supports, their own perceptual outlooks, and their own situational identities, they become less easily changed and less easily manipulated. As pointed out by Schein (1973), when individuals no longer have to balance their situational perspectives against the views of significant others within their settings, they become less susceptible to change and situational influences. Thus, movement through the three stages of job longevity can also be characterized, as shown in Figure 9-1, by relative shifts to more individual and less situational control.

As the locus of "control" shifts with increasing job longevity and individuals continue to stabilize their situational definitions, other important behavioral tendencies could also materialize. In particular, strong biases could develop in the way individuals select and interpret information, in their cognitive abilities to generate new options and strategies creatively, and in their willingness to innovate or implement alternative courses of action. Table 9-2 outlines in more detail some of the specific possibilities within each of these three general areas. Furthermore, it is the capacity either to prevent or overcome these kinds of tendencies that is so important to the long-term success of organizations; for, over time, each of these trends could lead to less effective performance and decision-making outcomes.

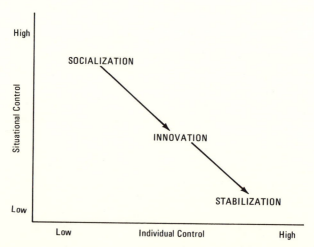

FIGURE 9-1 Situational versus individual control along the job-longevity continuum

Table 9-2 Representative Trends Associated With Long-term Job Longevity

---

Problem-solving processes
    Increased rigidity
    Increased commitment to established practices and procedures
    Increased mainlining of strategies

Information processes
    Increased insulation from critical areas
    Increased selective exposure
    Increased selective perception

Cognitive processes
    Increased reliance on own experiences and expertise
    Increased narrowing of cognitive abilities
    Increased homophyly

Problem-Solving Processes

It has been argued throughout this paper that as employees gradually adapt to prolonged periods of job longevity, they may become less receptive toward any change or innovation threatening to disrupt significantly their comfortable and predictable work practices and patterns of behavior. Individuals, instead, are more likely to develop reliable and effective routine responses (i.e., standard operating procedures) for dealing with their frequently encountered tasks in order to ensure predictability, coordination, and economical information processing. As a result, there may develop over time increasing rigidity in one's problem-solving activities—a kind of functional fixedness that reduces the individual's capacity for flexibility and openness to change. Responses and decisions are made in their fixed, normal patterns while novel situations requiring responses that do not fit such established molds are either ignored or forced into these molds. New or changing situations either trigger responses of old situations or trigger no responses at all. It becomes, essentially, a work world characterized by the phrase "business as usual."

Furthermore, as individuals continue to work by their well-established problemsolving strategies and procedures, the more committed they may become to such existing methods. Commitment is a function of time, and the longer individuals are called upon to follow and justify their problem-solving approaches and decisions, the more ingrained they are likely to become. Drawing from his work on decision making, Allison (1971) strongly warns that increasing reliance on regularized practices and procedures can become highly resistant to change, since such functions become increasingly grounded in the norms and basic attitudes of the organizational unit and in the operating styles of its members. Bion (1961) and Argyris (1969) even suggest that it may be impossible for individuals to break out of fixed patterns of activity and interpersonal behavior without sufficiently strong outside interference or help.

With extended job tenure, then, problem-solving activities can become increasingly guided by consideration of methods and programs that have worked in the past. Moreover, in accumulating this experience and knowledge, alternative ideas and approaches were probably considered and discarded. With such refutations, however, commitments to the present courses of action can become even stronger—often to the extent that these competing alternatives are never reconsidered.[7] In fact, individuals can become overly preoccupied with the survival of their particular approaches, protecting them against fresh approaches or negative evaluations. Much of their energy becomes directed toward "mainlining their strategies," that is, making sure their specific solution approaches are selected and followed. Research by Janis and Mann (1977) and Staw (1980) has demonstrated very convincingly just how strongly committed individuals can become to their problem-solving approaches and decisions, even in the face of adverse information, especially if they feel personally responsible for such strategies.

Information Processes

One of the potential consequences of developing this kind of "status-quo" perspective with respect to problem-solving activity is that employees may also become increasingly insulated from outside sources of relevant information and important new ideas. As individuals become more protective of and committed to their current work habits, the extent to which they are willing or even feel they need to expose themselves to new or alternative ideas, solution strategies, or constructive criticisms becomes progressively less and less. Rather than becoming more vigilant about events taking place outside their immediate work settings, they may become increasingly complacent about external environmental changes and new technological developments.

In addition to this possible decay in the amount of external contact and interaction, there may also be an increasing tendency for individuals to communicate only with those whose ideas are in accord with their current interests, needs, or existing attitudes. Such a tendency is referred to as selective exposure. Generally speaking, there is always the tendency for individuals to communicate with those who are most like themselves (Rogers and Shoemaker, 1971). With increasing adaptation to long-term job longevity and stability, however, this tendency is likely to become even stronger. Thus, selective exposure may increasingly enable these individuals to avoid information and messages that might be in conflict with their current practices and dispositions.

One should also recognize, of course, that under these kinds of circumstances, any outside contact or environmental information that does become processed by these long-tenured individuals might not be viewed in the most open and unbiased fashion. Janis and Mann (1977), for example, discuss at great length the many kinds of cognitive defenses and distortions commonly used by individuals in processing

---

[7]As shown by Allen's (1966) research on parallel project efforts, such reevaluations can be very important in reaching more successful outcomes.

outside information in order to support, maintain, or protect certain decisional policies and strategies. Such defenses are often used to argue against any disquieting information and evidence in order to maintain self-esteem, commitment, and involvement. In particular, selective perception is the tendency to interpret information and communication messages in terms favorable to one's existing attitudes and beliefs. And it is this combination of increasing insulation, selective exposure, and selective perception that can be so powerful in keeping critical information and important new ideas and innovations from being registered.

Cognitive Processes

As individuals become more comfortable and secure in their long-tenured work environments, their desire to seek out and actively internalize new knowledge and new developments may begin to deteriorate. Not only may they become increasingly isolated from outside sources of information, but their willingness to accept or pay adequate attention to the advice and ideas of fellow experts may become less and less. Unlike the socialization period in which individuals are usually very attentive to sources of expertise and influence within their new job settings, individuals in the stabilization stage have probably become significantly less receptive to such information sources. They may prefer, instead, to rely on their own accumulated experience and wisdom and consequently are more apt to dismiss the approaches, advice, or critical comments of others. As a result, adapted employees may be especially defensive with regard to critical evaluations and feedback messages, whether they stem from sources of outside expertise or from internal supervision.

It should also not be surprising that with increasing job stability one is more likely to become increasingly specialized, that is, moving from broadly defined capabilities and solution approaches to more narrowly defined interests and specialties. Without new challenges and opportunities, the diversity of skills and of ideas generated are likely to become narrower and narrower. And as individuals welcome information from fewer sources and are exposed to fewer alternative points of view, the more constricted their cognitive abilities can become. Essentially, there can be a narrowing of one's cognitive processes, resulting in a more restricted perspective of one's situation, coupled with a more limited set of coping responses. Such a restricted outlook, moreover can be very detrimental to the organization's overall effectiveness, for it could lead at times to the screening out of some vitally important environmental information cues.

Homophyly refers to the degree to which interacting individuals are similar with respect to certain attributes, such as beliefs, values, education, and social status (Rogers and Shoemaker, 1971). Not only is there a strong tendency for individuals to communicate with those who are most like themselves, but it is also likely that continued interaction can lead to greater homophyly in knowledge, beliefs, and problem-solving behaviors and perceptions (Burke and Bennis, 1961; Pfeffer, 1980). The venerable proverb "birds of a feather flock together" makes a great deal of sense, but it may be just as sensible to say that "when birds flock together, they become more of a feather." Accordingly, as individuals stabilize their work settings and patterns of communication, a greater degree of homophyly is likely to have emerged between these individuals and those with whom they have been interacting over the long tenure period. And any increase in homophyly could lead in turn to further stability in the communications of the more homophilous pairs, thereby increasing their insulation from heterophilous others. Thus, it is possible for the various trends to feed on each other. Finally, it should be mentioned that although individuals may be able to coordinate and communicate with homophilous partners more effectively and economically, such interactions are also more likely to yield less creative and innovative outcomes (Pelz and Andrews, 1966).

Longevity and Performance

These problem-solving, informational, and cognitive tendencies, of course, can be very serious in their consequences, perhaps even fatal. Much depends, however, on the nature of the work being performed and on the extent to which such trends actually transpire. The performances of individuals working on fairly routine, simple tasks in a rather stable organizational environment, for example, may not suffer as a result of these trends, for their own knowledge, experiences, and abilities become sufficient. Maintaining or improving on one's routine behaviors is all that is required—at least for as long as there are no changes and no new developments. However, as individuals function in a more rapidly changing environment and work on more complex tasks requiring greater levels of change, creativity, and informational vigilance, the effects of these long-term longevity trends are likely to become significantly more dysfunctional.

GROUP LONGEVITY

The degree to which any of these previously described trends actually materializes for any given individual depends, of course, on the overall situational context. Individuals' perceptions and responses do not take place in a social vacuum but develop over time as they continue to interact with various aspects of their job and organizational surroundings (Crozier, 1964; Katz and Van Maanen, 1977). And in any job setting one of the most powerful factors affecting individual perspectives is the nature of the particular group or project team in which one is a functioning member (Schein, 1978; Katz and Kahn, 1978).

Ever since the well-known Western Electric Studies (Cass and Zimmer, 1975), much of our research in the social sciences has been directed toward learning just how strong group associations can be in influencing individual member behaviors, motivations, and attitudes (Asch, 1956; Shaw, 1971; Katz, 1977). From the diffusion of new innovations (Robertson, 1971) to the changing of meat consumption patterns to less desirable but more plentiful cuts (Lewin, 1965) to the implementation of job enrichment (Hackman, 1978), group processes and effects have been extremely critical to more successful outcomes. The impact of groups on individual responses is substantial, if not pervasive, simply because groups mediate most of the stimuli to which their individual members are subjected while fulfilling their every-day task and organizational requirements. Accordingly, whether individuals experiencing long-term job longevity enter the stabilization period and become sub-jected to the tendencies previously described may strongly depend on the particular reinforcements, pressures, and behavioral norms encountered within their immediate project or work groups (Likert, 1967; Weick, 1969).

Generally speaking, as members of a project group continue to work together over an extended period of time and gain experience with one another, their pat-terns of activities are likely to become more stable, with individual role assignments becoming more well-defined and resistant to change (Bales, 1955; Porter et al., 1975). Emergence of the various problem-solving, informational, and cognitive trends, therefore, may be more a function of the average length of time the group members have worked together (i.e., group longevity) rather than varying according to the particular job longevity of any single individual. A project group, then, might either exacerbate or ameliorate the various trends (e.g., insulation from outside developments and expertise), just as previous studies have shown how groups can enforce or amplify certain standards and norms of individual behavior (e.g., Seashore, 1954; Stoner, 1968). Thus, it may be misleading to investigate the responses and reactions of organizational individuals as if they functioned as independent entities; rather, it may be more insightful to examine the distribution of responses as a function of different project teams, especially when project teams are characterized by relatively high levels of group longevity.

GROUP LONGEVITY:
AN EXAMPLE IN AN R&D SETTING

Over the past fifteen years or so, a plethora of studies have clearly demonstrated that oral communications, rather than written technical reports or publications, are the primary means by which engineering and scientific professionals collect and transfer outside information and important new ideas into their project groups (Allen, 1977; Menzel, 1966). Given the strategic importance of oral communica-tions in R&D settings, one should examine explicitly the effects of any variable purporting to influence the linkages between a project group and its outside tech-nological and work environments. In particular, the present example investigates the influence of group longevity on the *actual* amount of interaction between R&D project groups and their various outside sources of information and new ideas. As a group "ages" and becomes more stable in its membership, to what extent, if any, will its team members isolate themselves from external areas of information, influence, and feedback; essentially by communicating less frequently with profes-sional colleagues and peers outside their project team?

The present study was carried out at the R&D facility of a large American corporation. Geographically isolated from the rest of the organization, the facility employed a total of 345 engineering and scientific professionals, all of whom participated in our study. The laboratory's professionals were divided into seven departmental laboratories, which, in turn, were separated into 61 distinct project groups or work areas. These project groupings remained stable over the course of our study, each professional belonging to only one project team. The 61 project groups were organized around specific, long-term types of problems, such as fiber-forming development, urethane development, and yarn technology. The project groups ranged across three kinds of task areas: research, development, or technical service. Specific definitions of these project task areas can be found in Katz and Tushman (1979).

Methods

To measure actual communications, all the professionals were asked to keep track (on specially prepared forms) of all other professionals with whom they had work-related oral communication on a given sampling day. These sociometric data were collected on a randomly chosen day each week for 15 weeks with equal number of weekdays. Respondents were asked to report all contacts both within and outside the laboratory's facility (including whom they talked to and how many times they talked with that person during the day). They were instructed not to report strictly social interactions or written forms of communication. During the fifteen weeks, the overall response rate was 93%. Moreover, 68% of all reported communication episodes within the laboratory were reciprocally reported by both parties. These research methods, therefore, provided a relatively accurate log of the actual communications of all professionals within this laboratory.

Project communication is measured by the average amount of technical communication per person per project over the fifteen weeks. For the purposes of our study, three mutually exclusive communication measures were operationalized for each project group as follows:[8]

1. *Intraproject communication:* the amount of communication reported among all project team members.
2. *Organizational communication:* the amount of communication reported by project team members with other individuals outside the R&D facility but within other corporate divisions, principally marketing and manufacturing.
3. *Professional communication:* the amount of communication reported by project members with professionals outside the parent organization, including universities, consulting firms, and professional societies.

Project communication measures to these three independent domains were cal-

---

[8]Three other measures of communication were also operationalized but have not been included in this presentation because they were not associated with project performance either for projects in this site or in previous research studies. The three communication measures reported here have all been shown to be important for more effecive technical performance.

culated by summing the relevant number of interactions reported during the fifteen weeks with appropriate averaging for the number of project team members (see Katz and Tushman, 1979, for details). Finally, none of the pairs of measures of actual project communication were significantly intercorrelated at the $p < .10$ level of significance. Thus, these three distinct measures of project communication were independent both conceptually and empirically.

In addition to project communication, we also tried to measure the current technical performance of all project groups. Since comparable measures of project performance have yet to be derived across different technologies, a subjective technique had to be employed. Each department manager ($N = 7$) and laboratory director ($N = 2$) was separately interviewed and asked to evaluate the overall technical performance of all projects with which he was technically familiar. They were asked to make their informed judgments based on their knowledge of and experience with the various projects. If they could not make an informed judgment for a particular project, they were asked not to rate the project. Criteria the managers considered (but were not limited to) included: schedule, budget, and cost performance; innovativeness; adaptability; and the ability to coordinate with other parts of the organization. On the average, each project was independently rated by at least four managers on a seven-point scale, ranging from very low (1) to very high (7). As the performance ratings across the nine judges were highly intercorrelated (Spearman-Brown reliability = .81), individual ratings were averaged to yield overall project performance scores.

During the course of the study, demographic data were also collected from the professionals, including their age, educational degrees, and the number of years and months they had been associated with their specific project area. Group longevity or mean group tenure was calculated by averaging the project tenures reported by all project members. It is important to recognize, then, that group longevity is *not* the length of time the project has been in existence, but rather it measures the length of time project team members have worked together. Complete communication, performance, and demographic data were successfully obtained on a total of 50 project groups representing 82% of all projects within this R&D facility.

Results

In order to determine whether any clear pattern might emerge between group longevity and the various measures of project communication, the fifty project groups were divided into five quintiles according to the tenure categories shown in Table 9-3. The first interval, 0.0 to 1.5 years, corresponds to an initial "learning or team-building" phase as project members become socialized into their new project environments. In contrast, the last category of project groups represents teams whose members have worked together for a long period of time (i.e., for an average of at least 5 years).[9] This 5-year cutoff also reflects the time period commonly used to estimate the half-life of technical information (Dubin, 1972).

[9]The maximum group-longevity score for projects in this category was approximately 12 years.

Table 9-3 Mean Communication Frequencies as a Function of Group Longevity

Areas of Communication	Categories of Group Longevity (years)					All Project Groups
	0.0-1.5	1.5-2.5	2.5-3.5	3.5-5.0	5.0 or more	
Mean intraproject communications**	42.0	101.0	110.0	180.0	69.0	100.0
Mean organizational communications* (per person per month)	17.5	21.3	30.0	25.6	20.1	22.9
Mean external professional communications* (per person per month)	0.81	0.98	2.04	1.83	0.69	1.27
Number of projects	10	10	10	10	10	50

Notes: A one-way ANOVA test was used to test for significant mean differences across the five group-longevity categories *p < .10; **p < .05.

Because intraproject communication frequencies had to be adjusted for the number of possible interactions (see Katz and Tushman, 1979), intraproject communication scores cannot be linked to an absolute scale. To show relative intraproject differences across the various categories, however, the intraproject measures have been standardized to an overall sample mean of 100.

Table 9-3 shows the mean amounts of intraproject, organizational, and outside professional communication for all project teams in each of the five group-longevity categories. With respect to all three measures of communication, the long-tenured project groups reported much lower levels of contact than project groups falling within the 1.5 to 5.0 tenure categories; in fact, the levels of intraproject and outside professional interactions were significantly lower. These data, then, strongly support the hypothesis that project teams can become increasingly insulated from sources of information both within the organization and from sources outside the organization as project members continue to work together over an extended period of time. There may be, as a result, a significant tendency within this facility for members of project groups to isolate themselves from external technology; from other organizational divisions, especially marketing and manufacturing; and even from other fellow project members as the mean tenure of project membership increases to over 5 years.[10]

It is also important to point out that in the current organizational sample there was no clear trend in any of the communication patterns of individual engineers when they were examined as a function of job longevity. Only when the engineers were grouped according to their project teams was there a clear and obvious decrease in interaction as a function of mean project tenure. How individuals eventually adapt to their long-term tenure on a given project, therefore, is probably influenced to a great extent by their project colleagues.

Generally speaking, previous research has also shown that the overall technical performance of R&D project groups is strongly associated with its levels of project communication (Allen, 1977). Given the significant differences in the three measures of project communication along the group-longevity continuum, the next step is to examine the distribution of project performance as a function of group longevity to see if it follows a similar pattern. Accordingly, Table 9-4 presents the average performance scores of projects within each of the five tenure categories.

Table 9-4   Project Performance as a Function of Group Longevity

	Categories of Group Longevity (years)					All Project Groups
	0.0-1.5	1.5-2.5	2.5-3.5	3.5-5.0	5.0 or more	
Mean project performance[a]	4.29	4.89	4.87	4.82	4.07	4.59
Standard deviations	0.99	0.67	0.70	0.59	0.52	0.76
Number of projects	10	10	10	10	10	50

[a]Based on a one-way ANOVA test, the mean project performance scores are significantly different across the five group-longevity categories [$F(4, 45) = 2.89; p < .05$].

[10]One must be very careful in interpreting the data patterns reported here, for they are based on cross-sectional, not longitudinal-type data. Strictly speaking, we can only speculate about the tendency for communication activity to decline with high levels of group longevity.

The curvilinear association between project performance and mean project tenure within this facility parallels extremely closely the communication trends reported in Table 9.3. On the average, project performance was significantly higher and nearly identical across all three middle tenure categories. Contrastingly, average project performance was significantly lower for teams whose mean group tenure was either less than 1.5 years or more than 5 years. In fact, none of the 10 project groups in the long-tenured category were among the facility's higher-performing projects. All 10 groups had been rated as either average or below average in performance.[11] Further analyses of these data also demonstrated that it was tenure within the project team and not chronological age or organizational tenure that was more likely to have influenced project performance (see Katz and Allen, 1981, for details).

Even though the long-tenured project teams had comparatively lower performance ratings coupled with lower levels of intraproject, organizational, and external professional communication, one must be careful not to conclude that decays in all three areas of communication may have contributed significantly or equally to the decay in project performance. Indeed, previous research has shown that different categories of project tasks require significantly different patterns of communication for more effective technical performance (Allen, 1977; Katz and Tushman, 1979; Dewhirst et al., 1978). Research project groups, for example, have been found to be higher-performing when all project members maintained high levels of technical communication with outside professionals. Development project performance, on the other hand, has not been positively linked with direct project member communication to outside professionals; instead, they have been found to be higher performing when they maintained high levels of organizational communication, especially with individuals from manufacturing and marketing. Finally, both intraproject and outside professional communication have been significantly connected to the overall performance ratings of technical service project groups.

Because research, development, and technical service project groups differ significantly in the way they effectively communicate both internally and externally (i.e., with outside technological developments and information), one must also analyze the previous empirical trends by project type to see if the different kinds of project tasks have become insulated from their more critical information domains. Toward this end, Table 9-5 displays the correlations between group longevity and the various performance and communication measures for each project type during the interval in which the purported decays seem to take place (i.e., for projects whose group longevity scores exceed 2.5 years) (see Katz and Allen, 1981, for some detailed curve-fitting results). Of the 30 projects with a mean group tenure score of at least 2.5 years, 6 were categorized as research, 12 as development, and 12 as technical service projects (see Katz and Tushman, 1979, for details).

As shown in Table 9-5, all three project types revealed a significant deterioration

---

[11] It is important to point out that in rating project performance, higher-level management did not know which projects had high levels of group longevity; nor were they cued to our interests in the effects of group longevity.

Table 9-5   Correlations Between Group Longevity and Project Performance and Project Communication for Teams With Group Longevity of at Least 2.5 Years

Variables Correlated with Group Longevity	Research (N = 6)	Development (N = 12)	Technical Service (N = 12)
	Research *(N = 6)*	*Development* *(N = 12)*	*Technical Service* *(N = 12)*
Project performance	−.62*	−.39*	−.44*
Intraproject communication	−.26	−.14	−.72***
Organizational communication	.27	−.53**	−.12
Outside professional communication	−.51	−.23	−.39

*$p < .10$; **$p < .05$; ***$p < .01$.

in project performance with increasingly high levels of group longevity. Furthermore, there was the tendency, with one exception, for projects in each of these task categories to interact less often with individuals from the three communication domains. For each project type, however, the insulation trend was particularly strong to certain key areas. Specifically, with increasing group longevity, there was an obvious decay in the outside professional communication of research project groups, a significant decline in the linkage between development projects and other organizational divisions, and significantly lower levels of intraproject communication for the long-tenured technical service teams. Moreover, by using each of these key communication measures as control variables, partial correlational analyses were performed to confirm that for each project type, group longevity may affect project performance, at least in part, by operating through reductions in communication to its most critical information domains.[12]

Such findings suggest that it may not be a reduction in project communication per se that can lead to less effective or less creative project performance. Rather a deterioration in performance is more likely to stem from a project group's tendency to insulate itself from sources that can provide more critical kinds of evaluation, information, and feedback. Thus, overall performance may suffer when research project members fail to pay sufficient attention to events and information within their relevant external R&D community; or when development project members fail to communicate sufficiently with their client groups from marketing and manufacturing; or when members of technical service projects fail to interact sufficiently among themselves.[13]

[12] The partial correlations are reported in Katz and Allen (1981).

[13] Such findings should not be interpreted to mean that external developments in technology are unimportant to development projects. On the contrary, they are exceedingly important! It is simply that development project performance may not be adversely affected by having less direct member interaction with external professionals. This occurs because development groups, unlike research or technical service projects, are more effectively linked with their external technical environments through specialized boundary-spanning individuals labeled gatekeepers rather than through direct project member communication (Allen, 1977; Tushman and Katz, 1980).

CONCLUSIONS

What is suggested by this discussion of job and group longevities is that employee perspectives and behaviors, and their subsequent effects on performance, might be significantly managed through staffing and career decisions. One could argue, for example, that the energizing and destabilizing function of new team members can be very important in preventing a project group from developing some of the tendencies previously described for long-tenured individuals, including insulation from key communication areas. The benefit of new team members is that they may have a relative advantage in generating fresh ideas and approaches. With their active participation, existing group members might consider more carefully ideas and alternatives they might have otherwise ignored or dismissed. In short, project newcomers can represent a novelty-enhancing condition, challenging and improving the scope of existing methods and accumulated knowledge.[14]

The longevity framework also seems to suggest that periodic job mobility or rotation might help prevent employees from moving into a stabilization stage. As long as the socialization period is positively negotiated, employees can simply cycle from one innovation period into another.[15] Put simply, movements into new positions may be necessary to keep individuals stimulated, flexible, and vigilant with respect to their work environments. Within a single job assignment, the person may eventually reach the limit to which new and exciting challenges are possible or even welcomed. At that point, a new job position may be necessary. To maintain adaptability and to keep employees responsive, what might be needed are career histories containing sequences of job positions involving new challenges and requiring new skills (Kaufman, 1974; Dalton and Thompson, Chapter 8, this volume). As pointed out by Schein (1968), continued growth and development often come from adaptations to new or changing work environments requiring individuals to give up familiar and stable work patterns in favor of developing new ones.

As important as job mobility is, it is probably just as important to determine whether individuals and project groups can circumvent the effects of longevity without new assignments or rejuvenation from new project members. Rotations and promotions are not always possible, especially when there is little organizational growth. As a result, we need to learn considerably more about the effects of increasing job and group longevities. Just how deterministic are the trends? Can long-tenured individuals and project teams remain high-performing, and if so, how can it be accomplished? In the empirical example presented in this paper, none of the 10 long-tenured project groups were above the sample median in project performance. Nevertheless, different trends might have emerged with different kinds of

---

[14] As discussed by Van Maanen in Chapter 6 of this book, the socialization process of individuals can greatly affect the extent to which newcomers may be willing to try to innovate on existing "wisdoms."

[15] A discussion on effectively managing the socialization process is beyond the scope of this paper. The reader is referred to the descriptive theory presented in Chapter 6 as well as to the more normative presentations of Schein (1968), Kotter (1973), Hall (1976), Katz (1980), and Wanous (1980).

organizational climates, different personnel and promotional policies, differe economic and marketing conditions or even different types of organizational struc tures. Would matrix structures, for instance, allow long-tenured project groups to remain effective as long as their members remained strongly connected to their functional or technical specialty groups?

In a general sense, then, we need to learn how to detect the many kinds of changes that either have taken place or are likely to take place within a group as its team membership ages. Furthermore, we need to learn if project groups can keep themselves energized and innovative over long periods of group longevity, or whether certain kinds of organizational structures and managerial practices are needed to keep a project team effective and high-performing as it ages.

In response to this issue, Tom Allen and I have undertaken an extensive study in 12 different organizations involving over 200 R&D project teams of which 50 or so have group longevity scores that exceed 5 years. More interesting, it turns out that a large number of these long-tenured project groups were judged to be high-performing teams. Although we are still processing the data, preliminary analyses suggest that the nature of the project's supervision may be the most important factor differentiating the more effective long-tenured teams from the less effective ones. In particular, engineers belonging to the high-performing, long-tenured project groups perceived their functional supervision to be significantly higher (1) in disseminating technical information, (2) in being well-informed professionally, and (3) in being concerned about their professional development.[16]

Such findings suggest that a strong functional competency dimension may be especially important in the effective management of long-tenured project groups. With respect to R&D settings, this may imply that the presence of certain technical specialists, labeled gatekeepers by Allen (1977), may be especially important to the success of long-term R&D project teams.[17] Such a role requirement may be necessary because with long-term group longevity, many project members have become increasingly overspecialized and more "locally" oriented (i.e., more organizationally oriented), thereby making it increasingly difficult for them to communicate effectively with outside sources of technology or with keeping themselves up to date within their technical specialities.

In a broader context, we need to learn how to manage workers, professionals, and project teams as they enter and proceed through different stages of longevity. Clearly, different kinds of managerial styles and behaviors may be more appropriate at different stages of longevity. Delegative or participative management, for example, may be very effective when individuals are vigilant and highly responsive to their work demands, but such supervisory activities may prove less successful when

---

[16] For the 40 long-tenured project groups, the significant correlations between project performance ratings and project member perceptions of these three supervisory activities were .54, .58, and .44, respectively.

[17] It is interesting to note that in the data presented from the large R&D facility, none of the long-tenured development project teams had a technical gatekeeper as part of their team membership.

mployees are unresponsive to their job environments, as in the stabilization stage. Furthermore, as perspectives and responsiveness shift over time, the actions required of the managerial role will also vary. Managers may be effective, then, to the extent they are able to recognize and cover such changing conditions. Thus, it may be the ability to manage change—the ability to diagnose and manage between socialization and stabilization—that we need to learn so much more if we truly hope to provide careers that keep employees responsive and also keep organizations effective.

REFERENCES

Allen, T.J. "Studies of the problem-solving processes in engineering designs." *IEEE Transactions in Engineering Management*, 1966, *13,* 72-83.

Allen, T.J. *Managing the Flow of Technology.* Cambridge, Mass.: M.I.T. Press, 1977.

Allison, G.T. *Essence of Decision: Explaining the Cuban Missile Crisis.* Boston: Little, Brown, 1971.

Argyris, C. *Personality and Organization.* New York: Harper Torch Books, 1957.

Argyris, C. "The incompleteness of social psychological theory: examples from small group, cognitive consistency and attribution research." *American Psychologist,* 1969, *24,* 893-908.

Asch, S.E. "Studies of independence and conformity: a minority of one against a unanimous majority." *Psychological Monographs,* 1956, *70.*

Bales, R.F. "Adaptive and integrative changes as sources of strain in social systems." In A.P. Hare, E.F. Borgatta, and R.F. Bales, eds., *Small Groups: Studies in Social Interaction.* New York: Knopf, 1955, pp. 127-31.

Bion, W.R. *Experiences in Groups.* New York: Basic Books, 1961.

Burke, R.L., and Bennis, W.G. "Changes in perception of self and others during human relations training." *Human Relations,* 1961, *14,* 165-82.

Cass, E.L., and Zimmer, F.G. *Man and Work in Society.* New York: Van Nostrand Reinhold, 1975.

Chinoy, E. *Automobile Workers and the American Dream.* Garden City, N.Y.: Doubleday, 1955.

Crozier, M. *The Bureaucratic Phenomenon.* Chicago: University of Chicago Press, 1964.

Dewhirst, H., Arvey, R., and Brown, E. "Satisfaction and performance in research and development tasks as related to information accessibility." *IEEE Transactions on Engineering Management,* 1978, *25,* 58-63.

Dubin, S.S. *Professional Obsolescence.* Lexington, Mass.: Lexington Books, D.C. Heath, 1972.

Feldman, D. "The role of initiation activities in socialization." *Human Relations,* 1977, *30,* 977-90.

Graen, G. "Role-making processes within complex organizations." In M.D. Dunnette, ed., *Handbook of Industrial and Organizational Psychology,* Chicago: Rand McNally, 1976.

Hackman, J.R. "The design of self managing work groups." In B. King, S. Streufert, and F. Fielder, eds., *Managerial Control and Organizational Democracy.* New York: Wiley, 1978.

Hackman, J.R., and Oldham, G.R. "Development of the job diagnostic survey." *Journal of Applied Psychology,* 1975, *60,* 159-70.

Hall, D.T. *Careers in Organizations.* Pacific Palisades, Calif.: Goodyear, 1976.

Hall, D.T., and Nougaim, K.E. "An examination of Maslow's need hierarchy in an organizational setting." *Organizational Behavior and Human Performance,* 1968, *3,* 12-35.

Hall, D.T., and Schneider, B. *Organizational Climates and Careers.* New York: Seminar Press, 1973.

Homans, G.C. *Social Behavior: Its Elementary Forms.* New York: Harcourt, Brace and World, 1961.

Hughes, E.C. *Men and Their Work.* Glencoe, Ill.: Free Press, 1958.

Janis, I.L., and Mann, L. *Decision Making.* New York: Free Press, 1977.

Kahn, R.L., Wolfe, D.M., Quinn, R.P., Snoek, J.D., and Rosenthal, R.A. *Organizational Stress: Studies on Role Conflict and Ambiguity.* New York: Wiley, 1964.

Katz, D., and Kahn, R.L. *The Social Psychology of Organizations.* New York: Wiley, 1978.

Katz, R. "The influence of group conflict on leadership effectiveness." *Organizational Behavior and Human Performance,* 1977, *20,* 265-86.

Katz, R. "Job longevity as a situational factor in job satisfaction." *Administrative Science Quarterly,* 1978a, *10,* 204-23.

Katz, R., "The influence of job longevity on employee reactions to task characteristics." *Human Relations,* 1978b, *31,* 703-25.

Katz, R. "Time and work: toward an integrative perspective." In B. Staw and L.L. Cummings, eds., *Research in Organizational Behavior,* Vol. 2. Greenwich, Conn.: JAI Press, 1980, 81-127.

Katz, R., and Allen, T. "Investigating the not-invented-here syndrome." In A. Pearson, ed., *Industrial R&D Strategy and Management,* London: Basil Blackwell Press, 1981.

Katz, R., and Tushman, M. "Communication patterns, project performance and task characteristics: an empirical evaluation and integration in an R&D setting." *Organizational Behavior and Human Performance,* 1979, *23,* 139-62.

Katz, R., and Van Maanen, J. "The loci of work satisfaction: job, interaction, and policy." *Human Relations,* 1977, *30,* 469-86.

Kaufman, H.G. *Obsolescence of Professional Career Development.* New York: AMACOM, 1974.

Kiesler, S. *Interpersonal Processes in Groups and Organizations.* Arlington Heights, Ill.: AHM Publishers, 1978.

Kopelman, R.E. "Psychological stages of careers in engineering: an expectancy theory taxonomy." *Journal of Vocational Behavior,* 1977, *10,* 270-86.

Kotter, J. "The psychological contract: managing the joining-up process." *California Management Review,* 1973, *15,* 91-99.

Kuhn, T.S. *The Structure of Scientific Revolutions.* Chicago: University of Chicago Press, 1963.

Lawrence, P.R., and Lorsch, J.W. *Organizational and Environment.* Boston: Harvard Business School, 1967.

Lewin, K. "Group decision and social change." In H. Proshansky and B. Seidenberg, eds., *Basic Studies in Social Psychology.* New York: Holt, Rinehart, and Winston, 1965, pp. 423-36.

Likert, R. *The Human Organization.* New York: McGraw-Hill, 1967.

Maslow, A. *Toward a Psychology of Being.* Princeton, N.J.: D. Van Nostrand, 1962.

Menzel, H. "Information needs and uses in science and technology." In C. Cuadra, ed., *Annual Review of Information Science and Technology,* New York: Wiley, 1965.

Pelz, A., and Andrews, F.M. *Scientists in Organizations.* New York: Wiley, 1966.

Pfeffer, J. "Management as symbolic action: the creation and maintenance of organizational paradigms." In L.L. Cummings and B. Staw, eds., *Research in Organizational Behavior,* Vol. 3. Greenwich, Conn.: JAI Press, 1981.

Porter, L.W., Lawler, E.E., and Hackman, J.R. *Behavior in Organizations.* New York: McGraw-Hill, 1975.

Robertson, T.S. *Innovative Behavior and Communication.* New York: Holt, Rinehart and Winston, 1971.

Rogers, C.R. *On Becoming a Person.* Boston: Houghton Mifflin, 1961.

Rogers, E.M., and Shoemaker, F.F. *Communication of Innovations: A Cross-cultural Approach.* New York: Free Press, 1971.

Salancik, G.R., and Pfeffer, J. "A social information processing approach to job attitudes and task design." *Administrative Science Quarterly,* 1978, *23,* 224-53.

Schein, E.H. "Organizational socialization and the profession of management." *Industrial Management Review,* 1968, *9,* 1-15.

Schein, E.H. "The individual, the organization, and the career: a conceptual scheme." *Journal of Applied Behavioral Science,* 1971, *7,* 401-26.

Schein, E.H. "Personal change though interpersonal relationships." In W.G. Bennis, D.E. Berlew, E.H. Schein, and F.I. Steele, eds., *Interpersonal Dynamics: Essays and Readings on Human Interaction.* Homewood, Ill.: Dorsey Press, 1973.

Schein, E.H. *Career Dynamics.* Reading, Mass.: Addison-Wesley, 1978.

Scott, W.E., "Activation theory and task design." *Organizational Behavior and Human Performance,* 1966, *1,* 3-30.

Seashore, S.F. "Group cohesiveness in the industrial work group." Ann Arbor, Mich.: Survey Research Center, University of Michigan, 1954.

Shaw, M.E. *Group Dynamics: The Psychology of Small Group Behavior.* New York: McGraw-Hill, 1971.

Staw, B. "Motivation in organizations: toward synthesis and redirection." In B. Staw and G.R. Salancik, eds., *New Directions in Organizational Behavior.* Chicago: St. Clair Press, 1977.

Staw, B. "Rationality and justification in organizational life." In B. Staw and L.L. Cummings, eds., *Research in Organizational Behavior,* Vol. 2. Greenwich, Conn.: JAI Press, 1980, pp. 45-80.

Stoner, J.A. "Risky and cautious shifts in group decisions: the influence of widely held values." *Journal of Experimental Social Psychology,* 1968, *4,* 442-59.

Tushman, M., and Katz, R. "External communication and project performance: an investigation into the role of gatekeepers." *Management Science,* 1980, *26,* 1071-1085.

Van Maanen, J. "Police socialization." *Administrative Science Quarterly,* 1975, *20,* 207-28.

Wanous, J. *Organizational Entry.* Reading, Mass.: Addison-Wesley, 1980.

Weick, K.E. *The Social Psychology of Organizing.* Reading, Mass.: Addison-Wesley, 1969.

Wheeler, S. "The structure of formerly organized socialization settings." In O.G. Brim and S. Wheeler, eds., *Socialization after Childhood: Two Essays.* New York: Wiley, 1966.

Wortman, C.B., and Linsenmeier, J. "Interpersonal attraction and techniques of ingratiation in organizational settings." In B. Staw and G.R. Salancik, eds., *New Directions in Organizational Behavior.* Chicago: St. Clair Press, 1977.

10

Critical Functions: Needed Roles in the Innovation Process

EDWARD B. ROBERTS, Massachusetts Institute of Technology

ALAN R. FUSFELD, Pugh-Roberts Associates, Inc.

This article examines the main elements of the technology-based innovation process in terms of certain usually informal but critical "people" functions that can be the key to an effective organizational base for innovation. This approach to the innovation process is similar to that taken by early industrial theorists who focused on the production process. Led by such individuals as Frederick W. Taylor, their efforts resulted in basic principles for increasing the efficiency of producing goods and services. These principles of specialization, chain of command, division of labor, and span of control continue to govern the operation of the modern organization (despite their shift from popularity in many modern business schools). Hence, routine tasks in most organizations are arranged to facilitate work standardization with expectations that efficient production will result. However, examination of how industry has organized its innovation tasks—that is, those tasks needed for product/process development and for responses to nonroutine demands—indicates an absence of comparable theory. And many corporations' attempts to innovate consequently suffer from ineffective management and inadequately staffed organizations. Yet, through tens of studies about the innovation process, conducted largely in the last fifteen years, we now know much about the activities that are requisite to innovation as well as the characteristics of the people who perform these activities most effectively.

The following section characterizes the technology-based innovation process via a detailed description of a typical research and development project life cycle. The types of work activities arising in each project phase are enumerated. These lead in the third section to the identification of the five basic critical roles that are needed for effective execution of an innovative effort. Problems associated with gaps in the fulfillment of the needed roles are discussed. Detailed characteristics and specific activities that are associated with each role filler are elaborated upon in the fourth section. The multiple roles that are sometimes performed by certain individuals are observed, as are the dynamics of role changes that tend to take place over the life span of a productive career. The fifth section presents several areas of managerial implications of the critical functions concepts, beginning first with issues of manpower planning, then moving to considerations of job design and objective setting and to the determination of appropriate performance measures and rewards. How an organizational assessment can be carried out in terms of these critical functions dimensions is discussed in the sixth section, with the illustrative description of one such assessment in a medium-sized research and development organization. The final paragraphs summarize the chapter and indicate the transferability of critical functions to other kinds of organizations.

THE INNOVATION PROCESS

The major steps involved in the technology-based innovation process are shown in Figure 10-1. Although the project activities do not necessarily follow each other in a linear fashion, there is more or less clear demarcation between them. Moreover, each stage, and its activities, require a different mix of people skills and behaviors to be carried out effectively.

This figure portrays six stages as occurring in the typical technical innovation project, and sixteen representative activities that are associated with innovative efforts. The six stages are here identified as:

(1)   Pre-project
(2)   Project possibilities
(3)   Project initiation
(4)   Project execution
(5)   Project outcome evaluation
(6)   Project transfer

These stages often overlap and frequently recycle.[1] For example, problems or findings that are generated during project execution may cause a return to project initiation activities. Outcome evaluation can restart additional project execution

[1] For a different and more intensive quantitative view of project life cycles, see Edward B. Roberts, *The Dynamics of Research and Development* (New York: Harper & Row, 1964).

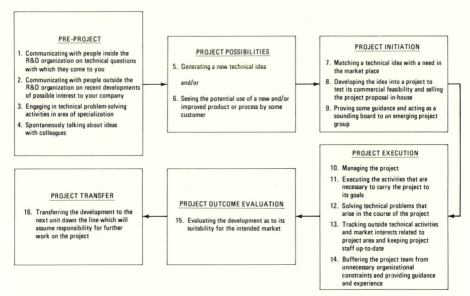

FIGURE 10-1 A Multistage View of a Technical Innovation Project

efforts. And, of course, project cancellation can occur during any of these stages, redirecting technical endeavors back into the pre-project phase.

A variety of different activities are undertaken during each of the six stages. Some of the activities, such as generating new technical ideas, arise in all innovation project stages from pre-project to project transfer. But our research studies and consulting efforts in dozens of companies and government labs have shown other activities to be concentrated mainly in specific stages, as discussed below.

(1) Pre-Project. Prior to formal project activities being undertaken in a technical organization, considerable technical work is done that provides a basis for later innovation efforts. Scientists, engineers, and marketing people find themselves involved in discussions internal and external to the organization. Ideas get discussed in rough-cut ways and broad parameters of innovative interests get established. Technical personnel work on problem-solving efforts to advance their own areas of specializaion. Discussions with numerous industrial firms in the United States and Europe suggest that from 30 to 60% of all technical effort is devoted to work outside of or prior to formal project initiation.

(2) Project Possibilities. Arising from the preproject activities, specific ideas are generated for possible projects. They may be technical concepts for assumed-to-be-feasible developments. Or they may be perceptions of possible customer interest in product or process changes. Customer-oriented perspectives may be originated by technical or marketing or managerial personnel out of their imagination or from direct contact with customers or competitors. Recent evidence indicates that many

of these ideas enter as "proven" possibilities, having already been developed by the customers themselves.[2]

(3) Project Initiation.   As ideas evolve and get massaged through technical and marketing discussions and exploratory technical efforts, the innovation process moves into a more formal project initiation stage. Activities occurring during this phase include attempts to match the directions of technical work with perceived customer needs. (Of course, such customer needs may exist either in the production organization or in the produce marketplace.) Inevitably, a specific project proposal has to be written up, proposed budgets and schedules have to get produced, and informal pushing as well as formal presentations have to be undertaken in order to sell the project A key input during this stage is the counseling and encouragement that senior technical professionals or laboratory and marketing management may provide to the emerging project team.

(4) Project Execution.   With formal approval of a project aimed at an innovative output, activities increase in intensity and focus. In parallel, someone usually undertakes planning, leadership, and coordination efforts related to the many continuing technical idea-generating and problem-solving activities being done by the engineers and scientists assigned to the project. Technical people often make special attempts to monitor (and transfer in) what had been done previously as well as what is then going on outside the project that is relevant to the project's goals. Management or marketing people frequently take a closer look at competitors and customers to be sure the project is appropriately targeted.[3] Senior people try to protect the project from overly tight control or from getting cut off prematurely, and the project manager and other enthusiasts keep fighting to defend their project's virtues (and budget). Unless canceled, the project work continues toward completion of its objectives.

(5) Project Outcome Evaluation.   When the technical effort seems complete, most projects undergo another often intense evaluation to see how the results stack up against prior expectations and current market perceptions. If a successful innovation is to occur, some further implementation must take place, either by transfer of the interim results to manufacturing for embodiment in its process or for volume production activities, or by transfer to later stages of further development. All such later stages involve heavier expenditures and the post-project evaluation can be viewed as a pre-transfer screening activity.

(6) Project Transfer.   If the project results survive this evaluation, transfer efforts take place (e.g., from central research to product department R&D, or

---

[2] Eric von Hippel, "Users as Innovators," *Technology Review, 80,* No. 3 (January 1978), 30-39.

[3] See Alan R. Fusfeld, "How to Put Technology into Corporate Planning," *Technology Review, 80,* No. 6, for issues that need to be highlighted in a comparative technical review.

development to manufacturing engineering).[4] The project's details may require further technical documentation to facilitate the transfer. Key technical people may be shifted to the downstream unit to transfer their expertise and enthusiasm, since downstream staff members, technical or marketing, often need instruction to assure effective continuity. Within the downstream organizational unit, the cycle of stages may begin again, perhaps bypassing the earliest two stages and starting with project initiation or even project execution. This "pass-down" continues until successful innovation is achieved, unless project termination occurs first.

NEEDED ROLES

Assessment of activities involved in the several-stage innovation process, as just described, points out that the repeated direct inputs of five different work roles are critical to innovation. The five arise in differing degrees in each of the several steps. Furthermore, different innovation projects obviously call for variations in the required role mix at each stage. Nevertheless, all five work roles must be carried out by one or more individuals if the innovation is to pass effectively through all six steps.

The five critical work functions are:

- *Idea generating:* Analyzing and/or synthesizing (implicit and explicit) information (formal and informal) about markets, technologies, approaches, and procedures, from which an idea is generated for a new or improved product or service, a new technical approach or procedure, or a solution to a challenging technical problem.[5]
- *Entrepreneuring or championing:* Recognizing, proposing, pushing, and demonstrating a new (his or her own or someone else's) technical idea, approach or procedure for formal management approval.[6]
- *Project leading:* Planning and coordinating the diverse sets of activities and people involved in moving a demonstrated idea into practice.[7]
- *Gatekeeping:* Collecting and channeling information about important changes in the internal and external environments; information gatekeeping can be focused on developments in the market, in manufacturing, or in the world of technology.[8]

[4] For further perspectives on project transfer, see Edward B. Roberts, "Stimulating Technological Innovation: Organizational Approaches," *Research Management, 22,* No. 6 (November 1979), 26-30.

[5] D. C. Pelz and F. M. Andrews, *Scientists in Organizations* (New York: Wiley, 1966).

[6] E. B. Roberts, "Entrepreneurship and Technology," *Research Management, 11,* No. 4 (July 1968), 249-66.

[7] D. G. Marquis and I. M. Rubin, "Management Factors in Project Performance," M.I.T. Sloan School of Management, Working Paper, Cambridge, Mass., 1966.

[8] T. J. Allen, *"Managing the Flow of Technology* (Cambridge, Mass.: MIT Press, 1977); and R. G. Rhoades, et al., "A Correlation of R&D Laboratory Performance with Critical Functions Analysis," *R&D Management, 9,* No. 1 (October 1978), 13-17.

- *Sponsoring or coaching:* "Behind-the-scene" support-generating function of the protector and advocate, and sometimes of the "bootlegger" of funds; the guiding and developing of less-experienced personnel in their critical roles (a "Big Brother" role).[9]

Lest the reader confuse these roles as mapping one-for-one with different people, three points need emphasis: (1) some roles (e.g., idea generating) frequently need to be fulfilled by more than one person in a project team in order for the project to be successful; (2) some individuals occasionally fulfill more than one of the critical functions; and (3) the roles that people play periodically change over a person's career with an organization.

Critical Functions

These five critical functions represent the various roles in an organization that must be carried out for successful innovation to occur. They are critical from two points of view. First, each role is different or unique, demanding different skills. A deficiency in any one of the roles contributes to serious problems in the innovation effort, as we illustrate below. Second, each role tends to be carried out primarily by relatively few individuals, thereby making even more unique the critical role players. If any one critical function-filler leaves, the problem of recruiting a replacement is very difficult—the specifics of exactly who is needed is dependent on usually unstated role requirements.

We must add at this point that another role clearly exists in all innovative organizations, but it is not an *innovative* role! "Routine" technical problem-solving must be carried out in the process of advancing innovative efforts. Indeed the vast bulk of technical work is probably routine, requiring professional training and competence to be sure, but nonetheless routine in character for an appropriately prepared individual. A large number of people in innovative organizations do very little "critical functions" work; others who are important performers of the critical functions also spend a good part of their time in routine problem-solving activity. Our estimate, supported now by data from numerous organizations, is that 70 to 80% of technical effort falls into this routine problem-solving category. But the 20 to 30% that is unique and critical is the part we emphasize.

Generally, the critical functions are not specified within job descriptions since they tend to fit neither administrative nor technical hierarchies; but they do represent necessary activities for R&D, such as problem definition, idea nurturing, information transfer, information integration, and program pushing. Consequently, these role behaviors are the underlying informal functions that an organization carries out as part of the innovation process. Beyond the five above, different

---

[9] Roberts, "Entrepreneurship and Technology," p. 252.

business environments may also demand that additional roles be performed to assure innovation.[10]

It is desirable for every organization to have a balanced set of abilities for carrying out these roles as needed, but unfortunately few organizations do. Some organizations overemphasize one role (e.g., idea generating) and underplay another role (e.g., entrepreneuring). Another organization might do just the reverse. Nonetheless, technical organizations tend to assume that the necessary set of activities will somehow be performed. As a consequence, R&D labs often lack sensitivity to the existence and importance of these roles, which, for the most part, are not defined within the formal job structure. How the critical functions are encouraged and made a conscious part of technology management is probably an organization's single most important area of leverage for maintaining and improving effective innovation. The managerial capabilities required for describing, planning, diagnosing problems, and developing the necessary teamwork in terms of the people functions demanded by an innovative program are almost entirely distinct from the skills needed for managing the technical requirements of the tasks.

Impact of Role Deficiencies

Such an analytic approach to developing an innovative team has been lacking in the past and, consequently, many organizations suffer because one or more of the critical functions is not being performed adequately. Certain characteristic signs can provide evidence that a critical function is missing.

Idea generating is deficient if the organization is not thinking of new and different ways of doing things. However, more often than not when a manager complains of insufficient ideas, we find the real deficiency to be that people are not aggressively entrepreneuring or championing ideas, either their own or others'. Evidences of entrepreneuring shortages are pools of unexploited ideas that seldom come to a manager's attention.[11]

Project leading is suspect if schedules are not met, activities fall through cracks (e.g., coordinating with a supplier), people do not have a sense for the overall goal of their work, or units that are needed to support the work back out of their commitments. This is the role most commonly recognized formally by the appointment of a project manager. In research, as distinct from development, the formal role is often omitted.

---

[10] One role we have frequently observed is the "quality controller," who stresses high work standards in projects. Other critical roles relate more to organizational growth than to innovation. The "effective trainer" who could absorb new engineers productively into the company was seen as critical to one firm that was growing 30% per year. The "technical statesman" was a role label developed by an electronic components manufacturer which valued the ability of some engineers to generate a leadership technical reputation through authorship and presentation of advanced concepts.

[11] One study that demonstrated this phenomenon is N. R. Baker, et al., "The Effects of Perceived Needs and Means on the Generation of Ideas for Industrial Research and Development Projects," *IEEE Transactions on Engineering Management*, EM-14 (1967), 156-65.

Gatekeeping is inadequate if news of changes in the market, technology, or government legislation comes without warning, or if people within the organization are not getting the information that they need because it has not been passed on to them. When, six months after the project is completed, you suddenly realize that you have just succeeded in reinventing a competitor's wheel, your organization is deficient in needed gatekeeping! Gatekeeping is further lacking when the wheel is invented just as a regulatory agency outlaws its use.

Inadequate or inappropriate sponsoring or coaching often explains projects that get pushed into application too soon, or project managers who have to spend too much time defending their work, or personnel who complain that they do not know how to "navigate the bureaucracy" of their organizations.

The importance of each critical function varies with the development stage of the project. Initially, idea generation is crucial; later, entrepreneurial skill and commitment are needed to develop the concept into a viable activity. Once the project is established, good project leading/managing is needed to guide its progress. Of course, the need for each critical function does not abruptly appear and disappear. Instead, the need grows and diminishes, being a focus at some point, but of lesser importance at others. Thus, the absence of a function when it is potentially very important is a serious weakness regardless of whether or not the role had been filled at an earlier, less crucial time. As a corollary, assignment of an individual to a project, at a time when the critical role that he or she provides is not needed, leads to frustration for the individual and to a less effective project team.

Frequently, we have observed that personnel changes that occur because of career development programs often remove critical functions from a project at a crucial time. Since these roles are usually performed informally, job descriptions are made in terms of technical specialties, and personnel replacements are chosen to fill those job vacancies, rather than on their ability to fill the needs of the vacated critical roles. Consequently, the project team's innovative effectiveness is reduced, sometimes to the point of affecting the project's success. Awareness of which roles are likely to be required at what time will help to avoid this problem, as well as to allow people performing functions no longer needed to be moved to other projects where their talents can be better utilized.

CHARACTERISTICS OF THE ROLE PLAYERS

Compilation of several thousand individual profiles of staff in R&D and engineering organizations has demonstrated patterns in the characteristics of the people who perform each innovation function.[12] These patterns are shown in Table 10-1, indicating which persons are predisposed to be interested in one type of activity more than another and to perform certain types of activity well. For example, a person who is theoretically inclined and comfortable with abstractions feels better suited

---

[12] The later section "Performing a Critical Functions Assessment" describes a methodology for collecting these data.

to the idea-generating function than does someone who is very practical and uncomfortable with seemingly discrepant data. In any unit of an organization, people with different characteristics can work to complement each other. Someone good at idea generating might be teamed with a colleague good at gatekeeping and another colleague good at entrepreneuring to provide necessary supporting roles. Of course, each person must understand his or her own expected role in a project and appreciate the roles of others for the teaming process to be successful. Obviously, as will be discussed later, some people have sufficient breadth to perform well in multiple roles.

Table 10-1 underlies our conclusion that each of the several roles required for effective technical innovation presents unique challenges and must be filled with essentially different types of people, each type to be recruited, managed, and supported differently, offered different sets of incentives, and supervised with different types of measures and controls. Most technical organizations seem not to have

Table 10-1   Critical Functions in the Innovation Process

Personal Characteristics	Organizational Activities
Idea Generating	
Is expert in one or two fields	Generates new ideas and tests their feasibility
Enjoys conceptualization, comfortable with abstractions	Good at problem solving
Enjoys doing innovative work	Sees new and different ways of viewing things
Usually is an individual contributor, often will work alone	Searches for the break-throughs
Entrepreneuring or Championing	
Strong application interests	Sells new ideas to others in the organization
Possesses a wide range of interests	Gets resources
Less propensity to contribute to the basic knowledge of a field	Aggressive in championing his or her "cause"
Energetic and determined; puts himself or herself on the line	Takes risks
Project Leading	
Focus for the decision making, information, and questions	Provides the team leadership and motivation
Sensitive to accommodating to the needs of others	Plans and organizes the project
Recognizes how to use the organizational structure to get things done	Ensures that administrative requirements are met
Interested in a broad range of disciplines and how they fit together (e.g., marketing, finance)	Provides necessary coordination among team members
	Sees that the project moves forward effectively
	Balances the project goals with organizational needs

Table 10-1 (continued)

Personal Characteristics	Organizational Activities
Gatekeeping[a]	
Possesses a high level of technical competence Is approachable and personable Enjoys the face-to-face contact of helping others	Keeps informed of related developments that occur outside the organization through journals, conferences, colleagues, other companies Passes information on to others; finds it easy to talk to colleagues Serves as an information resource for others in the organization (i.e., authority on whom to see and/or what has been done) Provides informal coordination among personnel
Sponsoring *or* *Coaching*	
Possesses experience in developing new ideas Is a good listener and helper Can be relatively more objective Often a more senior person who knows the organizational ropes	Helps develop people's talents Provides encouragement and guidance and acts as a sounding board to the project leader and others Provides access to a power base within the organization—a senior person Buffers the project team from unnecessary organizational constraints Helps the project team to get what it needs from the other parts of the organization Provides legitimacy and organizational confidence in the project

[a]Our empirical studies have pointed out three different types of gatekeepers: (1) technical, who relates well to advancing world of science and technology; (2) market, who senses and communicates information relating to customers, competitors, and environmental and regulatory changes affecting the marketplace; and (3) manufacturing, who bridges the technical work to the special needs and conditions of the production organization. See Rhoades et al., "Correlation of R&D Laboratory Performance."

grasped this concept, with the result that all technical people tend to be recruited, hired, supervised, monitored, evaluated, and encouraged as if their principal roles were those of creative scientists or, worse yet, routine technical problem-solvers. But only a few of these people in fact have the personal and technical qualifications for scientific inventiveness and prolific idea generating. A creative idea-generating scientist or engineer is a special kind of professional who needs to be singled out, cultivated, and managed in a special way. He or she is probably an innovative technically well-educated individual who enjoys working on advanced problems, often as a "loner."

The technical champion or entrepreneur is a special person, too—creative in his own way, but his is an aggressive form of creativity appropriate for selling an idea or product. The entrepreneur's drives may be less rational, more emotional than those of the creative scientist; he is committed to achieve, and less concerned about how to do so. He is as likely to pick up and successfully champion someone else's original idea as to push something of his own creation. Such an entrepreneur may well have a broad range of interests and activities; and he must be recruited, hired, managed, and stimulated very differently from the way an idea-generating scientist is treated in the organization.

The person who effectively performs project leading or project managing activities is a still different kind of person—an organized individual, sensitive to the needs of the several different people she is trying to coordinate, and an effective planner; the latter is especially important if long lead time, expensive materials, and major support are involved in the development of the ideas that she is moving forward in the organization.

The information gatekeeper is the communicative individual who in fact, is the exception to the truism that engineers do not read—especially that they do not read technical journals. Gatekeepers link to the sources of flow of technical information into and within a research and development organization that might enhance new product development or process improvement. But those who do research and development need market information as well as technical information. What do customers seem to want? What are competitors providing? How might regulatory shifts affect the firm's present or contemplated products or processes? For answers to questions such as these, research and development organizations need people we call the "market gatekeepers"—engineers or scientists, or possibly marketing people with technical background, who focus on market-related information sources and communicate effectively with their technical colleagues. Such a person reads journals, talks to vendors, goes to trade shows, and is sensitive to competitive information. Without him, many research and development projects and laboratories become misdirected with respect to market trends and needs.

Finally, the sponsor or coach may in fact be a more experienced, older project leader of former entrepreneur who now has matured to have a softer touch than when he was first in the organization. As a senior person he can coach and help subordinates in the organization and speak on their behalf to top management, enabling ideas or programs to move forward in an effective, organized fashion. Many organizations totally ignore the sponsor role, yet our studies of industrial research and development suggest that many projects would not have been successful were it not for the subtle and often unrecognized assistance of such senior people acting in the role of sponsors. Indeed, organizations are more successful when chief engineers or laboratory directors naturally behave in a manner consistent with this sponsor role.

The significant point here is that the staffing needed to cause effective innovation in a technical organization is far broader than the typical research and development director has usually assumed. Our studies indicate that many ineffective technical organizations have failed to be innovative solely because one or more of these five quite different critical functions has been absent.

Multiple Roles

As indicated earlier, some individuals have the skills, breadth, inclination, and job opportunity to fulfill more than one critical function in an organization. Our data collection efforts with R&D staffs show that a few clusters explain most of these cases of multiple role-playing. One common combination of roles is the pairing of gatekeeping and idea generating. Idea-generating activity correlates in general with the frequency of person-to-person communication, especially external to the organization.[13] The gatekeeper, moreover, in contact with many sources of information, can often synergistically connect these bits into a new idea. This seems especially true of market gatekeepers, who can relate market relevance to technical opportunities.

Another role couplet is between entrepreneuring and idea generating. In studies of formation of new technical companies the entrepreneur who pushed company formation and growth was found in half the cases also to have been the source of the new technical idea underlying the company.[14] Furthermore, in studies of M.I.T. faculty, 38% of those who had ideas they perceived to have commercial value also took strong entrepreneurial steps to exploit their ideas.[15] The idea-generating entrepreneuring pair accounts for less than one half of the entrepreneurs, but not the other half.

Entrepreneuring individuals often become project leaders, usually in what is thought to be a logical organizational extension of the effective selling of the idea for the project. And some people strong at entrepreneuring indeed also have the interpersonal and plan-oriented qualities needed for project leading. But on numerous occasions the responsibility for managing a project is mistakenly seen as a necessary reward for successful idea championing. This arises from lack of focus upon the functional differences. What evidence indicates that a good salesperson is going to be a good manager? If an entrepreneur can be rewarded appropriately and more directly for his or her own function, many project failures caused by ineffective project managers might be avoided. Perhaps giving the entrepreneur a prominent project role, together with a clearly designated but different project manager, might be an acceptable compromise.

---

[13] Allen, *Managing the Flow of Technology.*
[14] Roberts, "Entrepreneurship and Technology."
[15] E. B. Roberts and D. H. Peters, "Commercial Innovations from University Faculty," *Research Policy, 10,* No. 2 (April 1981), 108-26.

Finally, sponsoring, although it should be a unique role, occasionally gives way to a takeover of any or all of the other roles. Senior coaching can degenerate into idea domination, project ownership, and direction from the top. This confusion of roles can become extremely harmful to the entire organization. Who will bring another idea to the boss, once he steals some junior's earlier concept? Even worse, who can intervene to stop the project once the boss is running amok with his new pet?

All of the critical innovative roles, whether played singly or in multiples, can be fulfilled by people from multiple disciplines and departments. Obviously, technical people—scientists and engineers—might carry out any of the roles. But marketing people also generate ideas for new and improved products, "gatekeep" information of key importance to a project—especially about use, competition and regulatory activities—champion the idea, sometimes sponsor projects, and in some organizations even manage innovation projects. Manufacturing people periodically fill similar critical roles, as do general management personnel.

The fact of multiple role filling can affect the minimum-size group needed for attaining "critical mass" in an innovative effort. To achieve continuity of a project, from initial idea all the way through to successful commercialization, a project group must have all five critical roles effectively filled while satisfying the specific technical skills required for project problem-solving. In a new high-technology company this critical mass may sometimes be ensured by as few as one or two co-founders. Similarly, an "elite" team, such as Cray's famed Control Data computer design group, or Kelly Johnson's "Skunk Works" at Lockheed, or McLean's Sidewinder missile organization in the Navy's China Lake R&D center, may concentrate in a small number of select multiple-role players the staff needed to accomplish major objectives. But the more typical medium-to-large company organization had better not plan on finding "Renaissance persons" or superstars to fill its job requirements. Staffing assumptions should more likely rest on estimates that 70% of scientists and engineers will turn out to be routine problem-solvers only, and that most critical role-players will be single dimensional in their unique contributions.

Career-Spanning Role Changes

We showed above how some individuals fulfill multiple critical roles concurrently or in different stages of the same project. But even more people are likely to contribute critically but differently at different stages of their careers. This does not reflect change of personality, although such changes do seem partly due to the dynamics of personal growth and development. But the phenomenon also clearly reflects individual responses to differing organizational needs, constraints, and incentives.

For example, let us consider the hypothetical case of a bright, aggressive, potentially multiple-role contributor, newly joining a company fresh from engineering school. What roles can he play? Certainly, he can quickly become an effective routine technical problem-solver and, hopefully, a productive novel idea generator.

But even though he may know many university contacts and also be familiar with the outside literature, he cannot be an effective information gatekeeper, for he does not yet know the people inside the company with whom he might communicate. He also cannot lead project activities. No one would trust him in that role. He cannot effectively act as an entrepreneur, as he has no credibility as champion for change. And, of course, sponsoring is out of the question. During this stage of his career, the limited legitimate role options may channel the young engineer's productive energies and reinforce his tendencies toward creative idea output. Alternatively, wanting to offer more and do more than the organization will "allow," this high-potential young performer may feel rebuffed and frustrated. His perception of what he can expect from the job and, perhaps more important, what the job will expect from him, may become set in these first few months on the job. Some disappointeds may remain in the company, but "turn off" their previously enthusiastic desire for multidimensional contributions. More likely, the frustrated high-potential will "spin-off" and leave the company in search of a more rewarding job, perhaps destined to find continuing frustration in his next one or two encounters. For many young professionals the job environment moves too slowly from encouraging idea generating to even permitting entrepreneurial activities.

With two or three years on the job, however, the engineer's role options may broaden. Of course, routine problem solving and idea generating are still appropriate. But some information gatekeeping may now also be possible, as communication ties increase within the organization. Project leading may start to be seen as legitimate behavior, particularly on small efforts.[16] And the young engineer's work behavior may begin to reflect these new possibilities. But perhaps his attempts at entrepreneurial behavior would still be seen as premature. And sponsoring is not yet a relevant consideration.

With another few years at work, the role opinions are still wider. Routine problem-solving, continued idea generating, broad-based gatekeeping (even bridging to the market or to manufacturing), responsible project managing, as well as project championing may become reasonable alternatives. Even coaching a new employee becomes a possibility. The next several years can strengthen all these role options, a given individual tending usually to focus on one of these roles (or on a specific multiple-role combination) for this midcareer period.

Getting out of touch with a rapidly changing technology may later narrow the role alternatives available as the person continues to age on the job. Technical problem-solving effectiveness may diminish in some cases, idea generating may slow down or stop, technical information gatekeeping may be reduced. But market and/ or manufacturing gatekeeping may continue to improve with increased experience and outside contacts, project managing capabilities may continue to grow as more

---

[16] One study showed that engineers who eventually became managers of large projects began supervisory experiences within an average of 4.5 years after receiving their B.S. degrees. I. M. Rubin and W. Seelig, "Experience as a Factor in the Selection and Performance of Project Managers," *IEEE Transactions on Engineering Management, EM-14,* No. 3 (September 1967), 131-35.

past projects are tucked under the belt, entrepreneuring may be more important and for higher stakes, and sponsoring of juniors in the company may be more generally sought and practiced. This career phase is too often seen as characterized by the problem of technical obsolescence, especially if the organization has a fixation on assessing engineer performance in terms of the narrow but traditional stereotypes of technical problem solving and idea generating. "Retooling" the engineer for an earlier role, usually of little current interest and satisfaction to the more mature, broader, and differently directed person, becomes a source of mutual grief and anxiety to the organization and the individual. An aware organization, thinking in terms of critical role differences, can instead recognize the self-selected branching in career paths that has occurred for the individual. Productive technically trained people can be carrying out critical functions for their employers up to retirement, if employers encourage the full diversity of vital roles.

At each stage of his evolving career an individual can encounter severe conflicts between his organization's expectations and his personal work preferences. This is especially true if the organization is inflexible in its perception of appropriate technical roles. In contrast, with both organizational and individual adaptability in seeking mutually satisfying job roles, the scientist or engineer can contribute continuously and importantly to accomplishing innovation. As suggested in this illustrative case, during his productive career in industry the technical professional may begin as a technical problem solver, spend several years primarily as a creative idea generator, add technical gatekeeping to his performance while maintaining his earlier roles, shift toward entrepreneuring projects and leading them forward, gradually grow in his market-linking and project managing behavior, and eventually accrue a senior sponsoring role while maintaining senior project-program-organizational leadership until retirement. But this productive full life is not possible if the engineer is pushed to the side early as a technically obsolete contributor. The perspective taken here can lead to a very different approach to career development for professionals than is usually taken by industry or government.

MANAGING THE CRITICAL FUNCTIONS
FOR ENHANCED INNOVATION

To increase organizational innovation, a number of steps can be taken that will facilitate implementation of a balance among the critical functions. These steps must be addressed explicitly or organizational focus will remain on the traditionally visible functions that produce primarily near-term incremental results, such as problem solving. Indeed, the "results-oriented" reward systems of most organizations reinforce this short-run focus, causing other activities to go unrecognized and unrewarded.

We are not suggesting that employees should ignore the problem-solving function for the sake of the other functions. Rather, we are emphasizing the need for a balance of time and energy distributed among all functions. As indicated earlier, our impressions and data suggest that 70 to 80% of the work of most organizations is routine problem-solving. However, the other 20 to 30% and the degree of teamwork among the critical functions make the difference between an innovative and a noninnovative organization.

Implementing of the results, language, and concepts of a critical functions perspective is described below for the selected organizational tasks of manpower planning, job design, measurement, and rewards. If critical functions awareness dominated managerial thinking, other tasks, not dealt with here, would also be done differently, including R&D strategy, organizational development, and program management.

Manpower Planning

The critical functions concept can be applied usefully to the recruiting, job assignment, and development or training activities within an organization. In recruiting, an organization needs to identify not only the specific technical or managerial requirements of a job, but also the critical function activities that the job requires. That is, does the job require consulting with colleagues as an important part of facilitating teamwork? Or does it require the coaching and development of less experienced personnel to ensure the longer-run productivity of that area? To match a candidate with the job, recruiting should also include identification of the innovation skills of the applicant. If the job requires championing, the applicant who is more aggressive and has shown evidence of championing new ideas in the past should be preferred over the less-aggressive applicant who has shown much more technically oriented interests in the past.

As indicated above, there is room for growth from one function to another, as people are exposed to different managers, different environments, and jobs that require different activities. Although this growth occurs naturally in most organizations, it can be explicitly planned and managed. In this way, the individual has the opportunity to influence his growth along the lines that are of most interest to him, and the organization has the opportunity to oversee the development of personnel and to ensure that effective people are performing the essential critical functions.

Industry has at best taken a narrow view of manpower development alternatives for technical professionals. The "dual ladder" concept envisions an individual as rising along either "scientific" or "managerial" steps. Attempted by many but with only limited success ever attained, the dual ladder reflects an oversimplification and distortion of the key roles needed in an R&D organization.[17] As a minimum, the critical function concept presents "multiladders" of possible organizational contribution; individuals can grow in any and all of the critical roles while benefiting the organization. And depending on an organization's strategy and manpower needs, manpower development along each of the paths can and should be encouraged.

---

[17]For a variety of industrial approaches to the dual ladder, see the special July 1977 issue of *Research Management* or, more recently, *Research Management*, November 1979, 8-11.

Job Design and Objective Setting

Most job descriptions and statements of objectives emphasize problem solving, and sometimes project leading. Rarely do job descriptions and objectives take into account the dimensions of a job that are essential for the performance of the other critical functions. Yet availability of unstructured time in a job can influence the performance of several of the innovation functions. For example, to stimulate idea generating, some slack time is necessary so that employees can pursue their own ideas and explore new and interesting ways of doing things. For gatekeeping to occur, slack time also needs to be available for employees to communicate with colleagues and pass along information learned, both internal to and external to the organization. The coaching role also requires slack time, during which the "coach" can guide less experienced personnel. Table 10-2 elaborates our views on the different emphasis on deadlines (i.e., the alternative to slack time) for each of the critical functions and the degree of specificity of task assignments (i.e., another alternative to slack) for each function.

These essential activities also need to be included explicitly in the objective of a job. A gatekeeper would, for example, see his goals as including provision of useful information to colleagues. A person who has the attitudes and skill to be an effective champion or entrepreneur could also be made responsible for recognizing good new ideas. This person might have the charter to roam around the organization, talk with people about their ideas, encourage their pursuit, or pursue the ideas himself.

This raises a very sticky question in most organizations: Who gets the credit? If the champion gets the credit for recognizing the idea, not very many idea generators will be eager to let the champion carry out his job. This brings us to the next item, measures and rewards.

Performance Measures and Rewards

We all tend to do those activities that get rewarded. If personnel perceive that idea generating does not get recognized but that idea exploitation does, they may not pass their ideas on to somebody who can exploit them. They may try to exploit them themselves, no matter how unequipped or uninterested they are in carrying out the exploitation activity.

For this reason, it is important to recognize the distinct contributions of each of the separate critical functions. Table 10-3 identifies some measures relevant to each function. Each measure has both a quantity and quality dimension. For example, the objective for a person who has the skills and information to be effective at gatekeeping could be to help a number of people during the next twelve months. At the end of that time, his manager could survey the people whom the gatekeeper feels he helped to assess the gatekeeper's effectiveness in communicating key information. In each organization specific measures chosen will necessarily be different.

Rewarding an individual for the performance of a critical function makes the function both more discussable and manageable. However, what is seen as reward-

Table 10-2 Job Design Dimensions

Dimension of Job	Critical Function				
	Idea Generating	*Entrepreneuring or Championing*	*Project Leading*	*Gatekeeping*	*Sponsoring or Coaching*
Emphasis on deadlines	Little emphasis; exploring encouraged	Jointly set deadlines emphasized by management	Management identifies; needs strong emphasis	Set by the job (i.e., the person needing the information)	Little emphasis
Emphasis on specifically assigned tasks	Low; freedom to pursue new ideas	High; assignments mutually planned and agreed by management and champion	High with respect to overall project goals	Medium; freedom to consult with others	Low

Table 10-3 Measuring and Rewarding Critical Function Performance

Dimension of Management	Critical Function				
	Idea Generating	Entrepreneuring or Championing	Project Leading	Gatekeeping	Sponsoring or Coaching
Primary contribution of each function for appraisal of performance	Quantity and quality of ideas generated	Ideas picked up; percent carried through	Project technical milestones accomplished; cost/schedule constraints met	People helped; degree of help	Staff developed; extent of assistance provided
Rewards appropriate	Opportunities to publish; recognition from professional peers through symposia, etc.	Visibility; publicity; further resources for project	Bigger projects; material signs of organizational status	Travel budget; key "assists" acknowledged; increased freedom and use for advice	Increased freedom; discretionary resources for support of others

ing for one function may be seen as less rewarding, neutral, or even negative for another function because of the different personalities and needs of the role fillers. Table 10-3 presents some rewards seen as appropriate for each function. Again, organizational and individual differences will generate variations in rewards selected. Of course, the informal positive feedback of managers to their day-to-day contacts is a major source of motivation and recognition for any individual performing a critical innovation function, or any job for that matter.

Salary and bonus compensation are not included here, but not because they are unimportant to any of these people. Of course, financial rewards should also be employed as appropriate, but they do not seem to be explicitly linked to any one innovative function more than another. Table 10-3 identifies the rewards that are related to critical roles.

PERFORMING A CRITICAL FUNCTIONS ASSESSMENT

The preceding sections demonstrate that the critical functions concept provides an important way of describing an organization's resources for effective innovation activity. To translate this concept into an applied tool, one would need the capability for assessing the status of an R&D unit in terms of critical functions. Such an assessment could potentially provide two important types of information. The first is input for management decisions about ability to achieve organizational goals and strategy. The second is information that can assist management and R&D professionals in performance evaluation, career development, and more effective project performance.

Methods of Approach

The methodology for a critical functions assessment can vary depending on the situation—size of organization, organization structure, scope of responsibilities, and industry and technology characteristics. From experience gained with a dozen companies and government agencies in North America, the authors have found the most flexible approach to be a series of common questionnaires, developed from the replicated academic research techniques on innovative contributors, modified as needed for the situation. Questionnaires are supplemented by a number of structured interviews or workshops. Data are collected and organized in a framework that represents (1) the critical functions, (2) special characteristics of an organization's situation, (3) additional critical functions required in the specific organization, and (4) the climate for innovation provided by management. (See Table 10-4 for a sample of the approach used in one of the questionnaires.) The result is a measure of an organization's current and potential strengths in each critical function, an evaluation of the compatibility of the organization's R&D strategy with these strengths, and a set of personnel development plans for both management and staff that support the organization's goals.

Table 10-4   Sample of the Critical Functions Questionnaire

Each respondent is asked to rate statements such as those below according to three separate criteria: (1) the respondent's personal preference, (2) his or her perceived skills for performing each activity, and (3) each activity's importance in the person's present job. In the usual instrument three or four item sentences scattered throughout the questionnaire provide multiple indications for each critical role, thus assuring reliability of the assessment.

Working as an effective, contributing member of a team in carrying out a task with one or more colleagues. (A)

Creating or developing ideas that result in new programs or services. (B)

Being a "one-stop" question-answering service for others by maintaining an in-depth competence in a few areas. (C)

Acting as a link between my unit and users to ensure that users' needs are being met. (D)

Searching out or identifying unexploited ideas that can be developed into a new program or service. (E)

Bringing people together and developing them into a smoothly working team. (F)

Lending credibility or power to less experienced or less visible personnel so that they may be more effective in the organization. (G)

The letters shown in the examples above for the reader's guidance indicate perceived ties to the several critical functions:

A—Problem solving	E—Entrepreneuring or championing
B—Idea generating	F—Project leading
C—Technical gatekeeping	G—Sponsoring or coaching
D—Market gatekeeping	

Source: This sample is reprinted here with the permission of Pugh-Roberts Associates, Inc., which holds the copyright on the questionnaire.

This information is valuable for the organization and the individual. The organization first gains a complete and meaningful set of information on its own balance among the critical innovation skills. The match between the strengths and mix of these skills and the staffing requirements of present goals and strategy can then be evaluated. The assessment process also reinforces the explicit recognition of the need for performance of different types of innovation-enhancing skills in an effective R&D organization. For management this underlines the need for developing different expectations of a person's job and different ways of managing, motivating, and rewarding individuals in order to support the overall strategy. Finally, it gives the organization a framework for considering how the strengths of different individuals should be combined to be consistent with a productive long-range R&D strategy.

For the individual, the results provide a broader view of the role of a professional in an R&D organization, increased sensitivity to his own functioning and to his and his colleagues' relative strengths, and a very persuasive rationale for team-work—the use of multiple functions to move an idea forward. In addition, the assessment can assist the individual in eliminating or reducing a mismatch between his perceived skills and talents and the requirements of the job. (These mismatches are probably the single greatest factor lowering motivation of technical professionals.) The critical functions assessment helps by providing both managers and professionals working for them a clarified set of job dimensions appropriate to the innovation activity that can be used as a better base for performance evaluation, career planning, and the development of job expectations. It is then easier to recognize and work with individual differences and strengths that they may have already known existed, as well as being able to use new approaches and specific vocabulary to identify new strengths or personal goals.

One result of the assessment is a profile for the organization based upon the aggregate self-perceptions of the individual members. For validity, each of the self-reports is checked with the person's manager and with a set of colleague responses. Where differences exist they can then be reconciled.

Application of the Critical Functions Approach

To illustrate the kinds of empirical and managerial results deriving from a critical functions assessment, we present here some outcomes developed from one moderate-sized R&D organization. The analysis in this company included three main lines of inquiry:

1. Identification of the balance the company desired to have among the critical functions.
2. Identification of existing strengths in each function.
3. Identification of the factors supporting and inhibiting the performance of each function in the R&D organization.

Balance Among the Functions. Based upon careful examination of the organization's goals and requirements as discussed earlier, the management team determined what would be an "ideal" number of staff highly skilled at performing each function. This was accomplished by looking at each group and subjectively assessing the number required for each function, given the goals and human and physical resources of that unit. Table 10-5 presents the management group's assessment of the ideal number performing each function. Table 10-5 also shows questionnaire results on the number of people appearing to have the skills and strengths needed to perform each function well in addition to those actually carrying out the critical roles.

Table 10-5 "Ideal" versus Actual Distribution of Staff Performing Each Critical Function and Principal Strengths of the Staff[a]

	Idea Generating	Entrepreneuring/ Championing	Project Leading	Technical Gatekeeping	Market Gatekeeping	Sponsoring/ Coaching
"Ideal"	6	11	17	5	14	4
Actual	5	5	11	9	12	3
Strength	10	9	6	12	4	11

[a]Total population = 90 professionals.

Source: These data are drawn from Alan R. Fusfeld, "Critical Functions: The Key to Managing Teamwork in the Innovation Process," presented at Innovation Canada, 1976. Numbers of "actuals" and "strengths" are not additive because many of the individuals sampled performed or were strong in more than one critical function. Most of the professionals performed no critical functions.

Factors Affecting the Balance.   In addition, the R&D staff was asked to assess a number of factors affecting the performance of the critical functions. The data collection instrument designed for this purpose was called the "Innovation Climate Questionnaire." The results of these data provided substantial insights into the causes of discrepancies between the ideal and actual balance among the functions. For example, the staff's perception that they did not have management skills, (i.e., familiarity with management concepts and techniques) helps to explain why the "actual" number who are project leading is lower than the "ideal" number and the relatively few who report strengths in project leading. Another factor was the R&D staff's lack of understanding of what project leading/managing was expected in its new matrix organization. Market gatekeeping, on the other hand, was blessed with sufficient staff performing the function, but they seemed to be performing far in excess of their abilities. This was explained by the perception that this function was well recognized and well rewarded by upper management, who continually stressed the importance of being market-oriented.

Table 10-6 lists some of the factors serving to support and inhibit each of the critical functions in the organization studied.

Actions Taken.   As a result of the analysis, multiple actions were taken and it is useful to consider some of them. The first action was that every first-line supervisor and above, after some training, discussed with each employee the results of the employee's critical funtions survey. (In other companies employee anonymity has been preserved, data being returned only to the individual. In these companies employees have frequently used the results to initiate discussions with their immediate supervisors regarding job "fit" and career development.) The purpose of the discussion was to look for differences in how the employee and his boss each perceived the employee's job skills and to engage in developmental career planning. The vocabulary of the critical functions plus the tangible feedback gave the manager and the employee a meaningful, commonly shared basis for the discussion.

Several significant changes resulted from these discussions. A handful of the staff recognized the mismatch between their present jobs and skills. With the support of their managers, job modifications were made. Another type of mismatch that this process revealed was between the manager's perception of the employee's skills and the employee's own perception. Most of the time the manager was underutilizing his human resources.

The data also prompted action to improve the performance of the project leading function. The insufficient number who saw themselves performing the function and the perceived lack of skills resulted in several "coaching" sessions by upper management, further role clarification, and increased upper management sensitivity to the support needed for project leading. These activities also involved personnel from outside units to develop broader support outside the technical organization for the project leading role.

Important changes were made in how the technical organization recruited. To

Table 10-6 Organizational "Climate" Factors Affecting
the Critical Functions in One Company

Function	Factors Supporting the Performance of the Function	Factors Inhibiting the Performance of the Function
Idea Generating	Well-recognized function Reasonable freedom Good linkages with the market	Tight resources Focus on the short term
Entrepreneuring/ championing	Freedom to act Recognition of function	High cost of failure Limited reward for risk taking Receives poor coaching
Project leading/ managing	Strong management support Freedom to act Clear goals	Low acceptance by outside units Lack of management skills High cost of failure
Technical gatekeeping	Well known by peers Freedom to travel	Emphasis on measurable performance Emphasis on creating new ideas Physical design—distances Poorly recognized function
Market gatekeeping	Well-recognized function Ready market access	Poor customer credibility due to premature introduction of products
Sponsoring/ coaching	Clear business goals	Function not recognized Lack of company growth strategy "Firefighting" orientation

begin with, the characteristic strengths behind each critical function were explicitly employed in identifying the skills necessary to do a particular job. This led to a framework useful for interviewing candidates to determine how they might fit into the present organization and how they saw themselves growing. Also, upper management became conscious of the unintended bias in the recruiting procedure that was introduced by the universitites at which they recruited and by those who did the company's recruiting. Personnel primarily interested in idea generating (i.e., senior researchers) did most of the university interviewing. They tended to try to identify and favored hiring other people interested in idea generating, and described the organization in terms of interest to those people. As a result of the analyses, upper management was careful to have a mix of the critical functions represented by the people interviewing job candidates.

Other values resulted from the analyses which were less tangible than those listed above but equally important. Jobs were no longer defined solely in technical terms (i.e., the educational background and/or work experience necessary). For example, whether or not a job involved idea generation or exploitation was defined, and these typical activities were included in the description of the job and the skills needed to perform it well. The objectives of the job, in the company's management-by-objectives (MBO) procedure, were then expanded to include the critical functions. However, since all five functions are essential to innovation and it is the very rare person who can do all five equally well, the clear need for a new kind of teamwork was also developed. Finally, the critical functions concept provided the framework for the selection of people and the division of labor on the "innovation team" that became the nucleus for all new R&D programs.

SYNOPSIS

This chapter has examined the main elements of the technology-based innovation process in terms of certain usually informal but critical behavioral functions. The life cycle of activities encountered in an R&D project served to identify five critical roles as reoccurring: idea generating, entrepreneuring or championing, project leading, gatekeeping, and sponsoring or coaching. Organizational problems associated with weaknesses in the playing of each of these roles were described.

Each critical role was detailed in terms of representative activities during a project, and dominant characteristics of typical role players were presented from surveys conducted among many North American R&D/engineering organizations. Two key observations were that some unique individuals concurrently perform more than one of the critical roles, and that patterns of roles for an individual often change during a productive work career.

Managerial implications of the critical functions concepts were developed in regard to manpower planning, job design and objective setting, and performance measurement and rewards. These discussions provide a basis for design of a more effective "multiladder" system to replace many R&D organizations' ineffectual "dual-ladder" systems.

Techniques employed in carrying out a critical functions assessment were then described, together with the results obtained at one medium-sized R&D organization. A combination of survey questionnaires and management workshops were used to develop, interpret, and apply the critical functions data to organizational improvement.

The critical functions approach was conceived as embodying the essence of innovative work in a research and development process. But several years of development, testing, and discussion of this perspective have led to broadened views and applications. Computer software development was an early area of extension of the methods, as was their use in an architectural firm. Recent discussions with colleagues suggest an obvious appropriateness for marketing organizations, with more difficult translation expected in the areas of finance and/or manufacturing. To the extent that innovative outcome, rather than routine production, is the output sought, we have confidence that the critical functions approach will afford useful insights for organizational analysis and management.

WESTMAR COLLEGE LIBRARY